Social Media and Religious Change

Religion and Society

Edited by
Gustavo Benavides, Kocku von Stuckrad and
Winnifred Fallers Sullivan

Volume 53

Social Media and Religious Change

Edited by
Marie Gillespie, David Eric John Herbert
and Anita Greenhill

DE GRUYTER

ISBN 978-3-11-048857-9
e-ISBN 978-3-11-027048-8
ISSN 1437-5370

Library of Congress Cataloging-in-Publication Data
A CIP catalog record for this book has been applied for at the Library of Congress.

Bibliographic information published by the Deutsche Nationalbibliothek
The Deutsche Nationalbibliothek lists this publication in the Deutsche Nationalbibliografie;
detailed bibliographic data are available in the Internet at http://dnb.dnb.de.

© 2013 Walter de Gruyter GmbH, Berlin/Boston
Printing: Hubert & Co. GmbH & Co. KG, Göttingen
♾ Printed on acid-free paper
Printed in Germany

www.degruyter.com

———

For
Jean and Isobel

Margaret and Frank

Table of Contents

David Herbert and Marie Gillespie

1   Introduction:
Social Media and Religious Change

> Media professionals have been stripped of their exclusive narrative power, as a multiplicity of individual fans have emerged, wielding the unprecedented ability to publish their own understandings of celebrities online through a wide variety of public venues (Haughey and Campbell: 103).

> [R]eflexivity and plurality make it difficult for any public performance of the sacred not to evoke scepticism from sections of its public who regard it as inauthentic, instrumental or based on an inadequate form of the sacred (Lynch: 26).

How do religious and spiritually oriented groups use social media? What impact does this use have on their relationship with religious institutions? How are notions of the sacred being redefined with the advent of social media? How are discourses on religion and the sacred being re-positioned and mobilised in social media such as blogs, Facebook, Twitter and in virtual worlds? How do mass and social media interact? To what extent are social media catalysing religious change? These are the main questions addressed in this book. They were also the key issues debated at a symposium entitled 'Social Media and the Sacred', organised by the *Mediating Religion*[1] International Research Network, held on 28 – 29 June 2010 at The Open University's London Centre in Camden, on which this edited volume is based. The network forms an important plank of research at the Centre for Research on Socio-Cultural Change (CRESC).

CRESC's[2] 'mission is to understand how socio-cultural processes relate to our awareness and experience of technological innovation, economic instability and social inequality'. The specific aim of the *Mediating Religion* network is to further such understanding in the field of religion and media by engaging scholars from a range of disciplines—sociology, anthropology, cultural studies, media studies, religious studies and management studies are all represented in this volume. The collection pursues CRESC's mission in relation to the production of

---

1 www.mediatingreligion.org/ The network was founded by Marie Gillespie and David Herbert at CRESC's 2005 annual conference, and we would like to thank CRESC and the ESRC for their enduring support.

2 Details of the UK Economic and Social Research Council's Centre for Research in Socio-Cultural Change, co-hosted between the Open University and Manchester University can be found at: http://www.cresc.ac.uk/about-cresc (accessed 21 Sept 2012).

meanings around religion in relation to the shifting boundaries between the sacred and secular in contemporary mass and social media.

In this context, one key question linking socio-cultural processes with technological innovation and social inequality is raised by Haughey and Campbell in the first quotation above: to what extent have social media reduced the 'narrative power' of media professionals, challenging the 'highly centralised system of symbolic production' of the media industries, and hence demythologising what Nick Couldry has called the 'myth of the mediated centre' (2003: 45)? Or, to approach the issue from a slightly different angle (and again engaging Couldry), if the media are indeed the chief source of our knowledge of the world 'beyond our immediate locality', then to what extent has the growth of social media resulted in the redistribution of society's 'narrative resources' in the interests of a 'wider social justice' (Couldry 2011: 48–9)? Another key question raised by Lynch in the second quotation above is, what challenges face any public performance of the sacred in contemporary mass and social media rich societies? Does pluralism undermine public performances of the sacred? Does reflexivity produce disenchantment with conventional and institutionalized forms of religion, or can social media create and sustain shared and plural senses of the sacred beyond conventional religious definitions?

The contributions to this collection address these questions from different perspectives using various methodologies. There are studies which focus on mass media representations (Chapters 3–5), while others examine the use of social media to challenge mass media representations (Chapters 6 and 7). Some analyse the use of social media to challenge the monopoly of religious institutions in defining the meanings and contours of concepts of the sacred, rituals and rites of passage (Chapters 8, 9 and 11), while one (Chapter 10) examines attempts by religious leaders to control uses of the Internet among the Baha'í. Lynch's contribution (Chapter 2) differs in being a theoretical reflection on how best to conceptualise the sacred in contemporary societies, especially beyond conventional religious definitions and institutions, and how to locate and research the dynamic relationship between mediated sacred forms and wider socio-cultural processes.

In Chapter 2 Lynch develops a critical socio-cultural account of the category of the sacred through an evaluation of the so-called 'strong program' within cultural sociology, which argues the case for a meaning-centred social science (Alexander and Smith 2001). The idea of the 'strong program' has its roots in social studies of science (Latour and Woolgar 1986) and starts from the premise that scientific knowledge is always pre-structured by culturally embedded cognitive categories of meanings. Following this lead Alexander and Smith outline a research programme, the central features of which include: recognition of the autonomy of culture as an ontological given, acceptance of the methodological importance of 'thick description' of local cultural dynamics (requiring the heuristic bracketing out of wider, non-symbolic social relations), and acknowledgement of the central goal of producing a highly precise account of the causal impact of culture while 'anchor[ing] causality in proximate actors and agencies' (2011: 137). Alexander and Smith draw on various previous alternative accounts of cultural dynamics (e.g., Geertz, Bourdieu, Foucault, the Birmingham School of Cultural Studies), but in their view each falls short in nailing down causal processes that can explain cultural and social change.

One example of work inspired by the 'strong program' is Eyerman's (2008) *The Assassination of Theo van Gogh*, discussed by Herbert in Chapter 5, which displays both the strengths and the weaknesses of the approach. Herbert argues that Eyerman's 'strong program' approach is insightful if selective, emphasising as it does some aspects of Dutch cultural history (especially military defeats and humiliation) while ignoring others that are arguably equally significant (depillarisation, rapid secularisation, transformation in gender and sexual relations). The weakness of the approach, he argues, may well be a consequence of the 'bracketing out of wider, non-symbolic relations', leading to a lack of triangulation of evidence. This example also suggests that the bracketing out of 'wider non-symbolic processes', if not followed by an 'unbracketing' to allow structural processes back in, may result in a failure to connect important socio-cultural factors that can account for change. This in turn produces an unhelpful conceptual isolation of the category of culture. This tendency, argues Herbert, may well be reinforced by the polemic of 'strong program' against other 'weaker' approaches to culture, judging by Alexander and Smith's account of the 'strong program' (2001).

It is possible, however, to adopt the central tenets of the 'strong program' and to avoid such pitfalls. For example, its insistence on cultural autonomy encourages resistance to reductionism and technological determinism. Its advocacy of the use of thick ethnographic-style description promotes a thorough investigation of local and proximate cultural dynamics. And the quest for rigour in interrogating causal processes allows for complex multi-causal explanatory frameworks and explanations of the relationship between, for example, social media and religious change. If cultural dynamics are not reducible to structural factors but enjoy some autonomy in their own right, then it is still perfectly possible to factor into one's analysis a range of non-symbolic influences, interactions and processes. Indeed, to produce the best possible account of complex causal processes, a cultural sociology that embraces the 'strong program' with a focus on meanings and processes should be triangulated with approaches that can take into account the impact of social structures, political economy and power relations.

Lynch's account, to his credit, advocates the 'strong program' but without such isolationist tendencies towards cultural analysis. In Chapter 2 he analyses how the sacred is theorized within the 'strong program' and examines how it can help to illuminate the role of 'public media' in relation to sacred forms. Drawing on the further elaborations of the 'strong program' in Alexander's cultural sociology, Lynch develops an understanding of the 'immanent sacred' as 'operative forms of meaning and value in increasingly secularised or de-Christianised Western societies'. He provides a searching examination of the meanings of the sacred beyond institutional religion, developing a theoretical framework with which to map

> how the celebration and pollution of sacred forms gets acted out through particular social narratives and dramas, eliciting powerful emotional and collective responses at specific moments, and generating complex subjectivities and social interactions (Lynch: 21).

Such a framework is helpful in linking several themes raised across the volume. First, it sheds light on the power of the mass media evoked in Couldry's 'myth of the mediated centre' and challenged by Haughey and Campbell, for the 'centre' to which the (mass) media connects us is the Durkheimian sacred, representations of which, as Lynch describes, 'serve as focal points for the fusion of collective emotion, identity and moral community through the medium of meaningful and structured collective practices' (Lynch: 16). Couldry's purpose in *Media Rituals* is critical demythologising; he sets out to de-bunk the myth of the centre by exposing its artifice, its pretensions and the thrall it holds us in. Lynch's perspective enables social criticism; but it also provides a more nuanced perspective on the role of the mass media through Alexander's (2006) concept of 'civil repair', which posits that mass media, as well as exposing breaches of the sacred, can also provide the means through which restitution can be made. At the same time, Lynch underlines the fragility of any such restitution. Restitution is fragile because 'civil society ... is always grounded in practices of inclusion and exclusion, creating an irresolvable tension between the cultural role of sacred forms for collective and moral identification and the aspiration for an inclusive, global civil society' (Lynch: 23).

Second, by examining the relationship between social media on the one hand and mass media, religious institutions and change on the other, this collection raises the issue of the shifting meanings of and boundaries between the sacred and secular in contemporary, media-rich societies. One perspective on these issues is to suggest that mass media are taking over religion's role in mediating the sacred, whether or not this is conceptualised as linking us to the imagined centre of society, as in Couldry's account. Alternatively, media may be seen as performing a range of more diffuse 'functions', as for example in Hjarvard's influential conceptualisation of the 'mediatisation' of religion as a process through which

> the media have taken over many of the cultural and social functions of the institutionalised religions and provide spiritual guidance, moral orientation, ritual passages and a sense of community and belonging (2011: 124).

Hjarvard also argues that this process of mediatisation

> may both encourage secular practices and beliefs and invite religious imaginations typically of a more subjectivised nature (ibid.: 119).

In contrast to Hjarvard's substitution model (i. e., where media substitutes for religion by doing the work religion used to do), for Lynch the sacred is redistributed or partially relocated (extended to include certain values or categories of people or places as sacrosanct) rather than absorbed into the media, and the tension between sacred and profane is rearticulated rather than attenuated in this process.

The relationship between religious change and media institutions is more complex than Hjarvard's substitution account implies. This is reflected in the chapters in the volume that are based on empirical studies. For example, Thomas (Chapter 4) analyses responses among audiences and critics to two BBC television 'reality' series on contemporary monastic life and its appeals and challenges for 'lay audiences'. The methodology (content analysis of professional critical responses and semi-structured interviews with a group attending a monastic retreat) brings out the complexity of how audiences negotiate meaning. Rather than substituting for conventional religion, these series led some members of the audience to a deeper engagement with one of the religious institutions represented. And rather than accepting TV representations as authoritative, many of her interviewees demonstrated a highly critical awareness of the relationship between genre, modes of realism and producer intentions. Yet critical reflection did not produce a disenchanted disengagement with religion. Rather, varying degrees of narrative immersion and engagement with the monastery were evident. But this was an atypical audience and set of interviewees—committed enough to go on a monastic retreat and open to being interviewed about the experience. So one has to be cautious not to extrapolate too much and to caution that research results can be just as much a result of the research design as a genuine insight into how audiences-cum-interviewees respond to particular performances of religion. Nevertheless, this example suggests that critical appropriation of media resources can go hand-in-hand with involvement, engagement and pleasure.

Thomas' insights into the significance of gender for constructions of spirituality are particularly valuable. In particular, she argues that the significantly more critical response among professional and lay audiences to *The Convent* compared with *The Monastery* relates in part to gendered constructions of caring and spiritual work.

> *The Monastery*, which was hailed as a ground-breaking representation of religion, in fact reinforces existing norms of association of the spiritual with the masculine. ... [T]he caring characteristics which seem extraordinary in the monks become ordinary when associated with women (Thomas: 74).

While several contributions to this collection focus on the opportunities for social media and new media formats to challenge conventional media and religious narratives (see Chapters 7, 8 and 9), Thomas' analysis serves as a reminder of the power of conventional mass mediated narratives about religion (and the inequalities embedded in them) to reproduce themselves across new formats and audience segments.

In Chapter 3 Knott et al. analyse representations of Christianity, secularism and religious diversity in regional and national British media at two junctures, 1982–3 and 2008–9, looking in greater depth at particular media events, such as the deportation of Geert Wilders and the visit of Pope Benedict in their account of the second period. They use a concept called 'the secular sacred', which they define as 'those beliefs, practices and values that are explicitly non-religious but are nevertheless held to be non-negotiable and often referred to as "sacred" by those who hold them, e.g., freedom of speech and human rights' (Knott et al.: 44). The sacred here, then, refers to values that for some citizens should not be compromised and are in need of protection from being violated. The study sheds empirical light on arguments about the visibility and presence of religion as a topic in public discourse (Ward et al. 2008; Beckford 2010), demonstrating a huge increase in references to some religions. References to Islam, unsurprisingly, increased almost ten-fold across this period; references to atheism/secularism increased nine-fold; references to Hinduism increased seven-fold; references to Sikhism increased five-fold; and those to Judaism and Christianity increased by a more modest 5–10 %, although these started from a higher base. No categories of religion showed a decrease. The study provides empirical support for the contention that public exposure to reporting and opinion on religion and secularism/atheism has indeed increased, at least for British readerships and audiences. How are these topics represented? How are the debates framed? The story here is not straightforward, as the ambivalence shown in right-wing press representations illustrates. In their study of the Wilders case, they show that in the right-wing press tolerance of Islam was represented as submitting to Muslim demands, while Muslims were constructed 'mainly as hate preachers', although there was 'some acknowledgement of … more moderate Muslims'. In this context, Britain was constructed as a 'secular country' (challenged by Muslim threats to freedom of speech) and as a 'Christian country' (threatened by a perceived threat of 'Islamisation'). Yet in coverage of the papal visit, the accent in these newspapers turned against 'exclusive secularism and atheism', which were constructed as enemies of 'people of faith'. Here, in contrast with the Wilders case, religious diversity was seen as a positive force in society, with 'references to interfaith and its enrichment for the whole society' (Knott et al.: 55). There is a consistent tendency towards a positive framing of Christianity and a negative framing of 'extremist Muslims'. Religious diversity is sometimes framed positively, especially where there is co-operation between religions, while the discourse on secularism and atheism can flip from positive to negative depending on context. By providing a nuanced picture of media representations, Knott et al. help to shift debate beyond generalised claims about negative media framing of religion as well as giving empirical substance to claims about the 'return of public religion'.

Mass media framing is also central to Herbert's study (Chapter 5) of controversies around Islam and Muslims in the Netherlands. This chapter focuses on the turbulent period from 2001–2008, which witnessed several concerted anti-Islam media campaigns, two political murders of anti-Islam campaigners and the most extensive reversal of multicultural policies anywhere in Europe to date. Herbert seeks to relate mass media factors to the broader socio-cultural and political context in an attempt to explain why Dutch 'culture wars' became so intense and why Dutch multicultural reversals have gone so far. A key finding is that in contrast with Britain, where Knott et al. found that even the right-wing press tended to maintain a distinction between Islam and its interpretation by extremists, in the Netherlands, fed by the successive media campaigns of Fortuyn, van Gogh, Hirsi Ali and Wilders, Islam is 'Other' and identified as essentially in conflict with predominant European norms.

Even though mainstream news media were highly critical of Fortuyn and Wilders, the framing of Islam as essentially opposed to European values limited the discursive space available for alternative narratives to emerge about Muslims. Moderate-extremist dichotomies are of course problematic (Mamdani 2004; Geaves 2005), but at least they disrupt the logic that connects an essentialist notion of 'Islam' with problems of Muslim integration. Again compared with Britain, two other relevant factors include the high political profile given to interfaith activities by the British government (Beckford 2010), which may explain the favourable discourse on interfaith found in the right wing British press, and the

comparative openness of the Dutch political system to new personality-led political movements, whose opportunities are more restricted by the power of political elites in Britain's first-past-the-post Westminster electoral system.

Herbert also examines Muslim resistance to dominant media frames of Islam
and Muslims in the Netherlands, among both Dutch Muslims specifically and
broader-based social media activists. Social media usage is highest amongst
young Moroccan Dutch women, one of the country's least-represented groups
in mass media terms, and the chapter gives an example of this activism being
used to reach a broader public sphere in protests organised against Geert Wilders' campaign for a headscarf tax. This evidence suggests that for some minorities at least, social media do help to redistribute the balance of narrative resources, providing a sense of 'voice'. However, neither action in minority 'public
sphericules' (Gitlin 1998) nor more publicly visible protest necessarily shifts
the balance of narrative resources within mainstream public spheres, and
hence does not (at least as yet) serve to redress injustices in terms of broader
public recognition.

Haughey and Campbell's account (Chapter 6) of the way fans challenge
media representations of celebrities deploys a case study of a Michael Jackson
tribute. This also reflects on the nature of the relationship between mass
media and the resources (in this case narrative and symbolic) of religious institutions. On the one hand, the study could be interpreted as fitting Hjarvard's
substitution thesis, because 'implicit religious' activity takes place entirely on
a secular social media site. On the other hand, the fans' construction of Jackson
as martyr, saint and angel – in stark contrast to predominant media representations – shows a re-interpretation of these conventional religious categories
which does not dilute their transcendent dimension; hence Jackson becomes

> Michael the angel, depicted by fans as called by God to join him in the afterlife; Michael the
> otherworldly messenger, believed by fans to have been sent to spread love and hope to the
> world; and Michael the immortal spirit, depicted by fans as being continually resurrected
> by their eternal adoration (Haughey and Campbell: 110).

The role of religious institutions in promulgating an authoritative interpretation
of these terms is indeed usurped (substitution of media for religion), and religious imagination becomes more personalised/subjectivised; but this in no
way implies a secularisation of content or disenchantment.

Chapter 6 also contains discussion of the category of the sacred, this time in
relation to 'implicit religion'. Lord's definition of 'implicit religion', the authors
argue, shifts attention towards 'the mode of behaviour exhibited, rather than

the goal towards which the behaviour is directed' (2006: 206). It is then claimed that:

> From this perspective, a fresh understanding of religion shatters notions of a 'sacred versus secular' dichotomy, such that implicit religion is not deemed authentic because of a link to the 'recognisably holy', but is noted instead in the 'observable actions carried out by a person, whether random, habitual, impulsive or rational' (2006: 206). Therefore, in relation to this understanding, in order for celebrity worship to be considered implicit religion, fans' actions in veneration of celebrities must be analysed (Haughey and Campbell: 104).

What matters, they argue, in defining behaviour as religious is how the worshipper treats the object of devotion rather than the properties of that object. But it is not clear how this 'shatters notions of a sacred-secular dichotomy'. The rest of the chapter seems to depend precisely on such a distinction. For example, this is apparent in the argument that 'for celebrity worship to be regarded as implicit religion there must be significant evidence that fans apply their understanding of celebrities to their understandings of the greater world, and that their actions in reverence of celebrities create a religious experience' (Haughey and Campbell: ibid.).

If the distinction between sacred and secular were shattered, there would presumably be no alternative understanding to apply to the greater world, and hence nothing special about the ways in which fans respond to celebrities to create a religious experience. Rather, what this use of the concept of 'implicit religion' seems to do is to redirect attention away from the object of veneration to focus on the devotion of the worshipper. This leads the researcher to observe worship-like behaviour towards objects not previously regarded as 'recognisably holy', and in so doing extends the boundaries of the holy/sacred – perhaps beyond what some might regard as tenable. This interpretation would seem to be supported by the observation that 'the described reconstructions of the celebrity draw heavily from Christian belief', extending them beyond common (or at least orthodox) use to relate to new objects of veneration. This move has the effect of personalising/subjectivising and contesting the meanings of the sacred without the disenchantment that earlier theorists predicted would ensue as a result of the pluralisation of beliefs (Berger 1967).

Subjectivisation without disenchantment is also a feature of Nauta's examination (Chapter 7) of the phenomenon of Muslim martyrdom ('suicide bomber') videos. These are circulated via the Internet and present narratives explaining the actions of their protagonists, which challenge predominant media representations, both in the West and the Muslim-majority world. These narratives also challenge those produced by established (Islamic) religious institutions and bypass religious authorities by using DIY religious arguments to appeal directly to an imagined *umma*. The sharp re-articulation of the boundaries of the sacred and the profane, the pure (martyrs) and the polluted (world), is also very marked here, as it is in Pihlaja's study (Chapter 9) of the discursive construction of group identity amongst YouTube-based Evangelists. The media representations explored in Pihlaja's chapter present another form of direct appeal to congregations and adherents which bypass religious authorities. They are articulated in opposition to an essentialised secular world. The YouTube videos also deploy DIY theology, but this time to address an imagined Christian mission field. While the content is very different from that of Nauta's study, in both cases video clips are posted on social media to self-publicise a counter-cultural message which sharply divides the social world into the sacred and the profane, the saved and the unsaved, true religious adherents and infidels or apostates. In contrast to the dichotomous and confrontational constructions of sacred and profane in Nauta or Pihlaja's studies, both Abrams et al. (Chapter 8) and Greenhill and Fletcher (Chapter 11) show how conventional practices sanctioned by religious communities are adapted rather than displaced or transformed in online uses. Greenhill and Fletcher's study examines Internet-based memorial sites run by relatives of those who have suffered violent deaths and demonstrates that social media can enable a more active and on-going form of communal mourning than conventional institutions (whether media-based [death notices and obituaries], secular or religious [memorial services and bereavement support]) can provide. This may be seen as a case of supplementation rather than contestation of conventional forms; yet there is arguably something implicit in the discourse and practice constructed on these sites that critiques the adequacy of the narrative and ritual resources of mainstream religious institutions to address the needs of the bereaved. Similarly, a parallel process of renegotiation of meaning and challenge to authority is presented in Abrams et al.'s examination (Chapter 8) of 'post-denominational' Jews' efforts to generate new meanings, adopt different roles and create new forms of community (beyond those provided by established religious institutions) by using social media. Both these chapters and Lynch's theory challenge Hjarvard's argument that media replaces religion; rather, the process is more complicated, involving adaptations of traditions, challenges to authority and re-negotiations of meaning.

Campbell and Fulton (Chapter 10) focus on the other side of the dynamic between religious institutions and their adherents, that is on the attempts of a 'bounded' religious community (the Bahá'í) to regulate uses of social media among its members in order to maintain its boundaries and identity against what the authors describe as 'the social affordances of digital technology that can make it difficult to retain a cohesive identity structure'. To do so they use the 'Religious Social Shaping of Technology' (RSST) approach developed by

Campbell (2010) in relation to other bounded religious groups, which uses four
levels of analysis:

> (1) the history and tradition of the community, (2) its core beliefs and patterns related to
> media, (3) the specific negotiation processes it undergoes with a new technology, and ...
> (4) the communal framing and discourses created by them, which are used to define and
> justify the extent of their technology use (Campbell and Fulton: 188).

RSST sees the relationship between new technologies and bounded religious
groups as a dialectical one. Rather than simply rejecting new technologies, religious groups seek to regulate and shape their members' engagement with them
and, where they have the resources, influence the development of the technology
itself – as with Haredi Jews' shaping of 'kosher' mobile phone models (Campbell
2010). As a relatively small global religious organization, the Bahá'í's lack the resources to shape social media, so they must rely on appeals to their members to
follow the rulings of the 'House of Justice' and the social practice of 'shunning'
(excluding, rejecting) 'covenant-breakers'. Indeed, simply accepting a 'friend request' from someone who has set up an unauthorised Bahá'í website is 'seen as a
community violation, [as] being in association with a covenant-breaker' (Campbell and Fulton: 195).

The authors conclude that Bahá'í attitudes to the Internet reflect a tension.
Internet technologies resonate in some ways with Bahá'í beliefs – indeed they
can be welcomed in official documents as part of 'a development eagerly anticipated by The Guardian when he foresaw the creation of "a mechanism of world
intercommunication (...) embracing the whole planet"' (BIA [Bahá'í Internet
Agency] n.d). Yet members are warned that witnessing activity on social media
needs to 'be carried out in light of Bahá'í principles' (BIA 2007), requiring individual and institutional defensive action where necessary. The larger question of
whether the organisation can continue to successfully reproduce its core teachings in this plural discursive environment cannot be answered by a single case
study; but both this case study and those of Pihlaja and Abrams et al. suggest
that their participation in relatively open forms of social media activity does
not in itself have predictable consequences for sustaining religious identities
and community.

The RSST approach and Lynch's exposition of the 'strong program' are complementary in that both see the relationship between structural factors such as
technologies and culture as a dialectical one in which technologies provide 'affordances' for developments rather than dictating the direction of religious
change. Hence outcomes are as much shaped by culture and meaning as technological infrastructures. Technologies and social structures must be taken serious-

ly as independent variables capable of shaping the pathways along which technology is developed.

Has the growth of social media resulted in the redistribution of society's 'narrative resources' in the interests of a 'wider social justice' in the sphere of representations of the sacred and secular? Certainly, several case studies presented in this volume demonstrate a redistribution of resources from mass to social media to the extent that individuals and groups are using social media to generate alternative representations of sacred and secular to those of mainstream media (Haughey and Campbell; Nauta) and mainstream religious institutions (Abrams et al.; Pihlaja). But whether this wider redistribution of digital resources serves a 'wider social justice' is more questionable. First, it depends on how social justice is conceived (an issue beyond the scope of this volume), but the self-publicity of suicide bombers shows just how pernicious social media can be and confirms our main point that the meanings and consequences of social media do not inhere in the technology but in their uses.

Second, there is little evidence here that these experimental social media forms have yet had an impact on mainstream religious institutions, or indeed on mainstream public spheres. Rather, as Herbert's Dutch case study illustrates, it would seem that online social activism remains primarily a community resource, and the public action which has resulted from it does not (at least yet) appear to have translated into greater public sympathy or understanding. The consequences of social media for religious change will remain limited as long as access and use remain confined to the digitally empowered. The 'digital divide' continues to reproduce social inequalities, but generational differences in access to and use of social media and the demographic change in many parts of the developing world, especially the youth bulge, mean that the impact of social media on religious change is likely to gather pace in the future.

Case studies such as Greenhill and Fletcher's, Haughey and Campbell's and Abrams et al.'s demonstrate that social media are enabling the formation of networks or 'communities' providing the means with which to perform activities which appear to be valuable to their participants, but wider social impact is not evident. This, however, may simply be a question of scale (collectively, more case studies might provide some evidence of broader social impact) or possibly method; for example, it may be that, as Aupers and Houtman have argued in the case of New Age spirituality, existing methods have failed to capture the ways in which movements characterised by a rhetoric of radical autonomy and lacking official organisational hierarchies may nonetheless reproduce their discourse, ethos and practices 'by means of standardised legitimations' (2007: 201).

The question remains, however, as to whether religious change and senses of the sacred evoked by social media in chapters 6, 7, 9 and 11 can 'scale up' from 'shared' to 'public' levels and hence meet the challenges of pluralism and reflexivity to the public performance of the sacred as presented by Lynch. This is where Thomas' study is particularly valuable, because it shows that in spite of a range of publicly articulated criticisms, mainstream media representations of the sacred can still communicate a sense of authentic spiritual or religious experience to at least some of its audience, including critics. However, as a single case it remains indicative of a possible trajectory of development rather than evidence of a broader trend. Social media and mainstream media intersect in unpredictable ways rather than displace one another.

There is certainly enough evidence across the chapters to reject the idea that mainstream and/or social media are taking over the functions of established religions; rather, it would seem that religious activity is relocated and rearticulated rather than displaced through its mediation. But this is not to argue that the influential substitution version of mediatisation suggested by Hjarvard is wrong *per se*. It just does not offer a full account of the complex relations between media and religious change. To make sense of the case studies present here, a more dialectical model (such as Lynch's interpretation of the strong program in cultural sociology) is needed. Larger scale comparative studies which bring quantitative and qualitative data into dialogue would also help to establish how new media developments are shaping processes of religious change.

Social media embody the paradox of empowerment and surveillance. The advent of freely available software packages for analyzing our social media traces and trails—social media monitoring, data mining, natural language deciphering and sentiment analysis—mean that large-scale religious congregations using social media can be studied with greater accuracy and precision than ever before. Religious organisations can now monitor their congregations and their practices via analyses of 'big data' and thus exercise new kinds of powers. But useful as these software packages are for 'big data' analyses of, for example, digital sacred texts, they cannot analyse the quality of social media conversations and uses from a local or ethnographic perspective. But if we combine qualitative and big data sets, we can begin to get a much more complete and complex picture of the demographic and discursive aspects of these new spaces of communication and their implications for changing religious practices. We can bring the snail's eye and the bird's eye view into dialogue, or in Max Weber's terms, we can arrive at *verstehen*—understanding—*begreifen*—grasping the bigger picture.

References

Alexander, Jeffrey. 2006. *The Civil Sphere*. Oxford: Oxford University Press.
– and Philip Smith. 2001. "The Strong Program in Cultural Theory: Elements of a structural hermeneutics." In *The Handbook of Sociological Theory*, edited by Jonathan Turner, 135–150. New York: Kluwer.
Aupers, Stephanie and Dick Houtman. 2006. "Beyond the Spiritual Supermarket: The Social and Public Significance of New Age Spirituality." *Journal of Contemporary Religion* 21 (2): 201–222.
Beckford, Jim. 2010. "The Return of Public Religion: A critical assessment of a popular claim." *Nordic Journal of Religion and Society* 23 (2): 121–136.
Berger, Peter. 1967. *The Sacred Canopy: Elements of a Sociological Theory of Religion*. New York: Doubleday.
BIA [Bahá'í Internet Agency]. n.d. "Guidelines for Internet communication." Available at: http://www.bcca.org/bia/Guidelines%20for%20Internet%20Communication.pdf.
–. 2007. "Individual initiative on the Internet." Available at: http://www.bcca.org/bia/Individual-Initiative.pdf.
Campbell, Heidi. 2010. *When Religion Meets New Media*. London: Routledge.
Couldry, Nick 2003. *Media Rituals: A Critical Approach*. London: Routledge.
–. 2011. "Media and Democracy: Some missing links." In *Media and Social Justice*, edited by Sue Curry Jansen, J. Pooley, and L. Taub-Pervizpour, 45–54. London: Palgrave.
Eyerman, Ron. 2008. *The Assassination of Theo van Gogh: From Social Drama to Cultural Trauma*. Durham: Duke University Press
Geaves, Ron. 2004. "Who defines moderate Islam post 9/11?" In Islam and the West Post 9/11, edited by Ron Geaves, T. Gabriel, Y. Haddad, and J. Idelman Smith, 62–75. Ashgate: Aldershot.
Gitlin, Todd. 1998. "Public Sphere or Public Spherecules," In *Media, Ritual and Identity*, edited by Tamar Liebes and J. Curran, 168–174. London: Routledge.
Hjarvard, Stig. 2011. "The mediatisation of religion: Theorising religion, media and social change." *Culture and Religion* 12 (2): 119–135.
Latour, Bruno, and Steve Woolgar. 1986. *Laboratory Life*. Princeton, N.J.: Princeton University Press.
Lord, Karen. 2006. "Implicit religion: Definition and application." *Implicit Religion* 9: 205–219.
Mamdani, Mahmood. 2004. *Good Muslim, Bad Muslim: America, the Cold War and the Roots of Terror*. New York: Three Leaves/Random House.
Ward, Graham, and M. Hoelzl. 2008. *The New Visibility of Religion: Studies in Religion and Cultural Hermeneutics*. London and New York: Continuum.

Gordon Lynch
2 Media and the Sacred:
An Evaluation of the 'Strong Program'
within Cultural Sociology

In his influential book *The Invisible Religion*, Thomas Luckmann (1967) challenged sociologists of religion to move beyond their pre-occupation with traditional, institutional forms of religion to analyse the operative forms of meaning
and value in increasingly secularised or de-Christianised Western societies.
Some forty years on, Luckmann's call to study the 'new social form of religion'
beyond the structures of traditional religious institutions has still only been partially answered. In part, this is because mainstream religious traditions in North
America proved more robust than Luckmann had anticipated, albeit often in re-
structured forms (Wuthnow 1988; Miller 1999), and key research funders for the
sociology of religion in the United States remained primarily interested in the
changing nature of religious congregations and the role of religious institutions
as actors in civil society. In part, it is because the field of religious studies in
North America remains defined largely around the study of substantive religious
traditions, which provides little encouragement for thinking about the 'religious'
beyond mainstream traditions, despite the well-established critique of 'religion'
that underpins this disciplinary formation (see e. g., McCutcheon 2003). Partly, it
is because, in more secularised European contexts, the study of new religious
forms beyond traditional institutional structures has commonly focused on
new religious movements, the 'new age' or other alternative religions (e. g.,
Wicca, neo-Paganism) whose public profile belies the fact that only small frac-
tions of the population have any active involvement with them.[1]
    More recently, though, new possibilities have emerged for responding to
Luckmann's challenge to sociologists of religion, with the return to an interest
in theories of the sacred as a social phenomenon. For much of the twentieth century, the study of the sacred was framed by the work of scholars such as Rudolf
Otto (1923) and, most influentially, Mircea Eliade (1959), who argued that the 'sacred' referred both to a transcendent ontological reality and to the universal
human capacity to experience and represent this through common cultural
forms (i. e., myth, ritual, sacred space, cosmologies). The recent post-structuralist
and post-colonialist turn in the study of religion has led, however, to a sustained

---

1 For a fuller discussion of this, see Lynch 2007.

critique of this essentialised concept of the 'sacred', based partly on attempts to show how concepts in the study of religion more generally have emerged through a particular period of Western intellectual, cultural and political history (see e. g., King 1999; Fitzgerald 2000; Carrette 2007) as well as critiques of the political connotations of Eliade's views, which reference his early association with fascist politics in Romania (see e. g., McCutcheon 2003: 191–212). In the wake of this critique of Eliadean concepts of the sacred, there has been a growing interest in alternative ways of theorising the sacred, including the sacred as a boundary marker of identities and fundamental commitments (Anttonen 1999; Knott 2005), the sacred as that which is accorded ultimate value within a culture (Fitzgerald 2000, 2007) and the sacred as a powerful form of collective experience divorced from the framework of the cultural memory of traditional religions (Hervieu-Leger 2000). In the study of media and religion, the edited volume by Lundby, Summiala-Seppanen and Salokangas (2006) reflects the diverse ways in which the term 'sacred' is used in this field at the moment, from a synonym for 'religion', to denoting religious properties or significant moral commitments beyond institutional religion, to more developed theoretical accounts of the sacred in relation to cognition, emotion, collective identity and cultural practice.

Within this emerging field, the turn away from Eliade has created the conditions for a renewed interest in neo-Durkheimian understandings of the sacred. This theoretical tradition draws on the fundamental insights of Durkheim and Mauss' (1903) *Primitive Classification* and Durkheim's (1912) *The Elementary Forms of the Religious Life*, namely that the sacred (and its polluting profane) play a central role in structuring cultural systems of symbolic classification, and that representations of the sacred serve as focal points for the fusion of collective emotion, identity and moral community through the medium of meaningful and structured collective practices. Within the neo-Durkheimian tradition itself, there has been extensive critique of the limitations of the uses of Durkheim's work as a general theory of society (Alexander 1988b) in tending to emphasise social integration over conflict (Lukes 1975a), in failing to take account of the range of other, non-sacred forces in maintaining social bonds (Shils 1975) or indeed the evolutionary and ethnographic assumptions that underpin *Elementary Forms* (Lukes 1975b). At the same time, as this chapter will discuss, the emergence of a new approach to cultural sociology rooted in this Durkheimian tradition has made possible a theoretical account of the historically contingent nature of sacred forms; the relationships between the sacred, power, conflict and modern social institutions; the moral ambiguities of the sacred as a social force; and the place of the sacred within a wider theory of society. The aim of this chapter is to explore how a particular movement within cultural sociology – the 'strong program' – might support a constructive response to Luckmann's challenge by helping us to see the ways in which sacred forms intersect with media in contemporary society.[2]

1 The 'strong program' within cultural sociology

Over the past twenty years, 'cultural sociology' has become an increasingly significant sub-field within sociology, reflected in the growth of the culture section of the American Sociological Association becoming one of the largest sections in that organisation as well as the production of monographs, edited books and specialist journals (see Inglis et al. 2007 for an overview of these developments). The wider movement of cultural sociology includes a range of approaches, such as the sociological study of culture (in the sense of the defined social spheres such as media, the arts and creative industries) and the broader study of culture using existing sociological theories and methods. This has generated a range of theoretical and methodological perspectives on the sociological study of culture, including the ways in which cultural forms might be used to provide causal explanations of social life, such as Swidler's (1986) theory of 'strategies of action'. Within this broader interest in sociology and culture, a more specific body of work has developed which seeks to theorise the ways in which attention to cultural meaning might generate a distinctive approach to sociological analysis and interpretation.[3] The development of this 'strong program' of cultural sociology is particularly associated with the work of Jeffrey C. Alexander, as well as a network of other colleagues and former students of Alexander, focused around the Center for Cultural Sociology at Yale University (see Inglis et al. 2007; Cordero et al. 2008).

The 'strong program' is oriented around the claim that cultural meaning should not be seen as an epiphenomenon of an underlying 'reality' of social structures and material relations but as an 'independent variable' within socio-

---

2 In doing so, this chapter will bracket off discussion of another important academic trajectory in the discussion of media in relation to Durkheimian theory, namely the extensive discussion of media rituals set in motion by the work of Daniel Dayan and Elihu Katz (1992). For a discussion of the relevance of this literature for thinking about the performance and circulation of sacred forms through public media, see Lynch 2012.

3 Thus, whilst the 'strong program' shares Swidler's interest in the role of culture in sociological explanation, it diverges significantly from Swidler's primary focus on action (in which meaning and ideology is relatively untheorized) by focusing on the performance of cultural meaning-systems.

logical analysis. Culture is thus 'not a thing but a dimension, not an object to be studied as a dependent variable but a thread that runs through [...] every conceivable social form' (Alexander 2003: 7). Cultural meaning is therefore socially generative, shaping subjectivities, institutions, interactions and processes. One can therefore speak of the 'relative autonomy of culture' in the sense that culture is not simply determined by social structure; this autonomy is relative in that culture does not exist as free-floating symbolic systems or pure ideas, but always in relation to social and historical instances of agency, structure and practice (Alexander 2005: 21–3; Cordero et al. 2008: 527). The central aims of the 'strong program' include both the attempt to offer theoretical accounts of the role of meaning in social life and to provide empirical justification of the value of such theories for understanding the social. Beyond this, cultural sociology has also been presented as a form of 'cultural psychoanalysis', seeking to bring to awareness formative and deeply assumed cultural meanings: '[W]e must learn how [...] to reveal to men and women the myths that think them so that they can make up new myths in turn' (Alexander 2003: 4). To move beyond such cultural influences is never possible – social life is always conducted through meaning. But by being able to name these influences, the strong program seeks to identify the operative cultural structures that shape social life, better understanding both the implications when these are shattered through collective trauma and their role in social conflict as well as helping 'groups and actors separate themselves from an unthinking fusion with social performances' (Cordero et al. 2008: 528). The influence of semiotics, structuralism and post-structuralism on the 'strong program' is evident in its framing of culture in terms of language and text. Cultural sociology thus moves from a Parsonian emphasis on 'values' – critiqued as having limited explanatory value for understanding culture and society (Cordero 2008: 525; see also Swidler 1986) – to thinking of culture in terms of texts, constructed on the basis of wider symbolic codes (typically organised along lines of binary opposition). Such codes do not have any meaningful existence as disembodied symbol-systems but become social phenomena through their embodied performance by social actors. As such, these texts and codes are always historically situated, formed and performed in the context of particular social structures, conditions and processes. These cultural meanings are not immutable, but rather they are 'shifting cultural constructions' subject to the means of symbolic production which are 'fatefully affected by the power and identity of the agents in charge, by the competition for symbolic control, and the structures of power and distribution of resources' (Alexander 2003: 33). The task of cultural sociology then becomes to understand the cultural texts and codes that shape social life, thinking about these not in simplistically causal terms but in terms of their significance for interpreting structures, subjectivities, practices and processes within particular social contexts.

Although the 'strong program' bears the influence of a range of theoretical sources,[4] the later work of Emile Durkheim, from *Primitive Classification* and *The Elementary Forms of the Religious Life* onwards, remains of fundamental importance. In part, this Durkheimian legacy is rooted in the claim that Ferdinand de Saussure attended some of Durkheim's lectures on systems of classification around the time that he was beginning the work that later became known as the *Course in General Linguistics* (Smith and Alexander 2005). Durkheim and Mauss' interest in classificatory systems is thus seen as one source that fed the Saussurian linguistics which played a foundational role in the development of semiotics and structuralism. But more specifically, Durkheim's later interest in the sacred plays an important role for much work done through the 'strong program'. As Alexander (1988a: 3) wrote in the introduction to an important early collection of essays in cultural sociology:

> In a series of profound and probing discussions of education, politics, professional organization, morality and the law, Durkheim demonstrated that these modern spheres must be studied in terms of symbolic classifications. They are structured by tensions between the fields of the sacred and the profane; their central processes are ritualistic; their most significant structural dynamics concern the construction and destruction of social solidarities.

Although explicit reference to the sacred has become less evident in Alexander's most recent work – such as his major re-theorising of civil society, *The Civil Sphere* (Alexander 2006a) – this is not because the concept has become less important in his work. Rather it has become an increasingly assumed part of his theoretical work, evident in the gravitational pull that it exerts on other related concepts such as justice, social solidarity, pollution and the definition of exclusionary social and moral boundaries.

---

4 Alexander has cited the influential role that the symbolic anthropology of Clifford Geertz, Mary Douglas and Victor Turner played in his development of cultural sociology, an influence to which he became more open in the 1980s through the structuralist and semiotic theories of Claude Levi-Strauss, Roland Barthes and Marshall Sahlins (Cordero et al. 2008: 524–5). In addition to this, Alexander has also had a long-standing interest in the relationship between macro-level structures and micro-level practices and interactions, led by his engagement with symbolic interactionism and ethnomethodology (see e.g., Alexander 1988c; Cordero et al. 2008: 526). He has, however, been critical of the uses of the latter in sociology in ways that emphasise pragmatic, instrumental and individualist uses of culture, and which fail to recognise the influence of broader cultural meanings in shaping practice. Instead, he has turned to performance theory as a way of thinking about the enactment of culture (Alexander et al., 2006).

2 The concept of the sacred within the 'strong program'

In the context of Luckmann's call for sociologists of religion to attend to operative forms of meaning in contemporary society, the 'strong program' offers important theoretical insights into the nature of the sacred as a social phenomenon. Four points will be noted here.

Firstly, the sacred becomes a focal point in the structuring of cultural systems of meaning. There is, unlike Eliade, no notion here of a transcendent ontological reality, but rather the sacred is a type of signifier (or signification) associated with forms that are regarded as profound sources of meaning, truth, value or power within a particular cultural system. The content of what is regarded as sacred can therefore vary across and within societies, and as we shall note below, cultural forms can be subject to historically contingent processes of both sacralisation and de-sacralisation. The signifier of the sacred simultaneously constructs its other, the 'profane', a context-specific vision of the evil that threatens or pollutes the sacred form. Indeed sacred forms, which are often deeply assumed parts of cultural life, may come into consciousness particularly at moments when there is some kind of polluting breach of that form. Such pollution of the sacred is typically experienced as a painful wound, eliciting powerful, collective emotion and generating a desire for some form of restitution. The sacred and the profane therefore underpin cultural systems of classification, providing emotionally charged orientation towards constructions of good and evil in ways that shape interactions between individuals, groups and institutions. Whilst recognising the sociological significance of the cultural construction of the sacred, the 'strong program' does not make this the entire basis of its social analysis. Alexander has, for example, been critical of the idea that Durkheim's later interest in the sacred provides an adequate general theory of society and has argued instead that it is better understood as a 'special theory referring to specified kinds of empirical process' (Alexander 1988b: 190–191). There are, for example, other forces which hold societies together, such as the mundane influences of friendship, habit, the logics of local practices and assumed ties of kinship and nation (see e.g., Shils 1975).[5] The operation of the sacred also needs to be understood within a wider theory of society, in which due attention is given to issues of power, stratification and social differentiation, as discussed further below (see Alexander 2005). But within this wider context, the concept of

---

5 Nonetheless, such mundane ties can be problematic, in Alexander's view, when they establish hierarchies and exclusions that impede the extension of social solidarity (2006: 195).

the sacred provides a useful means for thinking about operative forms of meaning. Unlike notions of 'values', which appear to operate as a consistent and stable back-drop to social action, the concept of the sacred potentially provides a better framework for thinking about how the celebration and pollution of sacred forms gets acted out through particular social narratives and dramas, eliciting powerful emotional and collective responses at specific moments and generating complex subjectivities and social interactions. The recognition of the simultaneous presence of sacred forms in contemporary society also makes it possible to think about how these generate complex negotiations within the individual and between groups. It offers a way of thinking about both significant meanings operative at moments of particular cultural intensity and the ways in which these meanings are performed through particular ways of thinking, feeling and acting. As such, it adds considerable sociological texture to the more general concept of meaning used by Luckmann in *The Invisible Religion*.

Secondly, forms of the sacred are historically contingent. What is taken to be sacred in a given cultural context changes through time, through a process of interaction between social agents, operations of power, regulative and communicative institutions, social movements and wider social conditions. The historical contingency of sacred forms had been earlier recognised by Edward Shils (1975), who noted that the sacred significance of the coronation of Queen Elizabeth II was dependent upon the specific social conditions of a collectively oriented British society still deeply formed by the experience of the Second World War. Robert Bellah's (1967) notion of civil religion similarly recognised the historical particularity of the sacralisation of a particular vision of nationhood in the conditions of the formation of modern republics such as the United States and revolutionary France (see also Hunt 1988). Within the 'strong program', however, there has been more sustained attention to the ways in which sacred forms change through time. Particularly influential in this regard has been Alexander's discussion of the emergence of the Holocaust as a sacred moral symbol (Alexander 2003, 2009). In this, he describes a process which took place over a period of years following the liberation of the concentration camps in 1945, in which the weakening of anti-Semitism in Western culture allowed for greater identification with the Jews as human victims of the Holocaust and the emergence of the Holocaust as a unique cultural symbol of moral evil, compared to its initial framing as just one more war crime commissioned through the evil of German nationalism. Attention to the historical conditions through which particular sacred forms attract broader identification and come to shape social life thus represents an important part of the 'strong program's' treatment of the sacred. Inviting more collaborative work with social and cultural historians, such a focus may also help us to understand instances in which the relative power of different sacred forms changes over time within a given social context. One important such case is the ongoing controversy over the abuse and neglect of children in Catholic institutions in Ireland, which reflects the waning of forms of the sacred associated with the Catholic church in relation to the growing cultural influence of the sacralisation of the care of children through the twentieth century (see Zelizer 1985). Such historical sensitivity produces a more dynamic understanding of the sacred and social change than the more static understandings of meaning and value offered by Bourdieusian notions of habitus.

Thirdly, the 'strong program' recognises that the sacred is a morally and socially ambiguous force. The colloquial use of the 'sacred' as a synonym for religion and the Eliadean notion of a sacred ontological reality have tended to reinforce an implicit normative association between the sacred and the good. Even in Robert Bellah's work on civil religion there is an elision between the sacred and the normative good. Despite his early recognition of the possibilities for the discourses of civil religion to be used to legitimate the evils of American imperialism, Bellah remained convinced that civil religion at its best 'is a genuine apprehension of universal and transcendent religious reality as seen in or, one could almost say, as revealed through the experience of the American people' (Bellah, 1967: 12). The association of civil religion with morally repugnant practices was understood by Bellah either in terms of the 'demonic distortions' (Bellah 1967: 12) of its pure moral vision or the tragic structural failure of American society to live up to its high democratic vision (Bellah 1992: 184). The 'strong program' adopts a more critical stance than this. In general, the sacred is used as a descriptive category that does not carry intrinsic normative implications. Nazi anti-Semitism can, for example, be understood in terms of the operation of a particular sacred vision of the German nation and *Volk*. More specifically, though, there is recognition within the 'strong program' that the structural properties of sacred forms render them morally ambiguous. In his recent work on the civil sphere, for example, Alexander (2006a) argues that civil society is structured around cultural symbol-systems that define who is to be treated as a full person and citizen. Sacred visions of the 'public' which provide the symbolic content of civil society are, like any sacred signifier, constituted on the basis of the binary opposition of the polluting profane. At the same time as they enable moral and collective identification – the experience of solidarity – in the civil sphere, sacred visions of the public exclude individuals, groups and traits identified as profane. Civil society is therefore always grounded in practices of inclusion and exclusion, which have typically been accentuated in relation to the imagined collectivity of the nation-state (Alexander, 2006a: 196 – 8). The normative project of the 'strong program's' construction of the civil sphere is therefore always to be attentive to these processes of exclusion and to seek the extension of social solidarity. But a purely inclusive civil society is never possible, because the inclusive properties of sacred identifications on which the symbolic construction of the 'public' rests, and upon which the moral solidarity of the civil sphere depends, are structurally inseparable from their exclusion of the profane. As Alexander (2006a: 84) puts it, '[D]ichotomous evaluations of persons and events continue to be made, for pollution and purification are structural features of civil society as such'. There is, then, an irresolvable tension between the cultural role of sacred forms for collective and moral identification and the aspiration for an inclusive, global civil society. Whilst we might celebrate the extension of social solidarity represented, for example, by the women's movement or the civil rights movement for African-Americans, processes of exclusion inevitably remain intact, suggesting a fundamentally tragic propensity for conflict in human society. At its worst, the exclusionary nature of sacred forms means that 'civil society is, at its very origins, fragmented and distorted in what are often the most heinous ways' (Alexander 2006a: 202).

Fourthly, the 'strong program' uses the concept of the sacred in the context of a wider theory of society. As we have noted, Alexander sees the sacred construction of the public as central to the symbolic content of civil society. This observation functions within a broader theoretical understanding of the civil sphere as both symbolic and performed in relation to regulative institutions (i.e., the legal system and political structures) and communicative institutions (i.e., media and voluntary associations) in ways that are sedimented through time, space and social stratification in particular physical, cultural and social contexts (Alexander 2006a: 69–212). Beyond these institutions of civil society lie a range of 'non-civil' spheres – economics, science, religion, the family – which both challenge and are challenged by the symbolic performances of inclusion and exclusion within the civil sphere, and which also carry their own specific constructions of the sacred (e.g., the sacred as constructed in the symbol-systems of particular religious groups). Within this framework, social movements act as carriers of change in the civil sphere, mobilising in ways that provide a critical focus on injustices bound up with processes of symbolic exclusion or draw on expanded notions of solidarity in the civil sphere to critique injustice in non-civil spheres such as economic or domestic relations. Whilst still the subject of critical discussion and empirical exploration, Alexander's theory of civil society does important work in retrieving and defining the civil sphere as a relatively autonomous dimension of society, providing a framework for thinking about the nature of justice in real societies as opposed to the imagined social relations in the work of political philosophers such as Habermas and Rawls. More specifically, it situates an understanding of the sacred in relation to a broader theory of differentiated social institutions and social change in ways that may prove valuable for understanding the interaction of multiple sacred forms in complex modern societies.

3 The 'strong program' and the mediation of the sacred

Part of the challenge that Luckmann presented to sociologists of religion in *The Invisible Religion* was to revise the institutional focus of their work, to shift beyond the traditional interest in church, synagogue, mosque and temple, to think about a wider array of institutional structures through which significant contemporary meanings are mediated. The 'strong program', through its attention to the relationship between cultural meaning and broader social structures, provides one framework for developing this task. In particular, the 'strong program' has given sustained attention to the role of public media in this regard. In *The Civil Sphere*, for example, Alexander (2006a: 75–84) discusses both the role of fictional entertainment media and factual news media in the circulation of symbols and narratives which construct good and evil, and thus the boundaries of inclusion and exclusion, in particular civil societies. Fictional media, he suggests, have the potential both to circulate such categories in banal, assumed ways (for example, through representations of gender, sexuality and ethnicity in television sit-coms) as well as the capacity to generate narratives that powerfully dramatise the injustice of particular forms of exclusion in ways that can mobilise wider social movements (such as the role of Harriet Beecher Stowe's *Uncle Tom's Cabin* in mobilising support for the abolitionist movement). Factual media, whilst typically claiming an impartial perspective on actual events, are also involved in a fundamentally interpretative exercise, according to Alexander. Their roles in circulating symbols of the sacred and the profane are particularly important, given the role of news media as primary sources of everyday social knowledge. 'For most members of civil society, and even for members of its institutional elites, the news is the only source of firsthand experience they will ever have about their fellow citizens, about their motives for acting the way they do, the kinds of relationships they form, and the nature of the institutions they might potentially create' (2006a: 80). The immediacy and 'reality' of events to which news media refer can make the framing of these events in terms of the sacred and profane codes of a society particularly influential in evoking immediate responses from their audiences and stimulating broader social and political action. This is particularly the case given that dramatic breaches of sacred forms (such as the abuse of children, the denial of human rights or the undermining of democracy) are precisely those kinds of events that may be considered newsworthy.[6]

Beyond this broad interest in public and social media as a central structure for the circulation and negotiation of cultural meaning, the 'strong program' has also conceived of media in two more specific ways in relation to sacred forms. Firstly, within the recent turn to performance theory in the work of Alexander and others (Alexander et al. 2006), media are understood as playing a central role in the staging and circulation of sacred drama. This dramaturgical understanding of the performance of the sacred makes analogical use of the notion of scripts (cultural codes constructed around the sacred/profane), directors (elites seeking to shape codes or construct particular narratives through them), actors (the social agents drawn into the enactment of the sacred drama) and mis-en-scene (the particular social setting in which the drama is enacted). The public effects of such performances of the sacred are inseparable from their dissemination through media. For example, Alexander (2006b) discusses the attacks of 9/11 in terms of a drama enacted in relation to the construction of the sacred within a particular Islamist ideology, directed by influential figures within Islamist networks, enacted through the social agents of the attackers, their victims and a wider public audience, and staged at the particular sites of the attack. The symbolic force of this event was inseparable from the media coverage of the attack, a point of which the directors of the attack were well aware. Similarly, the sacred 'counter-performance' staged in identification with the victims through public speeches, vigils, charitable collections and re-telling of accounts of the attacks (including the recorded phone messages left by those trapped in the Twin Towers) was enacted and made possible through public media across the world. The performance of sacred dramas through public media in late modern society is not, however, uncomplicated. As Dayan (2010) and Katz (Katz and Liebes 2010) later acknowledged in relation to their theory of media rituals, audiences in pluralist and culturally reflexive societies are more likely to engage with such

---

6 The 'strong program's' recognition of the importance of public media in the circulation of sacred symbols has meant that case studies within this approach have often used media texts as data (Alexander 1990, 2009; Eyerman, 2008). One of the most detailed studies of public media within this approach has been Ronald Jacobs' (2000) *Race, Media and the Crisis of Civil Society*, which uses an analysis of African-American newspapers to demonstrate the role of such specialist news media in circulating the social interpretation of black writers and commentators whose views are rarely heard within a racially stratified society and media. Through his detailed analysis of media representation of the Watts uprising and the Rodney King case, Jacobs also demonstrates how the circulation of cultural meanings is tied not only to racial and class stratification but to physical and imagined geographies, the economics of the media industry and the practices and technologies of media professionals.

presentations of sacred drama in critical or detached ways. Alexander (2006b: 96) therefore argues that such reflexivity and plurality makes it difficult for any public performance of the sacred not to evoke scepticism from sections of its public audience who regard it as inauthentic, instrumental or based on an inadequate form of the sacred. Ritual leaders are no longer the 'unproblematic, authoritative disseminators of meaning that they were in the past' (Alexander and Mast 2006: 15). Such scepticism towards the performance of sacred drama through media is, in part, related to the media's own deconstruction of such dramas; the royal wedding of Charles and Diana (taken as an exemplary media ritual by Dayan and Katz) was, as we know, later followed by Martin Bashir's television interview with Diana, which presented a very different account of the marriage to its earlier, fairy-tale construction. It is also, to some degree, a result of the increasing segmentation of public media which makes possible a wide range of performances and critiques of different sacred drama. Audiences may prefer media that respect their sacred commitments – whether *The Guardian* or Fox News. But identification with a given sacred drama loses its taken-for-grantedness in social contexts in which many different sacred performances are enacted and forms of the sacred are plural and contested. In such a context, 'participation in, and acceptance of, ritual messages, are more a matter of choice than obligation' (Alexander and Mast 2006: 17).

A second important role for public media in relation to the sacred identified within the 'strong program' is that of the media acting as a structure for restitution of breaches of the sacred. A seminal discussion of this within the literature is Alexander's analysis of the role of the media in relation to the Watergate scandal (Alexander 1988b; 2003: 155–59; Alexander and Jacobs 1998). Here Alexander argues, with reference to a range of polling data, that public reaction to the Watergate break-in in June 1972 was relatively muted and, six months after the break-in, most Americans did not regard it as a crisis or believe that it had influenced their vote in the elections that year. Within two years, however, Watergate had become a deep crisis in American political and cultural life, leading to the eventual and unprecedented decision of the incumbent President, Richard Nixon, to resign. The capacity of Watergate to acquire the symbolic status of a crisis depended on a range of historically contingent factors (including the appeal of a new centrist rhetoric in the wake of the decisive defeat of the Left in the 1972 Presidential election and the post-election mobilisation of cultural elites previously alienated in Nixon's first term of office). But it was the live televising of the Senate Select Committee's hearings on Watergate that proved decisive in engaging a wider public audience in a drama in which the sacrality of American democracy had been polluted by the actions of Nixon and his political associates. Within the first two months of the televising of the hearings, the number of Americans regarding Watergate as a crisis significantly increased. In this context, then, public media, in collaboration with a coalition of political and cultural elites, functioned as a 'counter-centre' of the sacred, a structure through which it was possible to critique the breach of the sacred in other central institutions.[7]

Within the 'strong program', this case has been interpreted as illustrating the broader capacity of public media to critique breaches of the sacred in other areas of social life and potentially to provide means for restitution of this breach, or 'civil repair' (Alexander and Jacobs 1998; Jacobs 2000). Recent examples of public media acting in this way include media coverage of the expenses scandal involving British politicians in 2009, the ongoing role of public media since the 1990s in circulating stories about the physical and sexual abuse of children within Catholic institutions and even the global controversy sparked by Jade Goody's racist bullying of Shilpa Shetty on the UK's *Celebrity Big Brother*. Such a capacity for critique is increasingly understood, implicitly or explicitly, as an important element of news journalism by media professionals inspired by Murrow[8] and Woodward and Bernstein,[9] who conceive of their work as being honest brokers in holding other social actors to account for the breach of the sacred. Such an understanding of the media has been critiqued in terms of the way in which the media is accorded the status of giving privileged access and insights into the sacred centre of society (Couldry 2003). In pluralist societies, the tensions that broadcasters face between reproducing particular sacred forms and maintaining impartiality also generates controversy when their news coverage represents breaches of the sacred, but the broadcaster pulls back from supporting symbolic restitution (as illustrated in public anger over the decision by the

---

7 This notion of the 'counter-centre' was developed by Alexander in relation to Edward Shils' (1975) understanding of the relationship between the sacred (as a 'central values system') and key social institutions – where this association between the sacred and powerful social institutions created a symbiotic relationship of mutual legitimation and aura. Shils argued, however, that the routinisation of institutional life could produce a widening gap between institutional norms and practices and central sacred forms, leaving them vulnerable to others able to utilise the symbolism of those sacred forms to fashion a radical institutional and social critique.

8 Edward R. Murrow's television program on CBS in 1954 is seen as significantly contributing to the end of Senator Joseph R. McCarthy's communist witch-hunt in the USA (Hilliard and Keith 2005; see also CBS 1954).

9 Famous for the Watergate investigations from 1972–1976, the *Washington Post*'s Bob Woodward and Carl Bernstein brought to light a system of political 'dirty tricks' and crimes that led to the conviction of dozens of Republican party officials, including White House employees, and eventually to the resignation of President Richard Nixon (see Gettlin and Colodny 1991; Kutler 1997).

BBC not to broadcast a humanitarian appeal for those in Gaza during Israel's military assault in 2008/9; see Lynch 2012). Nevertheless, despite occasions when the media themselves become tainted by the pollution of the sacred, public media continue to be constructed both by media professionals and their audiences as counter-centres of the sacred at moments of political and cultural crisis. This role means that public media can reasonably be claimed to be a primary social institution engaged in the reproduction, celebration and contestation of sacred forms in late modern society.

4 The media, the sacred and the 'strong program': a critical evaluation

The 'strong program' therefore gives substance to Luckmann's (1967) claim that we should attend to the role of a much wider range of social institutions, beyond traditional religious structures, when thinking about the circulation of operative forms of meaning and significance. In particular, the 'strong program' provides a heuristic framework for thinking about the role of public media and sacred forms in ways that may help to interpret the intersections between cultural meanings, social agents, historical-contingency, the media and other institutions in the context of pluralist and stratified societies. In doing so, it provides a more theoretically advanced, and sociologically situated understanding of the sacred than that offered by those working within the post-Eliadean recovery of the sacred within the study of religion.

Whilst the theoretical development and heuristic value of the 'strong program's' understanding of media and the sacred are to be welcomed, a number of areas for critical reflection remain within this approach. Two particular issues will be noted here.

Firstly, there is some slippage in terms of the way in which the 'sacred' is used within the 'strong program'. At times, it is clearly used as a 'special theory referring to specified kinds of empirical process' (Alexander 1988b: 190), in which there is a fusion of classificatory categories, collective emotion and identification, moral sentiment and meaningful (ritualised) practice. Alexander's analysis of the response to the Watergate scandal and the emergence of the moral symbolism of the Holocaust are clear examples of this, situating sacred processes in historically situated empirical cases. At other points, however, the sacred is used in a far more limited, semiotic way, to refer to that which acquires sacred signification within a given system of cultural meanings – for example,

Alexander's (1990) semiotic analysis of the media construction of information technology in terms of the sacred and profane. Whilst both uses of the sacred are clearly meaningful within the interpretative project of the 'strong program', the problem with the latter, purely semiotic usage is that it can lead to the 'sacred' being treated simply as a synonym for the 'good'. Aside from Durkheim's observation that the distinction between the sacred and the profane is far more radical than the separation between good and bad, to treat the sacred simply as synonymous with the good is largely to empty its value as an analytical concept. The heuristic usefulness of the way in which the sacred has been thought about within the 'strong program' is precisely in its ability to make connections between cognition, moral sentiment, collectivities and practices in ways that help us to make sense of specific social interactions and processes. The concept of pollution and the ways in which the breach of the sacred is represented also provide a framework for thinking about interactions between symbols, emotion, institutions and action. The emphasis on cultural meaning within the 'strong program' distinguishes its contribution to sociological research, but the concept of the sacred functions most effectively within this approach when it is understood very specifically as a particular form of cultural meaning, associated with empirically-observable processes.

A more general problem here, though, is what criteria one uses to define whether a given cultural form should be considered sacred or not. Can 'nature' be considered a sacred form in contemporary society? The nation-state? The 'self' (and if so, the self in what regard)? Can gender categories be seen as invested with sacred significance? Is the family a sacred form, or more specifically the care and nurture of children? It is such apparent difficulty in defining the criteria for what constitutes a 'sacred' form that leads Hervieu-Leger (2000) to declare the sacred to be an impossible concept, unhelpful for sociological analysis because its applicability to specific social phenomena appears to lie entirely in the eye of the beholder. In one sense, such objections can overreach themselves. We can think, for example, about the sacred in terms of the particular *intensity* of the nexus of meaning, emotion, collectivity and action. To suggest, for example, that football teams represent sacred forms is unconvincing in this regard. People may kill for the nation-state or in response to the experience of the transgression of gender categories. People do not typically kill for their football team. I can experience profound shock and disgust at an account of the physical abuse of a child, but I would feel no sense of violation or pollution if someone were to dig up the turf in my team's stadium or even assault one of the players. Whilst this property of intensity is not something amenable to objective measurement – given that it is experienced through emotional structures that are culturally and historically specific, rather than immutable social realities – it is nevertheless one indicator of the kind of phenomena that we might think of as sacred. Furthermore, there is a sense in which such intensity is also necessarily associated with the subjectivity of the concept. When I have heard researchers from other countries present studies on sacred forms or moments in their cultures – for example, on media coverage of the murder of Anna Lindh in Sweden or the killing in China of a working-class student from a poor background as a result of careless driving by a young man from the new economic elite – I have been struck that there is an emotional content to these narratives which I can understand but do not experience as directly as the researchers themselves. Similarly, when talking to other researchers, our awareness of sacred moments in our own cultures is often tied to instances where we felt compelled to feel or act in extra-mundane ways – to grieve the loss of a public figure, or to engage in public protest at some instance of the violation of human rights. There is a sense in which an appreciation of sacred forms can involve a researcher's own emotional identification with those forms. This is not to say that the sacred is whatever a researcher wants to call the sacred. Rather, the researcher's own awareness of his or her cognitive, emotional, embodied response to particular social phenomena can provide evidence of the intensity that marks sacred forms which, when triangulated with other accounts or performances of such intense identification, may provide stronger grounds for using the concept of the sacred. This is, though, an initial proposal, and defining the criteria for identifying sacred forms will remain an ongoing task for the 'strong program'.

A second issue for critical reflection is the extent to which the 'strong program' takes adequate account of issues of aesthetics, materiality and embodiment. In its more strongly semiotic forms of expression, the 'strong program' risks reducing social interaction to a range of linguistic and textual concepts: code, symbol, langue, parole, text, script, binary distinction. Whilst supporting analysis of the content of cultural meanings present in a given situation, such linguistically derived concepts do not necessarily help to make connections between cultural meanings and subjectivity, materiality, embodiment or action. The use of performance theory has provided one way of thinking about the ways in which cultural texts are enacted, as has the use within the 'strong program' of speech-act theory. But there is scope for expanding an appreciation of the aesthetic and material within cultural sociology beyond this. Alexander has recently started to address this issue through developing the concept of 'iconic consciousness', which occurs when 'an aesthetically shaped materiality signifies social value', generating 'understanding by feeling, by evidence of the senses rather than the mind' (2008: 782). From this perspective, cultural signifiers are extended beyond the linguistic/cognitive to allow for the possibility of the experience of cultural meaning through aesthetic processes. Such processes do not reflect a deep engagement with the essence of material objects themselves in a Heideggerian sense, but rather 'the aesthetic construction of material surfaces and their experience via feeling consciousness' (Alexander 2008: 783). The aesthetic meaning of an object is not simply inherent in the materiality of the object itself but in the ways in which it is experienced aesthetically through cultural frameworks of meaning. Importantly, Alexander's position moves beyond an instrumental understanding of the material object as a carrier of pre-determined cultural meanings and recognises the ways in which cultural meanings themselves are always implicated in the qualities of particular material objects and sensuous forms of engagement with them. Whilst this represents a significant development in attempting to move beyond semiotics' relative failure to address the material and the aesthetic, there are still areas of ambiguity in Alexander's discussion. The use of the sacred/profane cultural binary is reflected in his tendency to use similar, generalised, aesthetic categories – the beautiful, the sublime, the banal. But, given his recognition of the specificities of material forms and aesthetic regimes, it would seem more profitable to make use of concepts from the study of religious mediation, such as the 'sacred gaze' (Morgan 2005) or 'sensational forms' (Meyer 2008), which provide a more flexible structure for thinking about how particular experiences of the sacred are implicated in particular cultural traditions, aesthetic practices and the material properties of media. Alexander is also cautious about placing too much emphasis on the effects of the material in structuring culture, reflecting the strong aversion to materialist theories of society within the strong program. He has, for example, argued that actor-network theory has little to offer cultural sociology because 'its ontology is relentlessly material [and] there is no symbolic imagining to speak of' (Alexander 2008: 783), rejecting it because of its over-emphasis on the concrete, pragmatics and immediate experience. But there is scope for asking whether this rejection is too strong. Could it be conceded that the nature and performance of sacred forms are shaped by the materiality of spaces, objects and technologies – not in a deterministic way, but in terms of the affordances that those material forms make possible? One example of such influence can be found in Jacobs' *Race, Media and the Crisis of Civil Society*, in which he argues that part of the reason for the ongoing marginalisation of the African-American press (and thus of cultural meanings grounded in the experience of black communities in America) relates to the information technology used by journalists. In a media age of tight copy deadlines, information technology is an essential journalistic tool for accessing data needed for a story, including previous stories published in the press. One of the main databases that support the search of media archives is *Lexis-Nexis*, which makes possible a range of different kinds of searches across thousands of news print media. African-American newspapers are not included in the *Lexis-Nexis* database, however, which means that the use of this very convenient data source by journalists in major commercial newspapers recursively reproduces the exclusion of black perspectives already reinforced by other sources of racial stratification. Although not simply determining the way cultural meanings circulate by itself, *Lexis-Nexis* as a technology embedded in a particular kind of cultural practice is implicated in the shape taken by such patterns of circulation. More generally, then, we might ask what role the affordances of different media play in the ways in which the sacred is encountered, celebrated, or contested in contemporary society. Alexander's emphasis on cultural meaning leads him only to acknowledge the 'illusion' of the agency of material objects at this point (Alexander 2008: 784), but the 'strong program' could reasonably expand its sense of the material and aesthetic further to allow that cultural meanings – and sacred forms – emerge in the context of fields of agency in which social actors, cultural symbols, material objects and aesthetic regimes all interact to shape the nature and significance of the mediated sacred (see Schofield Clark 2009; Miller 2010: 110–34).[10] Such attention to the material and the aesthetic has the potential both to add greater ethnographic richness to the ways in which the 'strong program' understands the relationship between cultural meaning and the practices of social life and to move beyond thinking about the representation of sacred forms in media texts to thinking about the experience of the sacred in the embodied and aesthetic uses of media.

References

Alexander, James C. 1988a. "Introduction: Durkheimian sociology and cultural studies today." In *Durkheimian Sociology: Cultural Studies*, edited by J.C. Alexander, 1–22. Cambridge: Cambridge University Press.

–. 1988b. "Culture and political crisis: 'Watergate' and Durkheimian sociology." In *Durkheimian Sociology: Cultural Studies*, edited by J.C. Alexander, 187–224. Cambridge: Cambridge University Press.

–. 1988c. *Action and Its Environments: Towards a New Synthesis*. New York: Columbia University Press.

–. 1990. "The sacred and profane information machine: Discourse about the computer as ideology." *Archives de Sciences Sociales des Religions* 69 (1): 161–171.

---

10 This would fit within the emphasis on multi-dimensionality in Alexander's social theory (see e.g., Alexander 2005: 22): 'The ambition of my cultural sociology has been to [...] provide the internal architecture of social meaning via concepts of code, narrative and symbolic action, so that culture can finally assume its rightful place as equivalent to, and interpenetrated with, other kinds of structuring social force'.

–. 2003. *The Meanings of Social Life: A Cultural Sociology.* New York: Oxford University Press.

–. 2005. "Why cultural sociology is not 'idealist': A reply to McLennan." *Theory, Culture and Society* 22 (6): 19–29.

–. 2006a. *The Civil Sphere.* Oxford: Oxford University Press.

–. 2006b. "From the depths of despair: Performance, counter-performance and 'September 11.'" In *Social Performance: Symbolic Action, Cultural Pragmatics, Ritual*, edited by J.C. Alexander, B. Giesen, and J. Mast, 91–114. Cambridge: Cambridge University Press.

–. 2008. "Iconic consciousness: The material feeling of meaning." *Environment and Planning D: Society and Space* 26: 782–94.

–. 2009. *Remembering the Holocaust: A Debate.* New York: Oxford University Press.

Alexander, James C., and R. Jacobs. 1998. "Mass communication, ritual and civil society." In *Media, Ritual and Identity*, edited by T. Liebes and J. Curran, 23–41. London: Routledge.

Alexander, James C., B. Giesen, and J. Mast. 2006. *Social Performance: Symbolic Action, Cultural Pragmatics and Ritual.* Cambridge: Cambridge University Press.

Alexander, James C., and Mast, J. 2006. "Introduction: Symbolic action in theory and practice: The cultural pragmatics of cultural action." In *Social Performance: Symbolic Action, Cultural Pragmatics, Ritual*, edited by J.C. Alexander, B. Giesen, and J. Mast, 1–28. Cambridge: Cambridge University Press.

Anttonen, Veikko. 1999. "Sacred." In *Guide to the Study of Religion*, edited by R. McCutcheon and W. Braun, 271–282. London: Continuum.

Bellah, Robert N. 1967. "Civil religion in America." *Daedalus* 96 (1): 1–21.

–. 1992. *The Broken Covenant: American Civil Religion in Time of Trial.* Chicago: University of Chicago Press.

Carrette, Jeremy. 2007. *Religion and Critical Psychology: Religious Experience in the Knowledge Economy.* London: Routledge.

CBS. 1954. "A Report on Senator Joseph R. McCarthy". *See It Now* March 9, 1954. Available at: http://www.lib.berkeley.edu/MRC/murrowmccarthy.html.

Cordero, Rodrigo, F. Carballo and J. Ossandon. 2008. "Performing cultural sociology: A conversation with Jeffrey Alexander." *European Journal of Social Theory* 11 (4): 523–42.

Couldry, Nick. 2003. *Media Rituals: A Critical Approach.* London: Routledge.

Dayan, Daniel. 2010. "Beyond media events: Disenchantment, derailment, disruption." In *Media Events in a Global Age*, edited by N. Couldry, A. Hepp, and F. Krotz, 23–31. London: Routledge.

Dayan, Daniel, and E. Katz. 1992. *Media Events: The Live Broadcasting of History.* Cambridge, MA: Harvard University Press.

Durkheim, Émile. 1912. *The Elementary Forms of Religious Forms.* Oxford: Oxford University Press.

Durkheim, Émile, and M. Mauss. 1903. *Primitive Classification.* Chicago: University of Chicago Press.

Eliade, Mircea. 1959. *The Sacred and the Profane.* New York: Harcourt.

Eyerman, Ron. 2008. *The Assassination of Theo van Gogh: From Social Drama to Cultural Trauma.* Durham, NC: Duke University Press.

Fitzgerald, Timothy. 2000. *The Ideology of Religious Studies.* New York: Oxford University Press.

–. 2007. *Discourse on Civility and Barbarity: A Critical History of Religion and Related Categories.* New York: Oxford University Press.

Gettlin, Robert, and Len Colodny. 1991. *Silent Coup: The removal of a President*. New York: St. Martin's Press.

Hervieu-Leger, Daniele. 2000. *Religion as a Chain of Memory*. Cambridge: Polity.

Hilliard, Robert L., and Michael C. Keith. 2005. *The Broadcast Century and Beyond*. Burlington, MA: Focus Press. 4th edition.

Hunt, Lynn. 1988. "The sacred and the French Revolution." In *Durkheimian Sociology: Cultural Studies*, edited by J.C. Alexander, 25–43. Cambridge: Cambridge University Press.

Inglis, David., A. Blaikie, and R. Wagner-Pacifici. 2007. "Editorial: Sociology, culture and the twenty-first century." *Cultural Sociology* 1 (1): 5–22.

Jacobs, Ronald. 2000. *Race, Media and the Crisis of Civil Society: From Watts to Rodney King*. Cambridge: Cambridge University Press.

Katz, Elihu, and T. Liebes. 2010. "'No more peace!' How disaster, terror and war have upstaged media events." In *Media Events in a Global Age*, edited by N. Couldry, A. Hepp, and F. Krotz, 32–42. London: Routledge.

King, Richard. 1999. *Orientalism and Religion: Post-Colonial Theory, India and the 'Mystic East'*. London: Routledge.

Knott, Kim. 2005. *The Location of Religion: A Spatial Analysis*. London: Equinox.

Kutler, Stanley. 1997. *Abuse of Power*. New York: Free Press.

Luckmann, Thomas. 1967. *The Invisible Religion*. London: MacMillan.

Lukes, Steven. 1975a. "Political ritual and social integration." *Sociology* 9 (2): 289–308.

–. 1975b. *Emile Durkheim: His Life and Work*. London: Penguin.

Lundby, Knut, J. Summiala-Seppanen, and R. Salokangas. 2006. *Implications of the Sacred in (Post)Modern Media*. Oslo: Nordicom.

Lynch, Gordon. 2007. *The New Spirituality: An Introduction to Progressive Belief in the Twenty-First Century*. London: IB Tauris.

–. 2012. *The Sacred in the Modern World*. Oxford: Oxford University Press.

McCutcheon, Russell T. 2003. *The Discipline of Religion: Structure, Meaning, Rhetoric*. London: Routledge.

Meyer, Birgit. 2008. "Religious sensations: Why media, aesthetics and power matter in the study of contemporary religion." In *Religion: Beyond a Concept*, edited by H. de Vries, 704–23. New York: Fordham University Press.

Miller, Donald. 1999. *Reinventing American Protestantism: Christianity in the New Millenium*. Berkeley: University of California Press.

–. 2010. *Stuff*. Cambridge: Polity.

Morgan, David. 2005. *The Sacred Gaze: Religious Visual Culture in Theory and Practice*. Berkeley: University of California Press.

Otto, Rudolf. 1923. *The Idea of the Holy*. Oxford: Oxford University Press.

Schofield Clark, Lynn. 2009. "Mediatization and media ecology." In *Mediatization: Concepts, Changes, Consequences*, edited by K. Lundby, 85–100. New York: Peter Lang.

Shils, Edward. 1975. *Center and Periphery: Essays in Macrosociology*. Chicago: University of Chicago Press.

Smith, Philip, and J.C. Alexander. 2005. "Introduction: The new Durkheim." In *The Cambridge Companion to Durkheim*, edited by J.C. Alexander and P. Smith, 1–40. Cambridge: Cambridge University Press.

Swidler, Ann. 1986. "Culture in action: Symbols and strategies." *American Sociological Review* 51 (2): 273–286.

Wuthnow, Robert. 1988. *The Restructuring of American Religion: Society and Faith Since World War II*. Princeton, NJ: Princeton University Press.

Zelizer, Viviana. 1985. *Pricing the Priceless Child: The Changing Social Value of Children*. Princeton, NJ: Princeton University Press.

Kim Knott, Elizabeth Poole and Teemu Taira
3   Christianity, Secularism and Religious Diversity in the British Media

Britain is a Christian, secular and religiously diverse country (Weller 2008). All three of these aspects are visible in the media portrayal of religious issues, but they are not covered equally and not treated in the same manner. This chapter examines these three aspects, their coverage in the British press and on television, and the way in which they are handled in particular news topics or media events. Based on the quantitative analysis and comparison of systematically collected media samples from 1982–3 and 2008–9, we show first that there is increased visibility of religious diversity, secularism and atheism in British society and the media. Two media events are then analysed in which Christianity, secularism and religious diversity were very considerably intertwined. The first of these is from February 2009 and concerns the deportation of the Dutch MP, Geert Wilders, who was refused entry to the UK to show his anti-Islamic film, *Fitna* (he was later admitted in 2010). The second is the Papal visit to Britain in September 2010. The representations of Christianity, secularism and religious diversity – and their interrelationships – are analysed and explained.

This chapter is based on research conducted in 2008–10 on 'Media portrayals of religion and the secular sacred' (in association with a major UK research programme on religion and society).[1] Data was collected from mainstream media, from a systematic sample of selected newspapers and television channels – *The Times*, *The Sun*, *The Yorkshire Evening Post*, BBC1, BBC2 and ITV1.[2] A broader selection of news material – from online sources as well as other newspapers and TV channels – was consulted for the analysis of the two key events.

---

1 'Media portrayals of religion and the secular sacred: A longitudinal study of British newspaper and television representations and their reception', AH/F009097/1, part of the AHRC/ESRC Religion and Society Programme, conducted at the University of Leeds from 2008–10 by Kim Knott, Elizabeth Poole and Teemu Taira.
2 The selection of media outputs was driven by the need to replicate the methodology used in an earlier study: 'Media portrayals of religion and their reception', conducted at the University of Leeds from 1982–3 by Robert Towler and Kim Knott (Knott 1984).

1 The rise of religious diversity and secularism in British society and the media

In their coverage of religion, the media do not aim to reflect with any exactitude the number of adherents of religious traditions in Britain, nor do they try to please those who claim to have no religion at all. But they cannot ignore transformations in the religious landscape. As statistics have shown, Britain has changed from being a broadly homogeneous Christian country to one that is more secular and increasingly religiously diverse (Office for National Statistics 2006). This has not led to a complete decline of Christianity or its role in public life. Neither has Christianity disappeared from the British media. Rather, in recent decades, conflicts and controversies between defenders of Christianity, secularists and adherents of religious minorities have become more visible in public discourse, including the media.

1.1 Changing religious patterns and their impact on media coverage

According to the Census in 2001 (Office for National Statistics 2006; cf. Weller 2008: 8–58), Christianity was by far the largest religious group, with 71.6 % of the British population claiming to be Christian (of whom approximately 67.5 % were Anglican, 13.8 % Catholic, 6.9 % Presbyterian and 3.1 % Methodist, with other denominations accounting for less than 1.2 % each). Muslims were the largest non-Christian religious group at 2.7 % of the population, with slightly more adherents than Methodism. Hindus accounted for 1 %, Sikhs 0.6 %, Jews 0.5 % and Buddhists 0.3 %. The category 'Other religion' (0.3 %) included mainly different kinds of Pagans (self-identified as Pagan, Wiccan, Druid and Asatru) but also Jains, Bahá'ís and Zoroastrians. Even though the majority of the population identified with a religious tradition (76.8 %), 15.5 % reported that they had no religion. The remainder, 7.3 %, did not answer the question. From these percentages we can deduce that somewhere between nine and fourteen million people in the UK (between 15.5 % and 22.8 %) in 2001 were non-religious.

However, it is important to remember that 2001 was the first time a religious question had been asked in the UK Census. The figures tell us how people wished to self-identify for public purposes. They give a notional sense of the size of broad religious groups or communities, but they reveal nothing about actual practice or belief, membership of religious organisations or degree of commitment at that time. It is not possible to predict how the religious landscape may have changed since then.[3]

Additional evidence of the presence and increase of religious diversity can be found in the number of places of worship. The number of mosques rose from 193 in the 1980s to 708 in 2004, and the number of Sikh *gurdwaras* from 90 to 190 in the same period. At the same time the number of Christian churches declined by 815 (Weller 2008: 32–42, 63). However, there were still more than 44,000 churches in the UK, illustrating that, despite the tendency towards increasing diversity, Christianity continues to dominate the landscape.

These statistics show that Britain is Christian, but significantly secular and increasingly religiously diverse. Christian denominations dominate just as they did at the time of our earlier research study in the 1980s, but to a lesser extent. Other religions now have a significant role in political and cultural life as well as in personal and community identities. Islam in particular, despite its relatively small numerical base in Britain, is increasingly on the national as well as global agenda in relation to debates about international policy, conflict and terrorism, and migration and integration. Furthermore, these changes have also had an impact on how religion is seen more widely in society and in the media. With an increase in the number of non-religious people or 'nones', the discussion of atheism, secularism and secularisation has risen up the media agenda at the same time that religion has again become more visible in public life. Secularism as well as religion is debated in discursive struggles over identities and privileges. And all of these issues are now addressed – directly and indirectly – in news reporting and commentary, editorials, cultural discussion, drama, comedy and entertainment.

The presence of British Muslims, in particular, began to be felt in the media following the Rushdie Affair in the late 1980s (Weller 2009; Knott 2010). As processes of globalisation and migration led to a reassertion of religious identities at a local level, it was then that the question about the loyalty of Muslims and their ability to integrate began to be raised. Since then, studies have demonstrated the increase in coverage of Islam and Muslims in the British press, a visibility that exploded post-9/11 (see Figure 1) (Poole 2002; Richardson 2004; Moore, Mason and Lewis 2008).

Our own study demonstrates the huge increase in references to Islam, from just 38 in the press and television sample in 1982–3, to 306 in 2008–9. Studies have repeatedly shown the emphasis on Muslims as a cultural issue and, more

---

3 The same religious question was asked in the UK population census in 2011. The results were released in 2012 but will not be analysed here.

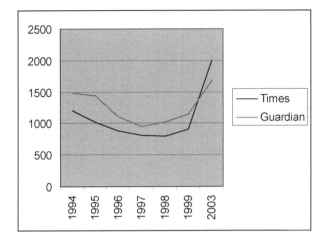

Figure 1: Articles on Islam in *The Times* and *The Guardian* 1994–2003 (Poole 2002)

recently in relation to British Muslims, as a security threat, with reporting largely focused on terrorism, conflict, extremism and cultural incompatibility. Coverage demonstrates the significance of Islam politically as nation states experience insecurities in the context of a changing globalised world.

Secularism and atheism have been present in the media in different ways. While secularism is a political doctrine or principle for organizing society rather than an identity as such, atheism is often expressed as an identity to be defended, promoted, represented and challenged in the media. Examination of the newspapers with the help of search engines shows that the words 'atheism' and 'secularism' have been used increasingly over the last decade. In addition, even though the numbers of references are far fewer, the rate of increase has been faster than it has been for related subjects, such as 'religion', 'faith', 'race' and 'ethnicity'.

The most obvious aspect of this new visibility has been the so-called New Atheism. Even though atheist books and pamphlets have been published throughout the past 200 years, none of them have had the impact of recent books by Sam Harris, Richard Dawkins, Daniel Dennett and Christopher Hitchens. Atheist, secularist and humanist interest groups have been revitalised, and membership rates have increased in the last few years. Whilst making clear they are not anti-religious, some politicians have now publicly admitted their atheism: Liberal Democratic leader Nick Clegg, for example (Bullivant 2010).

Atheism and criticism of religion have been popular topics in a variety of media. Television has aired documentaries such as *Atheism: A Rough History of Disbelief* (BBC Four 2004), *The Root of All Evil?* (Channel 4 2006) and *Faith School Menace?* (Channel 4 2010). BBC Radio 4's early morning slot, *Thought for the Day*, has not opened itself to non-religious voices, though this has often been debated (see BBC 'Should Thought Stay Sacred?' 2009). 2009 was important in other ways, too. The atheist bus campaign, in which the advertisement 'There's probably no God. Now stop worrying and enjoy your life' was placed on buses in Britain's major cities, took place in January and was soon copied in many European countries. Camp Quest UK, a summer camp for the children of atheists and non-religious people, was launched for the first time in Britain that summer. In November, public billboards – pointedly directed against religions – showed children saying, 'Please don't label me. Let me grow up and choose myself'. These events were widely covered in the mainstream media.

1.2 Changing media portrayals: the quantitative evidence

During our research in 2008–9 we collected and analysed references from a selection of British newspapers and terrestrial television channels and compared these to a similar sample from 1982–3. The selection in both periods included one month's newspapers from *The Times*, *The Sun* and the *Yorkshire Evening Post*, one 'broadsheet' or serious daily, one tabloid and one local paper. Also included was one week's television (excluding children's programmes) from BBC1, BBC2 and ITV1 (two other terrestrial channels, Channel 4 and Channel 5, were deselected for study in 2008 because they were not in existence at the time of the previous study in 1982).[4] Although our systematic sample was based on a relatively narrow selection of media sources, it had some evidential power and breadth and was supplemented with a broader selection of sources in the analysis of the two events (the Geert Wilders case and the Papal visit). Although we collected data on multiple key words relating to conventional religion, common religion and non-religion, our analysis below is restricted to the principal themes of Christianity, religious diversity (religious traditions other than Christianity) and secularism/atheism.[5]

The dominance of Christianity in the media coverage of religion, as well as the rise of secularism, atheism and religious diversity, can be seen in Figure 2 and Table 1 below. The first indicates clearly the fact that, in terms of religion,

---

4 Channel 4 began operating later in 1982, after our period of data collection had been completed.

5 For more discussion of media references to conventional and common religion, see Knott (1984), Taira et al. (2012).

references to Christianity still dominate the media. It also shows the significant rise in references to Islam (a key element of religious diversity). Furthermore, it offers evidence of the increased media visibility of secularism and atheism, even though the absolute number of references is far behind Christianity and Islam.[6]

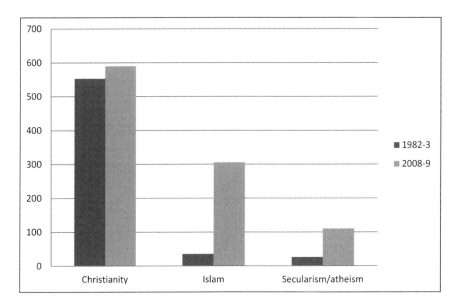

Figure 2: Media references to religion 1982–3 and 2008–9

Table 1 demonstrates that the increase in references to religious diversity is not limited to Islam, even though it is the most visible and most referenced religious tradition other than Christianity. It shows that references to atheism and secularism have increased more than references to Asian traditions, Judaism and New Religious Movements.

---

6 These totals for secularism/atheism include some references to other 'secular sacred' concerns such as humanism and secular spirituality. More than half of the references (59) were to secularism and atheism, however.

Table 1: The rise in the number of media references to religions and secularism/atheism, 1982–3 and 2008–9

	1982–3	2008–9
Atheism/Secularism	7	59
Islam	38	306
Judaism	88	91
Hinduism	5	35
Buddhism	2	43
Sikhism	3	13
Other World Religions[7]	5	20
New Religious Movements	10	36

These two charts provide evidence of the increase in references to religious diversity as well as atheism and secularism. Quantitative data has two significant limitations when it comes to interpretation, however. The increase in the number of references may not automatically mean that the theme has become more publicly significant. In our view, given the recent political climate, the increase in the number of references to Islam has been significant. But the same holds true in the case of atheism and secularism, much more than for Buddhism or Judaism, for example. The discussion of atheism and secularism is largely an elite debate covered in quality broadsheets rather than popular papers. References to atheism and secularism are found mostly in *The Times* (32 in 2008–9), with the discourse being almost entirely absent in *The Sun* and the local paper. It is spread more evenly among different television channels. Furthermore, the theme is not addressed lightly with passing references (which is sometimes the case in respect of terms denoting particular religions). When mentioned, atheism and secularism are often main issues in articles or television programmes. References appear generally in news and current affairs and in editorials and comments. Juxtapose this with the fact that, in 2008–9, Judaism was frequently referred to in obituaries (in *The Times*), and that approximately half of the newspaper references to Buddhism were in announcements/listings (in *The Times* and *Yorkshire Evening Post*). We suggest that, when compared with other increasingly referenced religions, there is a qualitative difference in how atheism and secularism are conceived and discussed.

Having provided statistical information and general data on media references to Christianity, religious diversity and secularism/atheism, we turn now to

---

7 In 1982–3 the category 'Other World Religions' included references to Shintoism, Confucianism, Bahai and Zoroastrianism. In 2008–9 it also included references to Taoism and Jainism.

our analysis of the first of two media events in which these themes were represented, the Geert Wilders event.

2 The Geert Wilders case, 2009

Geert Wilders, the Dutch Member of Parliament for the Party for Freedom (PVV), was thrust back into the public eye on 13 February 2009 when he was refused entry to Britain on public order grounds. He had been invited to a screening of his own film, *Fitna*, in the House of Lords by Lord Pearson of the UK Independence Party (UKIP).[8] The Home Office denied entry under an EU law which allows member states to do so on the grounds that the person constitutes a threat to public policy, security or health. The anti-Islamic film espousing Wilders' views, combined with his personal presence, was deemed by the then Home Secretary (Jacqui Smith) to be threatening community harmony and therefore public security. Despite being aware of this judgement, Wilders chose to fly into London Heathrow knowing he would be turned back at the airport, thus creating a huge publicity coup.

Since producing *Fitna*, Wilders' activities have been newsworthy for stimulating the expression of opinions and discourses about the role of religion in society and its relation to national identity. This salience is demonstrated by the amount of newspaper coverage of this event, 159 articles in all. In accordance with the media analysis of an earlier Papal visit (1982), all British national newspapers were analysed in addition to two local papers, *The Yorkshire Post* and the *Yorkshire Evening Post*. Articles published in the print edition and online as well as public letters and comments were included.

The event was largely interpreted as an issue of freedom of speech (a key value in what we refer to as the 'secular sacred'),[9] with different newspapers displaying different degrees of commitment to this. The event demonstrated dominant responses to increased religious diversity in the UK, particularly in relation to Islam, with different sections of society preferring to reinforce either Christian or secular identities. All the newspapers used the event to attack the New Labour Government's decision to ban Wilders.

---

8 In 2008, Wilders produced a short film, *Fitna* (variously translated, but in the UK press rendered as 'discord' or 'strife'), which juxtaposes violent images of extreme Islamism with verses from the Qur'an. It was widely and globally criticised as Islamophobic.

9 By 'secular sacred' we mean those beliefs, practices and values that are explicitly non-religious but are nevertheless held to be non-negotiable and often referred to as 'sacred' by those who hold them, e.g., freedom of speech and human rights.

2.1 Christianity

The case allowed the conservative press to illustrate what it saw as the increasing 'Islamification' of the UK, due to liberal policies of tolerance (equated by some journalists with submission and appeasement) and the resulting 'marginalisation' of Christianity. Whilst the newspapers distanced themselves from Wilders to avoid being labelled racist, the attention given to him and his arguments provided an outlet for saying the unsayable (about Islam) in the guise of claims of double standards and freedom of speech.

The construction of Wilders varied according to the degree of sympathy with his views. For *The Daily Mail* he was a 'democratically elected Dutch MP' (13/2/2009), but to *The Guardian* he was 'virulently anti-Islamic' (11/2/2009). For the conservative press, the attention to free speech appears to have been expedient, given their frequent demands to deport 'preachers of hate' and their stance on censorship in relation to other issues. Ironically, then, the curtailment of free speech was seen to have been brought about by liberal authoritarianism (in the form of political correctness). Liberal thought was therefore held to be responsible for the 'Islamification' of society and erosion of British, including Christian, values. Here, universal values (freedom) were localised and placed in opposition to Islam, which was constructed as naturally censorious (all of the papers highlighted the violent protests against the film, *Fitna*, across the Muslim world). In banning Wilders, the government was presented as submitting to the will of Muslims.

The preferential treatment awarded to Muslims at the expense of Christianity and British values was a common theme more generally. This was encapsulated by *The Daily Express* in Leo McKinstry's commentary, 'Why Christianity is on the ropes in Labour's Britain' (16/2/09). 'Elsewhere in the paper columnist Julia Hartley-Brewer argued that 'If we in the West fail to stand up for our own values of liberty, freedom of speech, tolerance and democracy, they will be swept away by the growing demands of Islam which, Wilders argues, is incompatible with European values....Wilders is not Abu Hamza. His film doesn't preach hate, it preaches that tolerance of the intolerant will ultimately lead to the end of tolerance and, with it, our civilization. Wilders may be wrong about a lot of things but he's not wrong about that' (*The Sunday Express* 15/2/09).

For *The Telegraph*, the main purpose of its coverage of Wilders was to focus attention on the diminishing role of Christianity and secondary treatment of Christians within the UK (whilst, according to the paper, Muslims are appeased). This was the theme of six articles. Its position is summed up in the editorial, 'The priorities of a Christian country':

> Although many state officials seem determined to forget it, Britain still has a state religion [...] That is why the stories that we publish today are so surprising, for they suggest that there is a concerted attempt by some officials to marginalise and to diminish the Christian faith [...] [F]or many state officials, the most important goal is to avoid offending any religious sensibility except Christianity [...] Christianity is and should be in a privileged position in Britain. (14/2/09)

This Christian identity was held most strongly by The *Daily Express, The Telegraph and The Daily Mail* (and is also evident at times in *The Sun*, but less so in coverage of this case). *The Times, Financial Times, Yorkshire Evening Post and Yorkshire Post* represented Britain as secular first, then Christian.

A discourse of 'Us' and 'Them' was constructed, with Wilders on the outside, but the conservative press largely reinforcing his views. By constructing Britain as a Christian country, Muslims were excluded. The emphasis on 'freedom of speech' by the conservative press was instrumental. It operated as a means of emphasising a cultural clash and further placing Muslims on the outside of British society.

2.2 Secularism

There were a few explicit references to secularism in the liberal press, but generally it was implicit in the text. For example, well-known secularists were invited to comment, as in the case of Johann Hari, who noted that 'generations of British people fought to create a secular space' (*The Independent* 13/2/09). A. C. Grayling depicted religion – but not secularism – as an identity position: 'all religions have their extremist minorities' (*The Guardian*, 13/2/09).

Overall, the press drew on liberal values to make sense of what had happened. Freedom of speech was given an almost absolutist position and treated as unconditional. *The Guardian*, whose poll encapsulated its coverage by formulating the question within the framework through which the event would then be interpreted, asked, 'On the grounds of free speech should he [Wilders] be let in?' (12/02/09); 84.4 % of *Guardian Online* readers voted 'Yes: It goes against the principles of free speech to ban him'. *The Guardian*'s commentary ran for a further nine days online following the last print article. Its website sets an industry standard in online news, providing extensive debate on a range of issues. However, it is the unevenness of this commentary that is of interest here. *The Guardian*'s position was that freedom of speech should be an absolute, with no exceptions: 'We cannot pick and choose what freedom we defend' (12/2/09 online). Its two editorials made this explicit; in one, 'Ban on Wilders was folly' (*The Observer* 15/2/09), it is claimed that 'Opinions, however odious, cannot in themselves be criminal', while the other is self-evident: 'Britain's political establishment has in an unwitting, collaborative effort of stupidity and democratic illiteracy presented itself as an accomplice to extremisms and enemy of free speech'.[10] However, there were no significant appeals for freedom of speech in response to the Phelps church, a virulently homophobic US Christian sect, which threatened to picket a play about the murder of a gay man in the UK. Another liberal paper, *The Independent*, did acknowledge the limitations to free speech. Its editorial on 13/2/09 argued, 'There are, it must be accepted, limitations on those freedoms. The Government has a responsibility to preserve the safety of minority groups in Britain'. However, it then went on to say that, in this case, the line had not been crossed.

Both these papers demonstrated greater inclusivity than others, with occasional Muslim voices and counter discourse. For example, *The Guardian* included an article from Lord (Nazir) Ahmed (a Muslim peer), 'Wilders ban is in Britain's best interests', in which he defended his own position of support for the ban and pointed out something largely ignored elsewhere in the press, that Muslims too have been banned (13/2/09). However, this further reinforced a dichotomising discourse whereby Muslim illiberalism was presented as at odds with liberal democracy, the core of British identity, again positioning Muslims as outsiders. In emphasising the value of freedom of speech and locating this as both British and secular, Britain was implicitly constructed as a secular country.[11]

2.3 Diversity

In the case of the reporting of the Geert Wilders case, religious diversity is not represented in a positive light. Whilst there are some acknowledgements of the possibility of moderate Muslims in the conservative press (two references each in *The Sun* and *The Daily Mail*), Muslims are mainly conceptualised in their extreme form as 'preachers of hate'. Lord Ahmed is named as the instigator who alerted the Home Office to the film screening (thus implying that Muslims are troublemakers); but he is also presented as having double standards in 'inviting an al Qaeda fundraiser into Westminster' (*The Sun* 13/2/09).

No Muslim voices featured at all in *The Times* or *The Daily Mail*. However, there is a distinction in *The Times* between ordinary Muslims and Islamists: 'There is a world of difference between Islam the great religion and Islamism

---

10 *The Observer* is *The Guardian*'s Sunday newspaper.

11 This construction can be compared to sections of the American press (*Newsweek, The New York Times*), where the case was interpreted as an attack on Muslims who should be defended (Poole, 2012).

the ideology of submission' (in a commentary by Michael Gove, 16/2/09). *The Telegraph* made a similar distinction in an article by Charles Moore (13/2/09). However, the rest of this piece was then used to attack the negative features of Islam:

> The unpleasant power of *Fitna* is that the atrocities it depicts and the preaching it shows are real and recent, and they were all carried out or uttered by Muslims acting, explicitly, in the name of their faith. You could not, in our age, compile any comparable clips of Jews or Christians. As a matter of plain fact, Islamic terrorism exists. Another plain fact about current Muslim culture is the use of the angry demonstration, the constant agitation to ban a book or insist on the veil, the bristling search for offence. So it would be silly to pretend that there is no problem about Muslim attitudes to a plural, free, democratic society. (*The Telegraph*, 13/2/09)

The two liberal broadsheets provided more space for Muslim voices, with five each, in *The Guardian* as writers and in *The Independent* as three writers and two sources. Yet, in its extensive coverage of this story, *The Guardian* made surprisingly little reference to Muslims. Is its way of dealing with promoting freedom of speech without offending Muslims to cancel them out of the discussion? Whilst these liberal newspapers are clearly not anti-Islamic, Muslims were problematised in their secular human rights stance (in which religious freedom was opposed at the expense of other freedoms). This 'exclusive liberalism' was more evident in *The Independent* and was demonstrated in a strongly anti-religious, pro-secularist, pro-freedom-of-speech piece written by regular commentator, Johann Hari. The purpose of the article was to defend an item he had written in *The New Statesman* in India on a similar topic, which provoked 'four thousand Islamic fundamentalists to riot outside their office' (13/2/09). This article clearly set up an opposition between the secular and rational who protect human rights and the religious and fanatical who abuse them: 'If we leave the basic human values of free speech, feminism and gay rights undefended in the face of violent religious mobs – many many more people will be hurt' (*The Independent*, 13/2/09). Whilst it cannot be said that this piece necessarily represented the stance of *The Independent*, it is an example of the kind of voice it provides space for.

In the reporting of this case, British values were clearly defined, and Muslims were repeatedly constructed in opposition to these. The press polarised the debate, choosing to ignore evidence that minorities may seek to be part of it. The lack of integration of Muslim minorities was represented as the result of incommensurable cultural and religious differences. For the press, the Wilders case highlighted the problem of Muslims in British society as one of a 'clash of cultures' (*The Daily Mail* 12/2/09). What was represented then was an anti-multiculturalist stance, aligned with an anti-immigration discourse. There were some explicit references to this. In *The Mail on Sunday*, John Laughland (15/2/09) declared himself to be incredulous regarding multiculturalism, which he interpreted as 'demanding [...] Britain renounce all traditions in favour of those of newcomers'. He went on: 'Multiculturalists may say you cannot impose your views on others but they are frighteningly good at imposing theirs on all of us'.

This story shows that immigration and religious diversity are still constructed as a problem for the UK. What is interesting is the convergence of views amongst liberals and conservatives. The secular liberal hegemony cannot accommodate the public and assertive nature of popular religious (Muslim) political agency within its conception of equality (which was previously based on race). The mirroring of the political activism of equal rights groups by Muslims has reopened questions about the place of religion in the public sphere, questions that were previously thought settled. In the reactions of these socio-political elites, various political hegemonies are reinforced in terms of either an exclusive nationalism or, amongst the secular elite, an exclusionary multiculturalism. Neither position is helpful to the workings of a multicultural democracy, given that they exclude Muslims from a conceptualisation of British citizenship. The reaction by the New Labour government was to replace multiculturalism with an assimilationist 'cohesion' agenda – witnessed in the citizenship policies introduced in the years following the inner-city disturbances of 2001. The political causes of the current situation at home and abroad were obscured as religio-cultural differences were brought to the fore and blamed in 'the clash of civilisations' discourse.

3 The Papal visit, 2010

If Christianity, secularism/atheism and religious diversity are the three key themes in the media coverage of religion generally, the media coverage of the Papal visit was no exception.

In September 2010 Pope Benedict XVI flew to Britain for a four-day state visit at the invitation of the government. This was the first Papal visit since 1982, when the previous Pope, John Paul II, had undertaken a six-day pastoral tour (the subject of an earlier study; see Knott 1984). During the 2010 visit, the full range of daily newspapers were collected systematically for six days – starting one day before the Pope's arrival and finishing one day after his departure. The primary material consisted of nearly 600 articles and more than 600 images. In addition, television programmes – almost 13 hours of live coverage by the BBC, four documentaries, and news and talk shows – were examined before and during the visit. Websites, particularly the official one for the Papal visit and the sites of interest groups such as the National Secular Society and the British Humanist Association, were also monitored.

The papal visit turned into a celebratory media narrative as pre-visit uncertainties and controversy melted away during the tour and finally transformed into sympathy, relief and joy: from a tale of doubt to one of success. One of the reasons for pre-visit reservations in 2010 was financial; many thought that, at a time of huge cuts, public funding could have been spent more wisely. Another reason for doubt was the Catholic child abuse controversy, which overshadowed the pre-visit coverage. It is telling that, of the six million British Catholics, more than half were in favour of the visit, whereas only 14 % of the nation at large supported the visit (*The Daily Mirror* 15/9/10).

One additional doubt was the personality of the Pope himself. If Benedict has been labelled as a Pope of content rather than image, it is partly because his predecessor John Paul II was thought to be a charismatic celebrity. However, all of the newspapers as well as the BBC deemed the 2010 visit to have been a success; 'God's Rottweiler' was overturned by the image of a 'warmer, more human and less rigid' Pope (*The Independent* 20/9/10). The whole trip was 'a resounding success' (*The Daily Telegraph* 20/9/10), 'beyond all expectations' (*The Times* 20/9/10). Some weeks after the visit *The Daily Telegraph* columnist, Christopher Howse, wondered what had changed and suggested it was the reputation of the Pope from a conservative and rigid man to one who was a little shy and thoughtful (23/10/10).

Even though the overall media coverage of the Papal visit was positive, there were some visible differences between newspapers. Some of these will be addressed in the following sections on the three key themes, but the general pattern was that the popular conservative British newspapers were also pro-Christian and pro-Pope. The conservative tabloids (the Labour-supporting *The Daily Mirror* being an exception) took a defensive stance towards critics of the Pope. They were keen to highlight the Pope's message on the marginalisation of Christianity in secular Britain. The most popular broadsheet, *The Daily Telegraph*, covered the visit with interest and adopted an extremely positive approach. *The Times* was mainly positive, though it dealt with some critical issues, too. Other broadsheets, whose circulation is smaller and whose political support is liberal or left wing, were more critical of the visit and of the Pope himself. *The Guardian* gave some positive coverage, but balanced it with critical commentary. By giving voice to the victims of child-abuse, *The Independent* was more directly critical (but stopped short of siding with public atheists like Richard Dawkins, as will be shown later).

We have noted that Christianity, secularism/atheism and religious diversity (particularly in relation to Islam) are key themes in the media coverage of religion generally. However, in each case these themes are made meaningful in different ways. We will now explore how the media emphasized these three themes during the Pope's visit.

3.1 The marginalisation of Christianity

According to the newspapers, the marginalisation of Christianity was Benedict's main message to Britain. The Pope said that he 'cannot but voice [his] concern at the increasing marginalisation of religion, particularly of Christianity', and continued that 'there are those who would advocate that the voice of religion be silenced, or at least relegated to the purely private sphere' (*The Daily Express* 18/9/10).

The main target of his complaint was understood to be 'aggressive secularism', but religions other than Christianity were also presented as a cause for concern. For instance, the Pope suggested that celebrating Christmas in a Christian way was under threat because it was seen to offend 'those of other religions or none' (*The Daily Express* 18/9/10). Some newspapers took the Papal view as evidence of diversity gone too far, but, in the tabloids particularly, his opinion was used to bash the 'political correctness' of 'atheist Left-wingers'. For example, *The Daily Express* (18/9/10) ran the headline, 'Pope's plea to help save Christmas from the PC brigade'.

Even though 'marginalisation' was sometimes printed with scare quotes, suggesting that the paper did not necessarily condone the expression, the idea gained surprising agreement in many papers. More secular-minded journalists thought that the warnings were far-fetched, but there was nevertheless strong support for the Pope's message. Nick Ferrari, a columnist from *The Sunday Express* (19/9/10), concluded with support for a society which 'embraces all peoples and allows them to celebrate their many religions and enjoy their Hanukkah, Eid, Diwali or whatever else it might be, while all the time accepting that this is a Christian country with Christian core beliefs and values'. Furthermore, *The Daily Star* (17/9/10) editorial suggested that 'we have a strong history for welcoming all cultures to our shores. But there's a growing sentiment across the country that our traditions are being slowly lost'. These views reinforced the difference and hierarchy between 'their cultures' and 'our Christian tradition', the latter being valued highly and seen to be in need of defence from marginalisation.

The Pope's defence of Christianity's role in public life led some in the media to desire equivalently authoritative British voices. A comparison was made with the Archbishop of Canterbury, Rowan Williams. *The Daily Mail* (20/9/10) argued that the Archbishop is 'so cowed by the forces of secularism that he no longer poses any threat to their bleak vision' and wondered 'if only the Archbishop dared to speak with a fraction of Benedict's authority'.

It is perhaps not surprising that there was no equivalent discourse on the marginalisation of Christianity at the time of the earlier Papal visit in 1982. Pope John Paul II's concerns about marginalisation were focused on the sick, elderly, handicapped and unemployed, not those in a hegemonic position in British society. The difference between the two Popes was certainly a matter of personality, but time and context made their own demands. By 2010 it was felt necessary to reclaim the position once held by Christianity and to justify it in public discourse against (real or imagined) threats posed by increasing diversity and more audible atheism and secularism.

3.2 Secularism and atheism: aggression and unholy warlords

Before the visit, campaigning secularists and atheists were responsible for repeated provocation in the media, the best-known example being the widely published call by Richard Dawkins to have the Pope arrested (originally printed on the front page of *The Times*, 11/4/10). These voices were further aroused on the eve of the visit, when Catholic Cardinal Walter Kasper was quoted as warning of the rise of a 'new and aggressive atheism' in Britain and of suggesting that arriving at Heathrow was like 'landing in a third world country'. This was taken as an offence against cultural and religious diversity. Most newspapers condemned Kasper's views and named him 'The Pope's Dope' (*The Daily Mirror* 16/9/10; *The Sun* 16/9/10). The statement was seen by right-wing, pro-Christian papers as 'a gift to the [...] left-wing atheists' (*The Daily Mail* 16/9/10). Furthermore, in his opening speech the Pope seemed to reinforce his Cardinal's point by referring to the 'atheist extremism of the 20th century', which – though unarguably a reference to Nazi Germany – was intended as a comment on the current British situation.

The day before the visit started, an 'atheistic protest letter', signed by Richard Dawkins, Stephen Fry, Terry Pratchett, Philip Pullman, Susan Blackmore, A.C. Grayling and 49 others, was published in *The Guardian* (15/9/10). It argued that the Pope should not have been given the honour of a state visit because the organisation of which he was head had been responsible for opposing equal rights. The letter was covered in many newspapers. There were follow-up articles dealing with these celebrities and public intellectual figures, accompanied by pieces on ordinary protesters (mainly the victims of child abuse and their representatives). The tabloids gave space to the topic but condemned the letter as 'spitting venom', 'a celebrity vendetta', written by 'the Left-wing chorus' and motivated by 'empty hatred'. All the anti-Papal voices were lumped together as atheist Left-wingers, multiculturalists and PC killjoys (see *The Sun* 18/9/10 to 20/9/10). They were undoubtedly far from homogeneous, but it is significant to note the manner and intensity with which the pro-Pope tabloids presented and condemned them, even though some columnists in the same papers found the Pope's references to aggressive atheism rather odd.

Even the broadsheets had ambiguous attitudes to the outspoken atheist and secularist criticism of religion. The views of Dawkins and others were published, but they were also criticised in the media – and not simply by avowedly religious journalists. For instance, Janice Turner, who spoke of a non-aggressive 'true secularism' which promotes an alliance with progressive and liberal religious groups against conservative voices, called Richard Dawkins, Christopher Hitchens and Stephen Hawking 'macho atheists' and 'unholy warlords' (*The Times* 18/9/10). A similarly well-known atheist, Julian Baggini, wrote in *The Guardian* (18/9/10) that campaigning does not work if it simply makes as much noise as possible without trying to bring dissatisfied Catholics along with the common cause. A similar message was voiced when *The Independent* (18/9/10) published a comment by Richard Ingrams, who suggested that 'atheism could do without Dawkins'.

Richard Dawkins often succeeds in getting his message across in the British media, despite the fact that his views are criticised by religious and non-religious journalists, readers and intellectual figures alike. On this occasion there was good reason for Dawkins and others to be criticised, as this directed more attention to those with genuine cause for acknowledgment; empathy was expressed for the victims of Catholic child abuse and their contrast with the self-promotion of celebrities and intellectual figures, making the arguments of the latter look even more hollow than in normal circumstances.

3.3 Religious diversity: from ecumenism to interfaith

The 1982 Papal visit had been framed principally in Christian terms. John Paul II offered an ecumenical approach, talked about the 'restoration of unity among Christians' and signed a declaration for improving Christian dialogue. In the official souvenir guide he was described as 'a pilgrim of Christian unity' (Knott 1984: 36). The Pope was seen as a wave in the tide of an ecumenical movement supported by all the newspapers. They gave him a 'Protestant welcome' but invited ecumenism as a positive and inevitable trend for overcoming disagreement between Catholics and Protestants (Knott 1984: 37–48).

This Christian ecumenical tone had altered to one focused on religious diversity and interfaith relations in the media coverage of the 2010 visit. A Sikh man was recorded as saying that the Pope spoke beyond Catholics and to be religious today was to be inter-religious (BBC1 16/9/10); BBC1's *Look North* ran a story about Muslim children who participated in the choir that sang for the Pope (15/9/10); *The Times* (15/9/10) published an article on Muslims welcoming the Pope to Britain; *The Daily Mirror* (18/9/10) ran the headline 'A Man for All Religions' and suggested that he 'speaks to us all [...] not just Catholics' (17/9/10). Furthermore, the Prime Minister, David Cameron, was quoted as saying that the visit was a 'unique opportunity to celebrate the good works of religious groups' (*The Daily Telegraph* 15/9/10) and one that furthered 'intercultural and interreligious dialogue for the enrichment of the entire community' (*The Guardian* 20/9/10). This emphasis was by no means evident from the Pope's general attitude or speeches. Crucially, it was the media that highlighted diversity and constructed this as an interfaith event.

The promotion of religious diversity and an interfaith attitude does not require full equality to be attributed to all traditions. Instead, it operates by making a distinction and favouring moderate (good) over extreme (bad) forms of religiosity. It is Islam that has been used as the prototypical media example of extremism, though discourse on Islam has focused on moderate as well as extreme dimensions. We can see this discourse at work in stories about the 'Muslim plot to kill Pope' (*The Daily Express* 18/9/10, front page).

On 18 September the media reported that the police had arrested six male cleaners suspected of attempting to assassinate the Pope. Their houses were searched, and they were released after the police had found nothing suspicious. The whole 'plot' turned out to be a false alarm, but it served as an opportunity to reinforce the connection between Islam and terrorism. Some papers were embarrassed to have exaggerated the story, while others hurried to defend themselves by claiming that there had been a serious threat. Nevertheless, most papers made news out of the 'plot'. Because there was little information, the actual story was filled with speculation, particularly about the ethnic origin and religiosity of the cleaners. *The Independent* was an exception. It did not feature the story on the front page and avoided sensational headlines when it reported on security issues, the arrests and the lack of evidence.

This case showed how eager the British newspapers were to demonise Islam when an appropriate occasion arose. But it was also a good example of the way in which the media handle the changing religious context and increased diversity. A positive image of religious diversity is constructed by including all religions whilst continuing to privilege Anglican Christianity and to exclude unacceptable (Islamist) extremism. But those who are included – moderate

Muslims, Hindus, Buddhists, Sikhs, Jews and other Christian denominations –
are presented in a fairly positive light, because they are seen as non-threatening
and potentially able to contribute to public policy ('the Big Society') through social action (cf. Beckford 2010).

4 Christianity, secularism and religious diversity: three themes, multiple discourses

In terms of the discursive representations of Christianity, secularism and religious diversity, how did the media coverage of the banning of Geert Wilders
and the visit of Pope Benedict compare?

In the Wilders case, Britain was constructed primarily as 'a Christian country' (in opposition to the 'Islamification of society' and the imagined preferential
treatment awarded to Muslims), especially by the right-wing papers. The liberal,
left-leaning press employed discourses of secularism in defence of liberalism in
general and freedom of speech in particular; they implicitly constructed Britain
as 'a secular society'. Wilders himself was labelled as both virulently anti-Islamic
and a voice against a censorious Islam, reflecting the location of the case within
a struggle over issues of religious diversity. In the right-wing papers, tolerance
towards Islam was interpreted as cowardly submission, and Muslims were constructed with reference to hate preachers, though there was some acknowledgement of the possibility of a moderate Islam. The case was also used to lambast
Labour government policy (in refusing entry to Wilders whilst letting Muslim
'preachers of hate' stay in the UK).[12]

These three themes were also significant in media coverage of the Papal
visit. Concern over the marginalisation of Christianity was expressed, and Britain
was constructed in the right-wing tabloids as a Christian country. Despite the fact
that they did not condone the most conservative aspects of the Pope's message,
these papers constructed an exclusive secularism and 'aggressive atheism' as the
enemies of 'people of faith' and as threats to people's hopes and enjoyment.
Contrary to the case of Wilders, religious diversity was represented as a positive
force for society through benign images of Catholics, Sikhs and Muslim children
and references to interfaith relations and their enrichment for the whole society.
The reporting of public statements by Prime Minister David Cameron helped to
endorse this message.

---

12 Labour were the political party in Government until the election of May 2010, when they
were superseded by a Conservative/Liberal Democrat coalition.

During the visit the media treatment of the three themes illuminated several broad changes in relation to discourse on religion: *Christianity* was seen, rightly or wrongly, as marginalised, thus reflecting a situation in which none of the traditions could be taken for granted as they must all justify themselves publicly. Identifying the 'enemies of religion' also contributed to the increased public visibility of *atheism and secularism*, barely acknowledged at the time of the previous Papal visit in 1982. Furthermore, at that time, public controversy had focused on relations between Protestants and Catholics, for which ecumenism was seen as the solution; *interfaith relations* had replaced ecumenism by 2010, reflecting the need to cope with increased diversity and make sense of it in terms of a common framework of 'faith' rather than 'religion' (Smith 2004).

All three themes have been witnessed – with two increasing in prominence since the 1980s – in the media representations of the role and place of religion in contemporary British society, though their meanings, functions and relationships vary, depending on both the case and the media standpoint. A concern for the marginalisation of Christianity at the time of the Wilders case was superseded by a reassertion of the visibility of Christianity during the Papal visit, though it could not to be said to have emerged covered in glory (with accusations of abuse and conservative anti-liberalism tempering more positive coverage). If the Wilders case highlighted the 'secular sacred' value of freedom of speech, during the Papal visit the focus shifted to human rights. The atheist agenda was also presented, whereas during the Wilders case it was secularism that merited coverage. And in terms of religious diversity, the two events were constructed very differently, with a negative Islamophobic media orientation in the earlier case and diversity and interfaith relations celebrated in the latter, partly – and somewhat ironically – in response to the Papal attack on British secular pluralism.

According to both the quantitative evidence and detailed exploration of these two recent events, the media continue to present Britain as Christian, but increasingly secular and religiously diverse. The dominant discourse in the popular media is of an engagement between traditional Christianity and moderate secularity, which allows for a certain degree of cultural, including religious, diversity. Although the common view (certainly among religious commentators) is of a secularist, anti-religious British media, this is not mirrored in actual media portrayals (except in some coverage in left-leaning newspapers). A broadly positive attitude towards religions is displayed, especially to Christianity, though less so to Islam. It is important to remember, however, as our analysis of these two events has shown, that the British media is not homogeneous; neither are its reporters, presenters and commentators when it comes to covering religion.

These findings offer further evidence that religion is back on the agenda of public life in Britain (Woodhead and Catto 2012) and that the media are increasingly interested in religion as well as its antithesis – secularism and atheism. This does not necessarily mean that the social significance of religion has increased or even that there is a resurgence of religion. Its increased visibility is connected to the changing configuration, role, place and function of religion and other ideological formations in society. Any glib assumptions about the direction of travel of religion in contemporary Britain – whether the decline of Christianity, the Islamification of society or the unrelenting process of secularisation – are challenged in a media environment that variously narrates the current context with reference to the three separate poles of Christianity, secularism/atheism and religious diversity.

References

BBC. 2009. "Should thought stay sacred?" Available at: http://news.bbc.co.uk/today/hi/today/newsid_8151000/8151113.stm

Beckford, James A. 2010. "The return of religion? A critical assessment of a popular claim." *Nordic Journal of Religion and Society* 23 (2): 121–136.

Bullivant, Stephen. 2010. "The new atheism and sociology: Why here? Why now? What next?" In *Religion and the New Atheism: A Critical Appraisal*, edited by Amarnath Amarasingam, 109–124. Leiden: Brill.

Knott, Kim. 1984. *Media Portrayals of Religion and their Reception: Final Report.* University of Leeds/Independent Broadcasting Authority.

–. 2010. "Theoretical and methodological resources for breaking open the secular and exploring the boundary between religion and non-religion." *Historia Religionum* 2: 115–133.

Moore, Kerry, Paul Mason, and Justin Lewis. 2008. *Images of Islam in the UK: The Representation of British Muslims in the National Print News Media 2000–2008.* Cardiff School of Journalism, Media and Cultural Studies. Commissioned by Channel 4.

Office for National Statistics. 2006. *Focus on Religion* (Census 2001). Available at: http://www.statistics.gov.uk/focuson/religion/. Accessed 29 July 2011.

Poole, Elizabeth. 2002. *Reporting Islam: Media Representations of British Muslims.* London: I. B. Tauris.

–. 2012. "Immigration, Islam and Identity in the UK and the Netherlands." In *The Oxford Handbook of Religion and the American News Media*, edited by Diane Winston, n.p. Oxford: Oxford University Press.

Richardson, John E. 2004. *(Mis)Representing Islam: The Racism and Rhetoric of British Broadsheet Newspapers.* Amsterdam: John Benjamin.

Smith, Greg. 2004. "Faith in community and communities of faith? Government rhetoric and religious identity in urban Britain." *Journal of Contemporary Religion* 19: 185–204.

Taira, Teemu, Elizabeth Poole, and Kim Knott. 2012. "Religion in the British media today." In *Religion and the News*, edited by Jolyon Mitchell and Owen Gower, Chapter 3. Farnham and Burlington, VT: Ashgate.

Weller, Paul. 2008. *Religious Diversity in the UK: Contours and Issues*. London: Continuum.

–. 2009. *A Mirror for Our Times: "The Rushdie Affair" and the Future of Multiculturalism*. London: Continuum.

Woodhead, Linda, and Rebecca Catto, eds. 2012. *Religion and Change in Modern Britain*. London and New York: Routledge.

Lyn Thomas
4   Religion for a Postsecular Society? Discourses of Gender, Religion and Secularity in the Reception of BBC2's *The Monastery* and *The Convent*

1 Introduction

In *The Monastery* (BBC 2005) the Benedictine monks of Worth Abbey in Sussex welcomed five 'ordinary men' into the monastery and their monastic routines for six weeks. The programme was a surprise success, attracting an average of 2.4 million viewers and a 10 % audience share across its three broadcasts (Deans 2005) and generating a follow-up programme, *The Monastery Revisited* (2006), and two 'sequels', *The Convent* (2006) and *The Retreat* (2007). A further programme, *The Big Silence* (2010), focused on the then Abbot of Worth, Christopher Jamison, introducing the concept and experience of silence to the lives of five men and women through sojourns at Worth and at a Jesuit Retreat Centre in Wales. An American remake of *The Monastery* was also broadcast on the 'Learning Channel' in 2006 (Tiger/Tigress Productions 2006). In this chapter I aim to analyse the meaning of this success and its significance in terms of debates about the relationship between religion (in this case, Christianity) and secularity in contemporary British culture.

My approach is premised on the view that the success of *The Monastery* is both a discursive construction and a real phenomenon, with thousands of viewers visiting the website of Worth Abbey after the broadcast and hundreds subsequently going on retreats at Worth. Here I focus on the discursive nature of the success through a study of the press reception of the programme, which is then contrasted with that of the sequel programme *The Convent*. This comparison introduces the important lens of gender to the discussion as well as an exploration of the relationship between gender and 'desirable' representations of religion. The second part of the chapter analyses a small group of engaged viewers in their appropriations of, and relationships to, these two programmes. 'Engaged' here is defined in part through the mode of recruitment at four retreat weekends at Worth Abbey held in May, June and July 2006, immediately prior to and during the broadcast of *The Convent* on BBC2; these respondents had all watched *The Monastery* and *The Convent* with high levels of interest and enthusiasm, and some of them described their presence at Worth as a direct result of watching

The Monastery. The responses analysed here take the form of talk and written text (emails and open-ended questionnaires), but the material dimension of the response to the programmes, in the form of journeys from all over Britain and Ireland to Worth Abbey, is also borne in mind. This discussion is thus, in this sense, concerned with a modern form of media-influenced pilgrimage (Couldry 2003).

My analysis here is based on Ward and Hoelzl's work (2008) on the new visibility of religion, defined as a 'new awareness of religion' rather than the re-emergence of traditional religions after a decline. It is also in this sense that I am using the term 'postsecular'; that is, not in terms of a return to religion after a secular age, but rather to suggest both that the postsecular is itself a construct and to describe a culture where a strong secular current is accompanied by a new visibilisation of religion. The emphasis is thus on visibility and the forms it takes, and my aim is to explore what Ward and Hoelzl (2008: 5) call 'the differences between the phenomena, the *seeing* of these phenomena, where they are being *seen*, who is making them *seen*, and how they are evaluated' through the study of the reception of two recent 'religious' programmes which achieved some measure of audience and critical success. How do these programmes and their reception make religion visible? How does gender inflect these representations and their reception? How do they participate in broader discourses and representations of religion and secularity in contemporary British culture?

2 The programmes

The Monastery, first broadcast in May 2005, was arguably a hybrid of reality television and documentary forms, even though its producers were strongly resistant to any connection with reality TV:

> There were no stunts, no contests, no votes, no faked scenes, no hidden cameras, no shooting scripts, essentially no formalised 'format' – all of which, more or less, are elements of what is known as 'Reality TV'. Indeed it was because we set our face against those modern TV tricks that we secured the confidence of, and access to the host organisations, and thus made the programmes possible. (Blake 2006)

Despite this, the five participants were required to leave their ordinary lives and the accoutrements of modern living, such as mobile phones, and, of course, to be filmed regularly over the six week period. Like *Big Brother* this was an experiment in living at close quarters with strangers, surrounded by cameras, with the crucial difference, as discussed elsewhere, that the experience and the relationships were mediated by the sensitive and caring interventions of the monks

(Thomas 2011: 558–572). The programme-makers attempted to differentiate this programme from reality TV formats and to inscribe it as 'quality' television by adopting high production values such as background music in the classical register (combined with the monks' ethereal chants), location filming of a landscape and setting worthy of a heritage film, and slow, lingering shots of the monks and men at prayer, objects such as candle flames and the Abbey Church. These effects were compounded by the middle-class educated language of the voice-over commentary, much of the monks' and the men's talk and the Abbot's reflections on the men's progress. The focus on 'quality' in the production of *The Monastery* suggests that class is one of the elements in its success – I will return to this theme later in the chapter.

Perhaps, however, the most innovative aspect of *The Monastery* is the filming of moments of silence; in the first programme of the series, one of the monks, Father Luke, asks the men to listen to the silence in the Abbey Church; the programme then develops this theme, which perhaps reaches its apogee in what was described by the viewers/retreatants I interviewed as 'Tony's white stone moment'. In this scene, in a final meeting with his mentor, Father Francis, Tony describes a strange state that he has never experienced before and that he can only comprehend as the presence of God. He says he is struggling to find words to describe this, and Father Francis advises him not to bother. The camera then focuses on Tony's expression of awe and wonder for several minutes, and nothing is said. Finally, Father Francis gives Tony a blessing. This is in sharp contrast to the constant verbalisation and movement required of participants in reality TV shows, who are often castigated for being too quiet or inactive by programme presenters and the press. Moments of silence are clearly unusual for the medium generally, and, as we will see, this daring scene was much remarked on.

The Convent was an altogether noisier programme than *The Monastery*, despite the nuns' spiritual and quiet lives. The men in *The Monastery* do indeed have conflicts, and even at one point a shouting match, but this is framed by the quietness I have described, which is present but more fragmented in *The Convent*. The four women participants in *The Convent* are represented as being at a crisis point in their lives, and there is a great deal of rule-breaking, soul-searching and crying. *The Convent* seems to be offering different pleasures, those of a high level of affective expression, rather than the tranquil scenes and settings of *The Monastery*; the 'soap opera' narrative of the women's lives and stay in *The Convent* is stronger here than the claims to 'quality' television we see in *The Monastery*. These differences are already indicated by the trailer for the programme, which billed it as 'detox for the soul' and constructed a pink and beauty-products-oriented version of femininity through images of 'pampering', which must have seemed a far cry from the realities of their lives to the nuns, ever busy with domestic duties or calls to prayer. The change in production team necessitated by the imperative to maintain an all-female environment at the convent may in part explain these differences.

Religion, then, becomes visible here in highly gendered form. The monks are not shown engaging in domestic tasks, whereas the nuns are; the monks officiate at mass, whereas of course the nuns must rely on the good offices of the local parish priest. The filming of the vast space of the Abbey Church and extensive grounds at Worth creates an image of austere but transcendent spirituality, traditionally associated with masculinity (Woodhead and Sointu 2008: 259–276). The nuns inhabit a smaller space and are more confined than the monks, who go out into the world as priests, teachers and nurses; a claustrophobic quality is conveyed through the filming of that space and of the women participants' rebellion against their confinement within it. In what follows I will consider the extent to which the reception of the programmes is marked and differentiated both by gender and class and how it participates in the construction of 'postsecular Britain'.

3 The press reception of *The Monastery* and *The Convent*

My analysis of the press reception of the two programmes is based on samples of newspaper reviews or short comments at the time of or immediately preceding the broadcasts, collected using the *Lexis Nexis* database. In this time frame, *The Monastery* was reviewed in nine national papers and six regional or Scottish ones, and there were in total 29 press reviews or short comments, with most (21) appearing in the national, mainly 'broadsheet' press. *The Guardian*, *The Telegraph*, *The Times* and *The Observer* all reviewed the programme four times, while *The Mirror* mentioned it only once, *The Mail on Sunday* published one review and *The Sun* ignored it completely. The 'quality papers' (*The Guardian*, *The Telegraph*, *The Times*, *The Observer* and *The Independent*) thus constitute 62 % of this sample of the press reception of *The Monastery* and also provide almost four-fifths of the positive reviews of the programme. Overall 22 of 29 (i.e., 76 %) of the reviews are positive, four are negative, and three are mixed or neutral (24 %). The negative reviews are concentrated in the regional and Scottish press: two in the *Glasgow Herald*, one in the *Evening Standard* and one in *The Scotsman*.

The theme of the quality of the programmes, and particularly their quality in relation to other examples of reality television, is present in 45 % of the pieces and thus is arguably the dominant discourse. Interestingly, most critics have few qualms about referring to *The Monastery* as reality television whilst simultaneously praising its quality features, unlike the programme-makers for whom, as we have seen, this was anathema. Mark Lawson (2005: 17) writing in *The Guardian* commented, for instance: 'Gabe Solomon's elegant and thoughtful series has already achieved a miracle: restoring the reputation of reality TV'. Here reality television has been elevated to a higher cultural status through the acquisition of a named *auteur*, the co-producer, Gabe Solomon. The then Abbot of Worth, Christopher Jamison, was also identified as a kind of *auteur* by critics; Lawson, for instance, described him as combining an 'actorish voice and looks with a kind of brain that has recently been more or less banned from television', while Kathryn Flett (2005: 20) in *The Observer* found the Abbot 'almost unbearably charismatic'. The programme was connected by critics with other 'quality' productions of various kinds; Mark Lawson suggested that, like *Brideshead Revisited*, *The Monastery* might result in an upsurge of recruitment to the Catholic Church. This comparison is clearly highly significant, since *Brideshead* was a landmark programme with all the characteristics of 'quality' TV: literary adaptation, classically inspired theme music, filming of heritage settings – Oxford and Castle Howard in Yorkshire – and 'serious' actors such as Jeremy Irons speaking Evelyn Waugh's original words in honeyed tones and perfect received pronunciation English. Kathryn Flett (2005: 20) commented that the Worth Abbey Church was 'lovely (as in *Grand Designs* lovely)', linking *The Monastery* to the Channel 4 programme about people (mostly middle-class professionals) building their own architecturally innovative houses. The mapping of the press reception thus far confirms that at one level the success of *The Monastery* is a discursive phenomenon – and that this discursive success is *classed*, that is, created by middle-class agents in papers read mainly by middle-class readers. In this sense we can see a match between the producers' intentions to distinguish themselves from 'modern TV tricks' and the critical reception, which essentially congratulates them on this.

The second most recurrent theme in the reviews was the adoption of a sceptical position in relation to religion – with a third of these critics adopting such a stance. This could be combined with praise or criticism of the programmes, but in either case, it allows the critic to identify him- or herself with a rationalist position, which in itself is a mark of education and status in many spheres of middle-class British culture. In this way, despite his obvious enthusiasm for the aesthetic pleasures of the programme, Mark Lawson retains his status as a liberal intellectual by arguing for a critical stance in relation to established religion:

'Like the coverage of the papal funeral, *The Monastery* tends to be too generous and gentle'. Nancy Banks-Smith (2005: 22) of *The Guardian* also adopted a sceptical position, maintaining her habitual irony: 'Worth has the feel of an excellent, if austere, public school. They teach silence, obedience and humility here'. Other critics adopted a more aggressively secularist stance, identifying strongly with modernity and science: 'What they're after is a kind of stealth proselytising [...] I am now doing whatever the atheist equivalent of praying for Tony's soul might be, since one doesn't like to see a man squander the priceless Darwinian gift of rationality like this' (Sutcliffe 2005: 46). In one review, published in a Scottish paper, the classed nature of the style of the programme (and perhaps its atmosphere of Englishness), as well as the religious content and aims, is remarked on and leads to rejection: 'I probably haven't got the hang of the spiritual life, but I can't help noticing the resemblance between Worth Abbey and a rather decent health farm. Stick a golf course on the place and you could call it a country club. A contemplative regime may have its rigours, but the Benedictine monks don't appear to have thought of testing their faith in the inner city' (Bell 2005: 19). However, this is very exceptional, and the majority of the reviews identify positively with the classed culture of the programme.

Alongside this sceptical position, there is also a significant positive response to the religious and particularly the spiritual content of *The Monastery*. One critic, who had a long history of visiting Worth Abbey, placed herself at the opposite pole to the rationalist position: 'I was seduced. I let go of the ways of thinking I had held so dear and allowed myself to be transformed through their mystical vision of God' (Ind 2005: 10). Another journalist spent two days at Worth just before the broadcast and wrote a positive account from the perspective of a fascinated and respectful outsider in *The Telegraph* (Brook 2005: np). The critics' interest in the spiritual dimension of the programmes is also expressed through the fact that several commented on Tony's spiritual experience (the 'white stone moment') in the final programme:

> Did you catch the last episode of *The Monastery* last week? It was amazing. The viewer observed what can only be described as a spiritual awakening, caught on camera. (Matthews 2005: 18)

Even Nancy Banks-Smith, after describing Tony as 'having the look of a small boy who has seen a spaceman and can't make anyone believe him', concluded that 'the intelligence, patience and gentle amusement of the monks was as soothing as the hypnotic swaying of their robes as they processed to church'. Only 'the odd chromosome' prevented her from 'giving it a go' (Banks-Smith 2005: 22). Here again, religion is represented as having a hypnotic and seductive quality that can only be resisted by the invocation of science and the materiality of human life. Stephen Pile of *The Telegraph* concluded that *The Monastery* was 'the best and most constructive piece of religious broadcasting in recent television history', and that 'Tony's final meeting with his spiritual advisor was remarkable for the fact that it contained prolonged periods of television silence as they wrestled with thoughts that were beyond words' (2005: 19). Like those adopting a secularist stance, this group of critics see religion as desirable, or potentially desirable, in the contemporary conjuncture, attributing powers of influence and persuasion to it; unlike them they see this as a force for the good, and its mysteries as benign. Alongside the need to demonstrate secular or even secularist credentials, we can then observe in these reviews a representation of religion as a seductive force, whose attractions lie in dimensions that cannot be explained by words: silence, mysticism and spirituality.

The positive response to spirituality in the press coverage of *The Monastery* is in itself representing the programme as evidence of a postsecular climate. While several reviews comment on the surprise success of the programmes, it is interpreted by some as an indication that 'spirituality is now in', or that 'there is still demand out there for what the Church offers' (Gledhill 2005: 26). Maggie Brown in *The Observer* surveys positive audience responses to a range of recent religious broadcasting, including *The Monastery*, under the headline: 'Viewers' prayers answered as religion enjoys a dramatic television comeback: From martyrs to monks, the appetite for spiritual topics is ravenous and the BBC aims to go on feeding it' (Brown 2006: np). The critic in the *Sunday Express* claimed that 'young people particularly are responding to the series' and quoted a spokesperson for the Catholic Enquiry Service: '[M]any young people are seeking direction in life and *The Monastery* has fed that hunger' (Fitzherbert 2005: 21). Alongside these images of spiritual hunger, the theme of 'spiritual journey' is also invoked in the reviews of *The Monastery*: 'It was twenty-nine year old Tony's *journey* from cynical soft pornographer to wide-eyed believer that captured the spirit of the experience' (Flett 2005: 18; emphasis added). The idea of the journey towards personal fulfilment and self-expression is, as I have discussed elsewhere (Thomas 2011), ubiquitous in lifestyle and reality television, particularly in a culture based on individualism and consumerism generally, and in this way the critics are making connections between this representation of religious experience and broader cultural trends. The reception thus illustrates both the continuing strength of the secular in British culture and the 'postsecular' moment, in that it combines this with a profound interest in these representations of spirituality. In this context the programme's high cultural qualities perhaps give permission for affirmation of the spiritual, of what is 'beyond words'.

The press reception of *The Convent* demonstrates how successfully *The Monastery* kindled the sparks of critical interest, since the sequel attracted significantly more press coverage: 54 as opposed to 29 reviews. The distribution of the reviews is very different from that of *The Monastery*, in that they are less concentrated in the quality press (43 % as opposed to 62 %), and there are correspondingly more reviews in the regional and tabloid press, which constitute 33 % and 24 % of the sample, respectively. This may simply be expressive of the broader interest in the sequel resulting from the earlier programme's success. However, the press reception of *The Convent* is far less positive than that of *The Monastery*, with 43 % of the reviews positive (as opposed to 76 %) and 24 % negative (as opposed to 10 %). The location of the positive reviews also contrasts with those of *The Monastery* in that only 22 % are in the national 'quality' papers, with most (43 %) in the regional press and 35 % in the tabloid press. Thus the most striking aspect of the comparison is that, unlike *The Monastery*, *The Convent* fails to capture the imagination of the 'quality' press but has a broader appeal than the former programme, with more positive responses in the regional and tabloid press. Clearly, this generally more critical reception by the press raises the question of why this representation of religion is deemed less desirable and how gender is informing this dynamic.

The discourse of a 'postsecular' society hungry for religion, present in the reviews of *The Monastery*, is reprised again here by some reviewers, with one critic asking, 'So could it be that society has reached a peak of excess and is ready to re-examine its values?' (Jones 2006: 6). The opposite pole, a secularist distrust of religion, is also expressed here: 'Alarming to see how quickly their new surroundings force these women to question their belief systems' (Proud 2006: 81). However, perhaps the most striking feature of the reviews of *The Convent* is the sense of disappointment – that it does not deliver the quality features or spiritual atmosphere of *The Monastery*. The notion that the second programme is an attempt to 'cash in' on the success of the first is one aspect of this trend: 'Television producers, as we know, cannot let a good idea lie [...] So it comes as no surprise that *The Monastery* – last year's quiet hit in which five blokes went to live among monks and reassess their approach to life and spirituality – has been adapted to feature women living in a convent' (Ridgway 2006: 42). Cynicism about the programme-makers' motivations was a theme in many articles on *The Convent*, particularly in terms of the choice of the women participants: 'They may well have all been on quests to find meaning in their lives, but one had the sneaking suspicion that they really had been chosen because the producer thought they were a lively mix and would make good television' (Matthew 2006: 65). Whereas *The Monastery* was reviewed as 'quality' television, or as 'quality reality', *The Convent* is pushed firmly back into the reality stable by reviewers:

> If *The Convent*'s makers hadn't already succeeded with a show entitled *The Monastery* [...] I reckon their newie might have been called Big Sister. [...] [T]hese self-same programme-makers evidently consulted Big Brother's Bumper Book of Rules, honing in on the first commandment of modern-day reality TV: ensure that your participants comprise a freak show. (Belcher 2006: 21)

As this comment suggests, criticism of the women participants is a major feature of the reception. Whilst the nuns are almost universally praised for their patience, kindness and wisdom, the women are variously described as 'petulant, paranoid, emotionally indulgent, neurotic, petty and self obsessed' (Heggie 2006: 44), 'naughty schoolgirls' (Johns 2006: 27) and guilty of 'wilful behaviour – a deliberate flouting of the rules' (Chater and Jackson 2006: 61). An ironic tone in describing the women is also prevalent: 'Iona – the only Christian of the group – was wetter than Wet Wet Wet singing "Raindrops keep fallin' on my head" underwater in Seaworld' (Virtue 2006: 29); 'Debi was abandoned by her mother as a sobbing five-year-old and is still a sobbing five-year-old, trying so hard to be a good girl' (Banks-Smith 2006: 32). The differences between the programmes that I have described must in part account for the more negative response to *The Convent*, which fails to appeal, particularly to the 'quality' press, because it lacks some of the aesthetic qualities of *The Monastery*. However, the vehement criticism and irony deployed in descriptions of the women participants are in sharp contrast to the positive and even affectionate terms used to comment on the male participants in *The Monastery*. In one review the women are compared to the men and found to be lacking in spiritual qualities: 'Unlike the men in *The Monastery* who took it all very seriously, these women seemed to have no spiritual component whatsoever' (Pile 2006: 19). The turning points in the 'spiritual journeys' of the women do not impress the critics in the same way as Tony's 'white stone' moment. In one instance (Thomas Sutcliffe in *The Independent*), the 'moment' is discussed as a televisual construction, rather than in spiritual terms, as had been the case for Tony: 'Iona's spontaneous moment of religious transcendence must have involved gaffers and cameramen clomping around switching lights on and off and directors cueing her up so that the long reverse zoom would end with the right framing' (Sutcliffe 2006: 22). Again, an ironic tone dominates in these reviews: '[D]oubtless they'll all be donning habits and sniffing incense by the end of the series' (Stephen 2006: 59); 'How about a second series called Vocation, Vocation, Vocation?' (Hitt 2006: 18).

The nuns, although spoken of in the main with respect by the press, are not seen as spiritual leaders in the same way as the monks, and a cultural reaffirmation of the connection between masculinity and spirituality and femininity and relational work seems to be evidenced in these receptions. More precisely, whilst the monks are seen as demonstrating unusual capacities for relational work, and praised for this, the nuns' kindness and patience do not suffice to 'lift' the programme to the level of success of *The Monastery* as a positive representation of religion: something seems to be lacking. In some reviews the nuns are described as excessively tolerant, for example in relation to one of the women participants who is married and in an 'open relationship', sharing her time between her husband and a lover. There is also the occasional hint in the reviews that the nuns' understanding of the women and the situation may be limited: 'The nuns' insight into the women, however, is rather simplistic. "It's not your fault" the Abbess told Debi, who had chosen her as her mentor. Well, blow me down with a rosary' (Stephen 2006: 59). There are only two physical descriptions of the nuns in the reviews, but both are in stark contrast to Lawson's evocation of the Abbot's 'actorish good looks'; Nancy Banks-Smith (2006: 32) in *The Guardian* refers to the nuns as 'brown as field mice in their habits', while Paul English in *The Daily Record* comments, 'there's always the chaste nuns with their beards and brown teeth' (English 2006: 31). Although this is not a dominant strand in the reviews, it is nonetheless significant that here religious women cannot escape being judged in terms of their appearance; the image of brown mice is particularly telling – associating the nuns with an image of humble, tiny creatures, reminiscent of a Beatrix Potter story. Whilst many reviews imply that the nuns' patience and tolerance stems from their spiritual lives when confronted with guests who flout the rules of the convent and even abuse their hospitality, only one makes a clear connection between the nuns and the kind of transcendent spirituality which Woodhead and Sointu (2008) argue is more frequently associated with masculinity: 'In last night's opener, the nuns came across as charming, gentle but tough, articulate, attentive, funny and without a trace of smugness – as though, in fact, they had access to a deep source of bliss denied the rest of us' (Heggie 2006: 44). However, even here the ironic tone rapidly returns, with the reviewer commenting that, if it was all an act for the camera, the nuns are good enough to get their own series: 'Spirit Doctor, maybe, in which they go round suburban homes teaching the transforming power of self-denial and silence?' (Heggie 2006: 44). This sentence concludes the paragraph and reinscribes the nuns in the domestic through the comparison with *House Doctor*, a series focusing on preparing houses for sale by 'dressing' them appropriately; the effect is further reinforced by the adjective 'suburban', which, with its links to 'housewife', connects the nuns to traditional female roles and to a devalued cultural context. This, again, is in sharp contrast to *The Monastery's* association with architecture and innovation through the *Grand Designs* comparison.

Despite the predominant praise of the nuns in the press, *The Convent* lacks the allure of the first series for the critics; there is no talk here of being swayed or seduced, and this representation of religion, which is more about the women's emotional lives and struggles, is perhaps less attractive because it is perceived as failing to provide the spiritual and aesthetic imagery which had attracted positive comments on *The Monastery*.

4 Retreatants' responses to *The Monastery* and *The Convent*

What then of the responses of viewers? To what extent do they mirror those of professional critics, both in terms of gender and the construction and expression of a 'postsecular moment'? The viewing figures suggest that the audience, like the critics, was less impressed by *The Convent* than *The Monastery*: the latter programme attracted 2.57 million viewers on its first broadcast, and retained 2.39 and 2.35 in the next two, whereas *The Convent* started well with 2.75, most probably because of its forerunner's reputation, but then dropped each week, to 1.8, 1.65 and 1.61 (BARB 2006). These figures, though still impressive in the context of religious broadcasting, seem to express something akin to the disappointment that dominates the press reviews. Clearly, however, they can tell us little beyond this in terms of the feelings and responses of viewers. In order to explore such responses, I attended four retreats at Worth Abbey in May, June and July 2006, after negotiations with the Abbot and Retreat Leader at Worth, Father Patrick Fludder. At these retreats I presented myself as a researcher but also as a participant, both in the time-honoured tradition of participant observation and as a fairly accurate reflection of my own position, for like many of the retreatants I had felt drawn to Worth by the experience of watching *The Monastery* (in my case on video, in January 2006). The retreats I attended – 'Finding Faith' and 'Finding Sanctuary' – were designed by the monks as a 'follow-up' to the programme, a way of responding to the wave of enquiries about coming to Worth which followed it. The retreats coincided with the broadcast of *The Monastery Revisited* and *The Convent*, and there was lively discussion of all three programmes, often in the informal spaces of the retreats, over coffee or at meals. However, as the retreats took place one year after the first broadcast, what is not captured here is the initial response to *The Monastery*. According to the then Abbot of Worth, Christopher Jamison, many retreatants who came to Worth immediately after the broadcast were entirely new to religion. My respondents, on the other hand, were mostly lapsed Catholics or Protestants, or practising Catholics or Protestants in need of spiritual renewal – fourteen of the respondents identified themselves as Catholic (including lapsed), and the rest included Church of England, Baptist and Quaker, or general Christian.

I offered several ways of participating in the research – a semi-structured interview or discussion group during the retreat (at a time when most people went for walks or had naps to recover from the early morning start), or an open-ended questionnaire, which some people filled in at the time and others emailed later. In these ways a total of nineteen responses were collected. Of these nineteen people, fourteen were women and five were men; eleven were White British, seven were Irish or British Irish and one was Lithuanian. The age range was quite broad, with four under 35, four in their 40s, six in their 50s, and five over 60. Most were in or had retired from upper or lower middle-class professions, and about two-thirds were educated to degree level or above. Again we can observe that *The Monastery* is a middle-class cultural success. The high percentage of women in the group (and attending the retreats generally) is consistent with other research, such as Heelas and Woodhead's (2005) findings on the significant numbers of women participating in both congregational religion and alternative spiritual practices. I have given a full account of these responses elsewhere (Thomas 2011); my discussion here revolves around the extent to which they are consistent with or in contrast to the press reception, and how they emerge from the context of the retreats.

Of course, whilst my nineteen respondents do not in any way represent 'the audience', they are an element of the engaged audience – those for whom, in most cases, the television broadcast has played some role in their decision to come to Worth on retreat. Some respondents made a very direct connection between watching the programme and making the journey to Worth:

> The Monastery programme has brought me closer to my Catholic faith and I was so influenced by the programme and the love emanating from the monks that I wanted to experience a retreat at Worth Abbey for myself (F, late 40s, White British, company director).

> I was absolutely hooked. It was the way the monks treated the men. There was something special about them. I thought it would be wonderful to be in their presence. [...] It was as though watching *The Monastery* seemed to draw me to Worth. It was a journey I somehow just had to make (F, early 70s, White British, retired secretary).

In these cases, retreatants seem to express a desire to enter the diegesis or narrative world created by the programme and to receive the same attention from the monks that the men in the programme benefited from. In this way, going on retreat at Worth becomes a form of pilgrimage to the filmed site, which acquires an added dimension of spiritual significance because it has been filmed and, perhaps more importantly, because of the way it has been filmed. The programme's high production values – the music, setting and slow pace of the filming – make this possible for these predominantly (though not exclusively) middle-class viewers; there is nothing here to offend or jar, and the programme corresponds to an aesthetic that appeals to their cultural backgrounds. If, as Nick Couldry (2003: 77) argues, media pilgrimages are 'an acting out in space of the constructed "distance" between "ordinary world" and "media world"', this is compounded here by the fact that the media site is also a sacred space, that is, one consecrated for worship, and in that sense is also extraordinary. Couldry (2003: 77) argues that we cannot fully make sense of such journeys unless we also consider their relationship to the 'domestic space from which the media pilgrim sets out'. Interestingly, the second respondent cited above explained to me that she had taken bed and breakfast accommodation for the night before and the night after the retreat. Her motivation was clearly practical in that her journey home was a long one by coach to the opposite end of the country, but at the same time, the B and B seemed to be providing a transitional space that would enable her to re-adapt to a less heightened reality, to ordinariness; she described its homely comforts and how the woman owner would be keen to talk to her about her experiences – perhaps providing some of the 'love' that my respondent had imagined coming from the monks.

Others, as I have described elsewhere, talked about their ordinary lives in terms of the exhaustion of working in a neoliberal regime, often in a caring role (Thomas 2011). The domestic spaces were not entirely havens but were invaded by struggles with bereavement, with personal and professional caring responsibilities and even, in the case of a (woman) vicar and a vicar's wife, with being, in some sense, professional Christians, never off-duty. The programme had allowed these retreatants to imagine a space where they could be cared for by the monks, like the men, but also a space of 'other-worldliness'. Once on the retreat, it was clear that many were fascinated by the monks, who were simultaneously available and not available, 'in the world but not of it'. This effect, clearly resulting from the monks' vocation, which placed clear boundaries around their interactions with retreatants, was intensified by the fact that they had also appeared on TV and thus also in this sense represented distance from ordinariness. The monks appeared from the closed space of the monastery at the offices, chanted ethereally and then disappeared, just as they had traversed the television screen. The retreat leader, Father Patrick, slept in the retreat house, and he and one or two other monks shared meals with the retreatants, so that ordinariness was at times restored in encounters over toast and cornflakes. Nonetheless, there was a shared feeling of being in a special place. Retreatants commented on the powerful atmosphere of the Abbey church, and some sat in the church late at night in the darkness; others were moved by recognising some of the chants from the programme or by seeing monks they recognised from the television at the offices. The experience of the retreat seemed to be intensified by being in the space where silence and mystery had been made 'visible'. Significantly, almost all the respondents singled out Tony's 'white stone moment', which was also remarked on by the press, as memorable:

> I was transfixed by each individual journey. Tony's moment was something which I still find extremely moving. (F, early 20s, Irish British; childcare worker)

> Tony's strange experience with Francis – the 'white stone' moment. (F, early 50s, Irish)

> Tony's revelation – very moving. (M, early 50s, Irish British)

> My favourite image however was the one when the monk gave one of the men the white stone and said it was something they did, following the book of revelations. That moment it felt like all the talk of faith which could seem alien to non-believers was made real. (F, early 30s, White British, administrator)

The last of these comments illustrates precisely how the programme has succeeded in making religious experience *visible* and real in a sometimes inimical cultural context. For the retreatants, as for some of the critics, the representation of spirituality and of mystery is a key element in making this representation of religion desirable.

For another respondent, watching the programme had put religion back on the agenda and acted as a reminder of a long-held desire to re-engage with Catholicism:

> I was also impressed with the intellectual capabilities of pretty much all the monks. At the point of watching I was very much a 'resting' Catholic having been unable to reconcile the rational historical nature of the studies I had been engaged in for some considerable time with the leap of faith needed to remain a believer. (F, late 50s, White British, administrator)

One of the striking features here is the comment on the intellectual abilities of the monks, which, along with the aesthetic qualities of the programmes, seem to give permission to be moved by the representation of faith (Thomas 2011). The secular, or even at times secularist, elements of the press reception are a significant aspect of the cultural context in which the middle-class believers and spiritual seekers interrogated here are operating. It is not surprising if they found in *The Monastery* a form of religion that they could match with middle-class taste and a source of support in secular cultural milieus:

> For myself I had many of my views reinforced. I was given permission to hold views I have only felt able to share with few people in the past. (F, early sixties, White British, retired social worker)

The programmes are used as a resource, not only in the sense of surviving in a predominantly secular world, but also in a spiritual sense; they can be watched over and over again because of their aesthetic and spiritual qualities:

> Initially I thought what beautiful grounds Worth is situated in, and then gradually I became impressed with the sincerity and gravitas of the monks. [...] Sprog also recorded the programmes and we have watched them many times since. I use them as a kind of chilling device. (F, late 50s, White British, administrator)

In contrast, *The Convent* is not seen as functioning in this way or as offering these pleasures and support. The retreatants are at least as critical, and in some cases more critical, of the programme than the press reviewers. Like the latter, they are almost entirely positive in their comments on the nuns but very critical of the women participants and of the programme-makers, whose motivations they distrust:

> I felt that the makers of *The Convent* were trying to create 'titillating TV' by putting in characters such as the woman who lived with two men and contrasting her with the nuns in the cloistered convent, i.e., trying to shock the nuns. Having these characters in the programme totally detracted from the good things that could have come out of the programme. (F, late 40s, White British, company director)

Feelings of irritation and anger with the women meant that the programme was the opposite of a 'chilling device'; for these retreatants, in search of spiritual space and nurture, watching four disturbed and at times rebellious women struggle with a regimented life was not relaxing. The phrase 'titillating TV' also suggests that *The Convent* has not met the requirements for quality television that *The Monastery* so amply delivered. Whilst the monks were seen as more than capable of dealing both with the programme-makers and the men (whose most rebellious moment was when two of them ran down to the village to buy sweets), the nuns were seen as vulnerable to exploitation:

> My daughter and I have discussed *The Convent* and we both felt irritated / angry with the women, respectful of the nuns, and slightly worried that the nuns, unlike the monks, were being exploited both by the female participants and the programme makers. (F, early 50s, Irish, consultant in health sector)

As alluded to in the press reviews, there was also a feeling that the nuns were not entirely in control of the situation:

> For their part, the nuns were out of their depth with these neurotic and manipulative women, so week by week the viewer had to watch the nuns floundering. The nuns were far too kind and compassionate when they needed to be firm and compassionate. (F, early 60s, White British, retired social worker)

Clearly, 'watching the nuns floundering' does not provide the experience of spiritual nurture that was found in *The Monastery*. A crucial element of that nurturing is the sense of structure and authority associated with the monks, and particularly the Abbot. This seems to result in part from the fact that the women participants do rebel more than the men – they are constantly late for offices, drink and talk in their rooms at night and even go to the pub. However, despite equally caring and cogent analyses of their guests' behaviour, the nuns are not seen as authoritative figures in the way the monks are; authority is thus associated with masculinity and found to be lacking in femininity.

5 Conclusion

As the analysis above suggests, both the representation of religion in these programmes and its reception are highly gendered; *The Monastery* offers an image of transcendent spirituality through a representation of masculinity that combines caring with power, whilst in *The Convent*, the nuns are equally caring but are seen as victims or potential victims of the programme-makers and their rebellious guests. This threat to the sacred space of the real and filmed convent is disturbing for some viewers, who are then unable to find in the programme the spiritual comfort and resource that they sought and found in *The Monastery*. In this sense *The Monastery*, which was hailed as a ground-breaking representation of religion, in fact reinforces existing norms of association of the spiritual with the masculine. Similarly, *The Convent* emphasises the cultural connections between femininity and affect verging on hysteria as well as between femininity and domesticity.

In some ways the programmes are grappling with a problem that is inherent in Christianity itself, that is, the gendered nature of Christian virtues: relational work is still women's work, and putting others before oneself is a requirement of many feminine roles. Thus the caring characteristics which seem extraordinary in the monks become ordinary when associated with women. In one review of *The Convent*, published in *The Guardian*, sociologist of religion Kristin Aune argues that the women participants' rebellion in *The Convent* is illustrative of a general trend of women being dissatisfied with the church because it does not provide spaces for anything other than traditional feminine roles: 'Since industrialisation, the church has operated alongside the private sphere of the home. Home-centred women without careers have been its backbone, running coffee mornings, visiting sick parishioners and teaching at Sunday school' (Aune 2006: 32). Both the experience of watching *The Monastery* and the retreats at Worth offered an escape from this domesticated participation in religion, which has traditionally been expected of women, to my mainly women respondents. Off-the-record conversations with some made it clear that feminist critiques of the patriarchal structure of the Catholic Church were being put 'on hold' in order to become immersed in the quiet and nurturing situation offered by the retreat experience. For these women, as Aune suggests, the realities of parish life may be less alluring than the 'extraordinary' spaces of the retreat and the programme. The latter are even more extraordinary because of their masculinity, which in time-honoured manner is associated with spirituality and, more innovatively, with caring (Thomas 2011).

Both programmes, then, raise the unresolved question of gender in spiritual lives and experiences in religious cultures in contemporary Britain; they also illuminate some of the tensions between secular and religious currents in British society. In particular, the press reception of *The Monastery* expresses a tension between the adoption of a secular (or even secularist), ironic mode and a discourse of 'being seduced by religion' and of finding something in the programme that is lacking in contemporary consumerist ways of life. The version of religion that is attractive to reviewers in the 'quality' papers and to my mainly middle-class retreatants is focused on prayer and silence, offering an escape from, or containment of, the affective excesses of much contemporary lifestyle and reality television; it is also aesthetically pleasing. This finding is consistent with the increase in attendance at cathedral services as opposed to ordinary parish services, where attendance is in decline (Thinking Anglicans 2011); it seems that a desirable version of Christianity in a context where a secular stance is often the mark of education and 'middle-classness' needs to be both spiritual and spectacular. The success of *The Monastery* with professional critics and audiences is in part explained by its combination of these two elements with caring masculinities.

References

Aune, Kirstin. 2006. [Comment and debate] "Sex, work and singleness: Women were once the backbone of the church. No more. A reality show in a convent shows why." *The Guardian* 1 July: 32.

Banks-Smith, Nancy. 2005. "TV Review: Animal magic." *The Guardian* May 11: 22.

–. 2005. "TV review: Kitchen sink drama." *The Guardian* 25 May: 22.

–. 2006. "How would four troubled women cope with the rigours of convent life?" *The Guardian* June 15: 32.

BARB [Broadcasters' Audience Research Board]. 2006. "The Convent." Viewing Figures: Weeks Ending June 18 / 25 / July 2 / 9. Available at: http://www.barb.co.uk/report/weeklyTopProgrammesOverview. Accessed: 11 November 2011.

Belcher, David. 2006. "When nuns shall pass muster." *The Glasgow Herald* 5 June: 21.

Bell, Ian. 2005. "Series that moves slower than a Sunday in the Western Isles." *The Glasgow Herald* 18 May: 19.

Blake, John. 2006. (Executive Producer, BBC2's The Monastery and The Convent) Private Correspondence with Lyn Thomas.

Brooke, Simon. 2005. "The first 30 years are the hardest: The life of a Benedictine monk has been a surprise television hit, reports Simon Brooke, the only journalist allowed to share their monastery." *The Telegraph* 24 May: 15.

Brown, Maggie. 2006. "Viewers' prayers answered as religion enjoys a dramatic television comeback." *The Observer*. Available at: http://www.guardian.co.uk/media/2006/may/21/raceandreligion.religion. Accessed: 18 November 2011.

Chater, David and Jackson, J. 2006. "TV Choice." *The Times* 24 June: 61.

Couldry, Nick. 2003. *Media Rituals: A Critical Approach*. London: Routledge.

Davies, Matthew. 2005. "Matthew Davies Column." [North-East] *Evening Gazette* 31 May: 18.

Deans, Jason. 2005. "BBC gets into the habit with convent reality show." *The Media Guardian* online. September 21. Available at: http://www.guardian.co.uk/media/2005/sep/21/realitytv.bbc. Accessed: 11 November 2009.

English, Paul. 2006. "Cars, cash or kisses? Nun of the above: The Convent, BBC2, Wednesday." *The Daily Record* 15 June: 31.

Fitzherbert, Henry. 2005. "Seeking peace in the cloisters." *The Sunday Express* May 22: 21.

Flett, Kathryn. 2005. "Review." *The Observer* 15 May: 20. Available at: http://www.guardian.co.uk/theobserver/2005/may/15/features.review27.

–. 2005. "Brotherly love island." *The Observer Review* 29 May: 18. Available at: http://www.guardian.co.uk/theobserver/2005/may/29/features.review27.

Gledhill, Ruth. 2005. "All of Europe will fall into anguish if we forget God, says Catholic leader." *The Times* 26 May: 26.

Heelas, Paul, and Linda Woodhead. 2005. *The Spiritual Revolution: Why Religion is Giving Way to Spirituality*. Oxford and Malden: Blackwell.

Heggie, Iain. 2006. "Who knew nuns made such great TV stars." *The Scotsman* 15 June: 44.

Hitt, Carolyn. 2006. "Big sister could become a habit." *Western Mail* 12 June: 18.

Ind, Jo. 2005. "Why this place is worth becoming a man." *Birmingham Post* 12 May: 10.

Johns, Ian. "Day one in big sister house." *The Times* 15 June: 27.

Jones, Catherine. 2006. "From a £200,000 diamond-encrusted crucifix to a reality show with a point." *Western Mail* 6 June: 6.

Lawson, Mark. 2005. "Lawson on TV: Get the abbey habit." *The Guardian* 9 May: 17.

Matthew, Christopher. "Leaving us nun the wiser." *Daily Mail* 15 June: 65.

Pile, Stephen. 2005. 'Pile on TV: Do you know the way, Saint Jos?' *Daily Telegraph* 28 May: 19.

–. 2006. "No such thing as clean dirt." *The Daily Telegraph* 8 July: 19.

Proud, Danielle. 2006. "Watch this: The Convent." *The Guardian* 10 June: 81.

Ridgway, Imogen. 2006. "Pick of the night." *The Evening Standard* 14 June: 42.

Stephen, Jaci. 2006. "Club 18–30? I'd rather be a nun." *The Mail on Sunday* 18 June: 59.

Sutcliffe, Thomas. 2005. "Last Night's TV: Give me the Abbey over Abi any time." *The Independent* 18 May: 46.

–. 2006. "Reviews: They can't curb their enthusiasm." *The Independent* 29 June: 22.

Tiger Aspect for BBC2. 2005. *The Monastery*. 2005. Producers Gabe Solomon and Dollan Cannell. Edited by Martin Cooper and directed by Dollan Cannell. Transmitted on BBC2 from 15 May 2005 (4 episodes).

Tiger Aspect for BBC2. 2006. The Convent. 2006. Producer/Director Rebecca Ciallella. Transmitted on BBC2 from 7 June 2006 (4 episodes).

Tiger/Tigress Productions for the Learning Channel, US. The Monastery. 2006. Producers Chester Dent and Kevin Jarvis. Transmitted on the Learning Channel from October 22, 2006 (5 episodes).

Thomas, Lyn. 2011. "Changing old habits? 'New Age' Catholicism, subjectivity and gender in BBC2's *The Monastery* and its reception." *European Journal of Cultural Studies* 14 (5): 558–572.

Thinking Anglicans. 2011. *Cathedral Attendance Statistics*. Available at: http://www.thinkinganglicans.org.uk/archives/004974.html.

Virtue, Graeme. 2006. "Poor Clares … having to put up with this lot." *The Sunday Herald* 18 June: 29.

Ward, Graham, and M. Hoelzl. *The New Visibility of Religion: Studies in Religion and Cultural Hermeneutics*. London and New York: Continuum.

Woodhead, Linda and E. Sointu. "Holistic Spirituality, Gender, and Expressive Selfhood." *Journal for the Scientific Study of Religion* 47 (2): 259–276.

David Herbert

5 Paradise Lost? Islamophobia, Post-liberalism and the Dismantling of State Multiculturalism in the Netherlands: The Role of Mass and Social Media

In the first decade of the twenty-first century, politics and everyday life in the Netherlands became polarized, under the influence of several conservative and populist movements that reflected a growing distrust of government and 'politics as usual', and a xenophobic and cultural conservative attitude towards migrants and migration, more specifically of Muslims and Islam. Politics took on the shape of a cultural war. (Boomkens 2010: 307)

The liberal center, not just the illiberal periphery, believe Muslim minorities still give their loyalty to their country of origin, not the one they now live in. (Sniderman and Hagendoorn 2007: 42)

[By] November 2006 [...t]he new policy of the Dutch government had become so imbued with Fortuyn's points of view that the 'familiar' image of the open and tolerant Netherlands, such as in the case of the aliens' policy and social security, was no longer recognised abroad (Margry 2007: 130)

Despite similar rhetorical rejections of multiculturalism by leading politicians elsewhere in Europe,[1] the 'cultural war' (Boomkens 2010) in the Netherlands has arguably had the most far-reaching political consequences. These have included the formation of three political parties on a principally anti-Islamic platform since 2000 (*Leefbar Nederland* [Livable Netherlands], *List Pim Fortuyn* and *Partij voor de Vrijheid* [PVV – Freedom Party]), each of which has enjoyed considerable electoral success and influenced the mainstream political agenda (Margry 2007), resulting in the dismantling of key aspects of institutional multiculturalism (Vertovec and Wessendorf 2010: 3–4), including (remarkably) the cessation of ethnic monitoring of labour market participation, the withdrawal of national-level funding for minority group organisations and the introduction of immigration processes which discriminate against social conservatives (Meer and Modood 2009: 474; Butler 2008: 3). Given the Netherlands' international reputation for tolerance and social progressivism (Cherribi 2010: 3), this turn of events is both troubling and puzzling.

---

1 These include the French, German and British leaders, Sarkozy (*France24* 2011), Merkel (Weaver 2010) and Cameron (*New Stateman* 2011).

It will be argued here that Dutch anti-Islam mobilisation has a distinctive profile. Successive populist Islamophobic campaigns (led by Fortuyn, van Gogh and Hirsi Ali, and Wilders) have come not from the traditional far right, but rather from figures who represent themselves as defenders of secular, liberal values– including being explicitly pro-gay– in contrast not only to American but also to other European anti-immigrant groupings (Vossen 2010: 27). Indeed, these figures are difficult to place in conventional political categories, including the labels 'conservative' and 'populist' used by Boomkens' above (Vossen 2010: 27); here, the term 'post-liberal' will be preferred, since these leaders are self-identified liberals, yet their attitude toward Muslim migrants is illiberal. Similarly, amongst the wider Dutch public, suspicion of Muslim minorities is not confined to traditional supporters of the far right but arguably extends to the 'liberal center' (Sniderman and Hagendoorn 2007: 42), meaning a wider and more influential support base, which may help explain why the reversal of institutional multiculturalism has extended further here than elsewhere. Such evidence suggests that the Netherlands is manifesting a new, 'post-liberal' politics of prejudice, with the potential to spread elsewhere amongst increasingly secular European populations (Norris and Inglehart 2011: 153).

It will be further argued that modern mass and social media are central to the rise and spread of post-liberal, Islamophobic attitudes, but also to their contestation. Thus social media are integral to contemporary journalistic practice, for example providing the means through which targeted advance publicity for broadcasts or features can be circulated and dominant cultural memories can be articulated and refreshed (Cherribi 2010: 146; Margry 2007). But they are also vital to the articulation of discourses of resistance and to the organisation of counter-cultural solidarities (D'Haenens 2007; Leurs et al. 2012).

Methodologically, this chapter seeks to advance the study of social media by situating them in the context of their interconnections both with mass media and with broader social and political processes. It does so through a *retroductive analysis* (Danemark et al. 1997: 96–106) of a range of alternative explanations that have been advanced for the rise of Islamophobia and the dismantling of multiculturalism in the Netherlands, triangulating these with evidence on the role of mass and social media to conclude that media play a much more central role than most commentators think, and by implication may do so elsewhere.

First, it will be useful to clarify some key terms. 'Religion' in this account features both as an ascribed identity, constructed by the mainstream media, and as a 'resistance identity' (Castells 1996: 356–7), articulated in response to dominant representations but not reducible to a reaction to them. The controversial term 'Islamophobia' (Iqbal 2010; Bleich 2011) is used here to mean 'indiscriminate negative attitudes or emotions directed at Islam or Muslims' (Bleich 2011:

1581). Hence it does not mean just any criticism of Islam or Muslims (however well- or ill-founded), but only the indiscriminate attribution of negative characteristics on the basis of an ascribed identity. 'Secularisation' is used here to mean a decline in the social significance of religion, a process connected in the Dutch case with the collapse of the Dutch pillar (*verzuiling*) system. In the relatively short period since the 1960s, Christianity in the Netherlands shifted from a key principle of social organization to a factor considered personally important by only an eighth (12.5 %) of the population, roughly a quarter of the figure for British (21 %) and half that for American (47.4 %) populations respectively (van der Veer 2006; World Values Survey 2006 – 9 wave, henceforward WVS 2006 – 9).

Four uses of the contested term 'multiculturalism' are distinguished here. First, 'empirical multiculturalism' refers to the simple fact of cultural diversity, in this case in Europe, primarily as a result of labour markets and immigration policies since the 1960s. Second, 'institutional multiculturalism' refers to (primarily) state-led responses to cultural diversity and is understood as 'a range of institutional initiatives [...] aiming to: reduce discrimination; promote equality of opportunity and overcome barriers to full participation in society; allow unconstrained access to public services; recognise cultural identities (as opposed to assimilation), and foster acceptance and cultural understanding of all groups' (Vertovec and Wessendorf 2010: 3 – 4). Third, 'philosophical multiculturalism' consists of philosophical arguments which seek to justify and define the legitimate scope of such initiatives (e. g., Taylor 1994). Fourth, what Gilroy (2006) calls 'everyday multiculture' refers to the unplanned product of social interaction in contexts ranging from work to education to leisure and sport, including both face-to-face and virtual encounters. The focus in this chapter is mostly on the second use.

1 Possible causes of the Dutch culture wars

Commentators disagree passionately about the causes of the Dutch culture wars. Some dismiss media factors, arguing that 'the media [...] do not have the power to set an agenda that is not [already] broadly shared by their audience' (Enztinger 2009: 827), whereas others assign media a central role (Shadid 2006; Cherribi 2010). Some argue that multicultural policies have generated popular resistance because they have failed to promote integration, either producing communal separatism by subsidising linguistic and cultural difference (Koopmans 2010: 1) or provoking majority resentment by over-emphasising identity claims (Sniderman and Hagendoorn 2007). Others argue that Dutch and international commentators have exaggerated the extent and generosity of the Dutch multiculturalism and ignored the strength of institutional and societal racism (Vasta 2007: 713). The importance of the legacy of the Dutch pillar system is also contested, with some challenging the widespread view that it provided a model for post-1960s immigrant integration (Vink 2007: 337), arguing that instead of integration on equal terms, new migrants were subordinated in a system of 'minorisation' (Rath et al. 1999). Some have stressed the role of cultural memory in Dutch reactions (Eyerman 2008), others the rapid secularisation of Dutch society (van der Veer 2006), and still others the responsibility of politicians in setting the tone of public debate, producing a negative spiral in which elite discursive polarisation feeds popular demands for assimilationist policies (Shahid 2006: 20).

Following a critical assessment of these arguments, this chapter will argue that while the media are often mentioned and discussed in depth in particular cases (Uitermark and Gielen 2010; Cherribi 2010), their overall impact has been underestimated and under-theorised. It will then be argued that the media (both mass and social, in interaction) play two key roles:

1. Influencing the agenda of public discussion by providing a negative framing of Islam and Muslims;
2. Personalising politics in a way that has enabled independent populist politicians (from Fortuyn to Wilders) to have a significant impact on national politics.

These media processes are common across many contemporary societies, but in the Dutch case they have had a particularly powerful impact on the political system because of their articulation with two specific features of the Dutch context, namely:

1. The openness and responsiveness of the Dutch political system means that populist politicians can have a rapid and significant impact. Although the institutionalisation of new political parties has been subject to the same weaknesses and limitations as elsewhere (e. g., the collapse of *List Fortuyn*), they have been able to exert an unusual degree of political pressure through significant electoral successes.
2. The unusually high value placed on personal and cultural autonomy (in global and even Western European terms) and general scepticism of any form of external authority amongst the Dutch (WVS 2006–9 wave) has made the Dutch particularly susceptible to accepting the media framing of Islam as the archetypical heteronomous and illiberal religion. This cluster of values may in turn be related to an unusually rapid, thorough and recent experience of secularisation (van der Veer 2006). But it may also be a sign of things to come elsewhere, as attitudes which are widespread across the

Dutch population are becoming more common amongst younger cohorts elsewhere in Western Europe (Norris and Inglehart 2011: 153).

The interaction of these four factors has enabled the agenda of 'new realist' (Prins and Suharso 2008: 365) anti-multiculturalism and Islamophobic ideas to affect Dutch politics to an unusual degree, leading to once marginal political ideas being implemented by mainstream parties of government (Margry 2007: 130).

2 Accounts of the dismantling of Dutch institutional multiculturalism: a critical appraisal

[M]ulticultural policies, which grant immigrants easy access to equal rights and do not provide strong incentives for host-country language acquisition and interethnic contacts when combined with a generous welfare state, have produced low levels of labour market participation, high levels of segregation and a strong overrepresentation of immigrants among those convicted for criminal behaviour. Sweden, Belgium and the Netherlands, which have combined multicultural policies with a strong welfare state, display relatively poor integration outcomes. (Koopmans 2010: 1)

It is necessary, proponents of multiculturalism contend, to go beyond "mere" tolerance because the heart of the matter is that the majority honor the claims of minorities to their own identities. This ordering of tolerance and identity, we will argue, gets things wrong all the way down. Bringing issues of identity to the fore undercuts support for the right of religious minorities to follow their own ways of life. (Sniderman and Hagenhoorn 2007: 16)

To assess the significance of media factors on the rise of Islamophobia and the reversals in context, it is necessary to locate them in relation to other factors that may be involved. As the above quotations illustrate, some empirical studies support the argument of post-liberal politicians that reversals in Dutch multicultural policies are justified because such policies are failing to achieve their aim of promoting integration. Thus Koopmans (2010) argues that multicultural policies inhibit immigrant integration by reducing incentives for language acquisition and labour force participation, while Sniderman and Hagendoorn (2007: 16) contend that multicultural policies undercut majority support for minorities by highlighting differences rather than commonalities through their focus on identity. This section will critically examine these arguments, arguing that the limitations exposed point to the role of media factors. It will also consider alternative accounts, including those based on 'cultural trauma' (Eyerman 2008) and rapid secularisation/de-pillarisation (van der Veer 2006).

First, how extensive was Dutch institutional multiculturalism? While this is contested (Vasta 2007; Rath et al. 1999), a fair summary would seem to be that while it never amounted to the Dutch state's funding of a fifth 'pillar' (*zuil*) for immigrants to Dutch society (Rath et al. 1999: 59), the 1983 Minorities Memorandum initiated a series of measures which meant that, by the late 1990s, the Netherlands had one of the highest levels of institutional multiculturalism in the world. These included extension of the same rights to public subsidy as other 'identity groups' in the areas of broadcasting, education and other aspects of welfare, including subsidised broadcasting for Muslims in 1985 and Hindus in 1994, Muslim (1988) and later Hindu primary schools, and the involvement of specified (ethnic and national) minorities in government consultations on a regular basis, formalised in the Law on the Consultation of Minority Policy (1997). In employment, the Equal Treatment Act of 1994 established a powerful Equal Treatment Commission, and in 1998 the Labour Market Stimulation Act provided for the employment of 'corporate minority advisors' to work with the national employment service, with the goal of achieving more equal minority representation across the labour market. Hence the recent reversals represent significant policy shifts.

So, was Dutch institutional multiculturalism too generous? As indicated above, Koopmans (2010) points to international comparative data which associate lower integration with higher levels of welfare provision and institutional multiculturalism. However, in the Dutch case, trend data points to a convergence between minority and majority Dutch attainment on several indicators (education, labour participation, Dutch language) between the mid-1990s and mid-2000s, suggesting increasing integration (Musterd and Ostendorf 2009: 254). So it seems difficult to explain increased hostility to institutional multiculturalism during this period purely on the grounds of policy failure, as integration (at least on key measures) actually seems to have been improving.

Second, there are problems with some of the indicators Koopmans uses to measure integration and segregation. For example, he uses residential concentration of minority population as a measure of segregation. Yet residential concentration alone tells us little about contact with the majority population or participation in society. In fact, in the Dutch case, researchers have not found a negative effect of living or being educated in areas/schools with high minority concentrations on the social career, educational achievement or self-image of minority Dutch (Karsten et al. 2006; Gramberg and Ledoux 2005: 19–24). Rather, it may be argued that high minority concentrations may be helpful, both for minorities seeking resources to aid settlement, integration and cultural support and for authorities seeking to address disadvantage (Simpson 2005: 665).

But if Dutch institutional multiculturalism does not seem to have failed so spectacularly in terms of conventional measures of integration as to explain the attacks on it, might another explanation be that it has undermined public support by highlighting differences rather than commonalities between minority and majority populations, as Sniderman and Hagendoorn (2007) contend? Drawing on a telephone survey conducted in 1998, they provide evidence of majority Dutch negative perceptions of Islam and Muslims, even before 9/11, Fortuyn's anti-Islam campaign (2001–2) and the killing of Theo van Gogh by a Dutch Muslim immigrant in 2004. Thus a majority (53.6 %) agreed or strongly agreed (30.5 %) with the proposition that 'Western and Muslim ways of life are irreconcilable', almost 90 % agreed that Muslim men in the Netherlands dominate their women, and 75.9 % agreed that Muslims in the Netherlands raise their children in an authoritarian way. In addition, they found that 'a third of the Dutch population view immigrant groups as criminal, dishonest and violent – a negative image to say the least' (Sniderman and Hagendoorn 2007: 48). This prejudice is distributed across the political spectrum (Sniderman and Hagendoorn 2007: 70), while 'threat' to culture is perceived as twice as important as any other single factor, including individual or societal economic well-being (Sniderman and Hagendoorn 2007: 89). Overall, they conclude that:

> Substantial numbers of the majority intensely dislike immigrant minorities. There is nothing subtle about their feelings towards minorities, or the positions they take based on them. Prejudice, our findings make plain, has the power to induce people to reject publicly the most fundamental form of equality for minorities – not equal outcomes or even equal opportunities, but equal rights. (Sniderman and Hagendoorn 2007:66–7)

But where does this negativity and hostility come from? First, they argue that negative perceptions of 'the Other' are reciprocated between majority and Muslim minority populations, from which one may hypothesise a negative spiral of mutual misperceptions (Entman and Rojecki 2001: 120). However, their evidence on Muslim attitudes is undercut by the poor construction of the questions to their Muslim sample and does not, in any case, provide much evidence of minority hostility (Herbert, forthcoming). So how else might majority negativity arise?

An important clue – though not an inference drawn by the authors – is found in their study of the volatility of majority opinion. Part of their survey examined 'how much support could be generated for extremist policies if a politician attempted to mobilize support for a policy beyond the pale', using the hypothetical example of a 'legally segregated school' in which majority and minority children were forbidden to sit together (Herbert, forthcoming: 107). The research question was, 'How much support can be won for a policy [....] by appealing to authority?' (Herbert, forthcoming: 108). The hypothesis was that those who value social conformity more highly would be more likely to change their mind under some kind of appeal to authority than those with low social conformity scores. They found that while appeals to authority produced a 4 % change for low social conformists, this rose to 18 % for high conformists. This finding is significant for two reasons. First, it suggests that public opinion can be manipulated by changing the information available – thus highlighting the role of the media in forming public opinion. Second, it sheds light on how populist figures, such as Fortuyn and Wilders, might influence public opinion through rhetorical appeals to authority and be especially influential amongst certain segments of the population.

However, it is not only high social conformists who are subject to media influence. Sniderman and Hagendoorn (2007) also identify a body of opinion amongst their respondents as 'critical liberal'. This is a politically significant group because they are relatively affluent and politically engaged, hence likely to be disproportionately influential in political agenda setting, as compared with those who simply dislike Muslims and immigrants and who tend to be poor and politically marginal. Critical liberals express no 'global hostility' to Muslims as such, but object to (what they perceive to be) Muslim norms. In spite of these objections, they tend to support the right of Muslims to follow their own way of life in the Netherlands; there is more than a 90 % chance that they will do so, almost the same as among those who do not object to Muslim norms (Sniderman and Hagendoorn 2007: 38–9). Their differentiation between Muslims (no hostility) and their practices (disapproval) is quite robust and holds up even under experimental conditions where interviewer reaction is controlled for (so they tend to be low social conformists) (Sniderman and Hagendoorn 2007: 35). However, compared with those with no objection to Muslim norms, critical liberals are more than twice as likely to think that immigration should be made more difficult (Sniderman and Hagendoorn 2007: 31), four times as likely to regard Muslim immigrants as 'politically untrustworthy' (Sniderman and Hagendoorn 2007: 41) and twice as likely to support assimilation, with a more than a 50 % chance that they will do so (Sniderman and Hagendoorn 2007: 38).

The authors' interpretation of these findings is that this group is basically tolerant and would be natural supporters of a culturally diverse society, if it were not for the undue attention drawn to cultural differences by a multicultural ideology which 'insists on fundamental differences between majority and minority' (Sniderman and Hagendoorn 2007: 42). But is this the most likely explanation? First, it is difficult to see how multicultural policies could have sufficient practical impact on the lives of critical liberals to make them question the political loyalty of Muslims or wish to seek to restrict their immigration. Given their residential locations, occupations and social class profiles, critical liberals and Moroccan and Turkish immigrants are unlikely to be in any regular contact, let alone enough to discuss politics or observe domestic gender differentiation. Indeed, one of the benefits of residential segregation research has been to reveal just how isolated white groups, especially middle classes, are in empirically multicultural societies (Simpson 2005: 666). Therefore, it is important to attend to the mediating processes through which groups' opinions are formed.

However, before turning to the media directly, other explanations of Dutch 'cultural wars' require review. Using a theory of 'cultural trauma' derived from the recent work of Jeffrey Alexander, Ron Eyerman argues that 'to gain a deep understanding of reactions to the murder of van Gogh one has to grasp the emotional effects of significant events in Dutch history, at least since the Second World War' (2008: 167). Dutch identity has been constructed, he argues, from narratives that reflect the complex legacy of that conflict (suffering, resistance, collaboration, loss of most of the Jewish population), the loss of colonial possessions and forced repatriation of Dutch civilians, pride in economic recovery and success, and the failure of Dutch UN peacekeepers to protect the Muslim population of Srebrenica in 1994. He contends that the significance of these events is best understood through this theory of cultural trauma, defined as 'a tear in the fabric of the social order precipitated by a shocking occurrence that sets up a meaning struggle that demands reparation' (2008: 163). Van Gogh's murder by a Dutch Moroccan Muslim can thus be read as another event in this historical series, finding supporting evidence in Fortuyn and van Gogh's comparison of Islam with fascism.

Eyerman's account is useful in highlighting the importance of an analysis of Dutch identity in understanding the public response to the traumas of the early noughties, but there are at least two critical problems with his argument. One is timing: as Sniderman and Hagenhoorn (2007) show, the Dutch public showed widespread suspicion and dislike of Muslims at least as far back as 1998, before these traumatic events. The second is selectivity: he presents a highly selective account of the formation of Dutch identity. In particular, while the 'traumatic' loss of colonies is mentioned, the legacy of specifically Dutch and more generally European colonialism for Dutch perceptions of Muslims is not. Neither is the very dramatic change in Dutch public attitudes toward gender roles and sexuality since the 1960s, nor the similarly dramatic decline in church attendance and the public influence of Christian religion, whether Catholic or Protestant, from the same date.

Fortunately, each of these factors has been taken up by van der Veer (2006). Noting that 'most discussions in the Netherlands [...] have been about the nature of Islam and global terrorism', he argues rather that:

> What needs to be explained is the aggression of the Dutch against a Muslim minority that forms some 7 percent of the Dutch population and is by and large a socially and culturally marginal group (van der Veer 2006: 112).

He locates the origins of this 'aggression' in the legacy of the 1960s, a 'turning point' in Dutch culture, during which 'Holland [sic] was transformed from a highly religious to a highly secular society' (van der Veer 2006: 118). The *verzuiling* system of tightly integrated pillars– 'when I grew up during the 1950s and 1960s, I was raised as a Protestant, and we had our own church, political party, sports teams, schools, shops and welfare organisation' (van der Veer 2006: 118)– fell apart. He identifies the key factors in this collapse as 'the sexual revolution, the student revolt, and the rise to power of postwar babyboomers' (van der Veer 2006: 118). Seen in this context, the Dutch problem with socially conservative Muslim immigrants, with their restrictions on young people, headscarves, demands for prayer rooms and regular mosque attendance, is that:

> Muslims stand for theft of enjoyment. Their strict sexual morals remind the Dutch too much of what they have so recently left behind. There is indeed very little difference between strict Christian ideas about sexuality and enjoyment and strict Muslim ideas about these matters (van der Veer 2006: 119).

Mepschen et al. (2010) add another layer to this cultural analysis by arguing that Dutch gay politics ceased to be 'queer' (that is, oppositional) when Dutch homosexuals achieved equal civil rights in the 1980s; as a result, Dutch gay society has been largely assimilated within Dutch 'heteronormativity', enabling the mobilisation of Dutch gay identity in the cultural othering of non-European immigrants, especially Muslims, in a process they describe as 'the instrumentalisation of gay rights':

> In order to criticize Muslims as backwards and as enemies of European culture, gay rights are now heralded as if they have been the foundation of European culture for centuries (Mepschen et al. 2010: 965).

So is the reason for widespread Dutch aversion to Islam and Muslim culture its social conservatism, which reminds the Dutch of their recent, religious and socially conservative past? The World Values Survey would seem to provide some support for at this contention.

Compared with two other advanced industrial Western societies – the US and the UK – the Netherlands emerges as the most secular in a number of ways. For example, it is has the fewest respondents saying that religion is important in their lives (12.5 %, compared with 21 % in Britain and 47.4 % in the US) (WVS 2006 Wave) and the lowest levels of confidence in the churches (WVS 2006 Wave). Similarly, fewer Dutch respondents considered someone for whom tradition is important to be like or very much like them (24.4 %, compared with 43.5 % US and 47.8 % in Britain). This perhaps suggests that Dutch society has less cultural capital available to draw on for an empathetic response to those for whom religion or tradition is important. Also fitting the pattern of cultural change sketched by van der Veer (2006) and Mepschen et al. (2010), the Netherlands has the lowest levels of prejudice against homosexuals, with less than 5 % objecting to living next door to homosexuals, compared with 18.8 % for Britain and 26 % for the US. Yet in the neighbour test for 'living next door to people of a different race', the Netherlands (8.5 %) comes out as less tolerant than Britain (5.4 %) and the US (4.1 %), with similar patterns emerging for 'different religion' (Britain 2.1 %, US 2.6 %, Netherlands 3.2 %) and 'different language' (Britain 6.3 %, Netherlands 10.7 %; US 11.1 %). This evidence (WVS 2006 Wave) would seem to confirm that Dutch tolerance of diverse sexualities is unusual even amongst Western societies; but this tolerance does not apply to the same extent to racial, religious or linguistic diversity.

In attitudes towards social conformity and authority the Netherlands also stands out, and here a plausible link to dislike of attitudes characteristic of social conservatism and authoritarianism may be made. As noted, the Dutch identify less than British or Americans with those for whom tradition is important and have the least confidence in the churches; this also goes for government, the armed forces and the police (WVS 2006 Wave). They also have the lowest proportion prepared to fight for their country (the only one with less than 50 %; all others were above 60 %), trust their family least (63.4 % trust them completely, compared with 72.5 % for the US and 85.9 % for Britain) and are most likely to give 'protecting free speech' as their first choice personal aim (43.4 %) (WVS 2006 Wave).

In this context Islam, with its social conservatism and family-oriented culture, is likely to be regarded skeptically. Van der Veer's (2006) cultural analysis of the significance of rapid and recent secularisation triangulates well with these results; Eyerman's (2010) cultural trauma thesis fits less so – for example, it is dissonant with the low value placed on tradition and patriotism. We now turn to consider the processes through which such attitudes have been produced, and in particular the production of Dutch social knowledge of Islam and Muslims.

3 Media and the stigmatisation of Islam and Muslims in the Netherlands

In 2008 the European Commission against Racism and Intolerance (ECRI) concluded that Muslims in the Netherlands are:

> [...] the subject of stereotyping, stigmatising and sometimes outright racist political discourse and of biased media portrayal, and have been disproportionately targeted by security and other policies. They have also been the victims of racist violence and other racist crimes and have experienced discrimination. (ECRI 2008: 36 – 7)

This section will consider more precisely the role of the mass media in the production and circulation of 'stigmatising' and 'biased' representations of Muslims and Islam. A range of mostly US-based research has pointed to the role of the media in the production of 'ethnicized ways of seeing' (Entman and Rojecki 2001: 120), meaning stereotypical representations in which out-group members are seen to 'possess fundamentally different traits', such that 'it becomes difficult for in-groups to empathize with them' (Entman and Rojecki 2001: 120).

In the Netherlands such a sense of fundamental difference is produced and perpetuated by the media's use of words such as *tuig* (literally 'harness' but meaning 'lesser breed') and *Islamieten* (perjorative term; no English equivalent) to describe Muslims (Cherribi 2010: 142, 148), by 'the painful overexposure in the Dutch media of Moroccan-Dutch individuals who break the law', such that Moroccans and criminality become reflexively linked in the public imagination (Leurs et al. 2012: 165), and by a whole series of ways of representing minority (especially Muslim) groups as a threat. For example, minority self-organisation through social media is described as 'ghettos on the web' (Hulsman 2005: 33) and is linked with radicalisation (Ostveen 2004: 38) and hate speech (Pietersen 2008). Moreover, ethnicisation arguably extends beyond the media to mainstream political and official public discourse:

> [T]he terminology of 'autochthonous' (read white) people versus 'allochthonous' (read black, migrant, refugee) people, steadily maintained by Dutch politicians, government officials and mainstream news outlets, is fraught with meaning as an exclusionary practice. [... T]he label 'allochthonous' allocates positions to groups of people considered non-Dutch others, and, like a long tail that cannot be shed, the label is not only applied to first-generation migrants but also to the subsequent generations that are born in the Netherlands. (Leurs et al. 2012: 156)

A detailed study of newspaper coverage of Geert Wilder's video compilation, *Fitna*, shows that coverage of Islam and Muslims tended to be negatively represented by politicians, experts and citizens (Scholten et al. 2008: 4, Table 1). However, the same study also cautions against seeing the media as uncritically supporting Islamophobic perspectives; Wilders and the video were often more negatively portrayed than Islam and Muslims (Scholten et al. 2008: 4), and earlier Fortuyn had also experienced a hostile press much of the time (Margry 2007: 111: Oosthoek 2005: 112–114). Indeed, a perception that media characterisation of Fortuyn as a far-right extremist had contributed to his death fuelled public anger in its wake (Margry 2007: 111).

Media scholarship has long established that conflict makes stories more newsworthy (Fiske 2006), but the Dutch case suggests that recent trends in news production and public relations – especially 'pro-active news-making' and the mediatisation of politics – may further increase the conflictual framing of news (Cherribi 2010: 139–140), as the following examples will show.

3.1 Proactive newsmaking: The El-Moumni affair

Arguably a key event in the launch of Fortuyn's political career was the El-Moumni affair. On May 3 2001 the late-night current affairs programme *Nova*, the flagship news discussion programme on public broadcasting channel Nederland 3, aired a much-trailed, pre-recorded interview with the Rotterdam-based imam Khalil El-Moumni. The interview had been arranged on the topic of crime involving Moroccan youth, but the interviewer gave additional questions: 'What do Muslims think about homosexuality?', to which El-Moumni replied, 'It is a sickness', followed by a question on gay marriage, to which the imam replied, 'If men continue to marry men, and women marry women, then Dutch society will disappear' (cited in Cherribi 2010: 144). Over the following days a 'snowball effect' occurred, in which the stance of Muslims on homosexuality was widely (and negatively) represented, from the liberal daily newspaper *NRC Handelsblad* to the populist daily *De Telegraaf*, which opined that the imam's views could only be found in the 'medieval deserts of North Africa' (8 May 2001, in Mepschen 2010: 967).

Thus the episode came to be represented as an attack by a Muslim spokesman on gay rights, even by academics writing much later. For example, in a widely cited article on the Dutch retreat from multiculturalism, Joppke wrote:

> [...] only when *provoked* by a prominent Dutch-Moroccan Imam's statement that homosexuality was a 'disease' did Fortuyn *retaliate* that Islam was a 'backward' culture (2004: 249, emphasis added).

Yet El-Moumi's statements were a spontaneous response to unexpected questions in an interview ostensibly about something else. It is also decidedly odd to depict Fortuyn as acting in self-defense, since in 1997 he had already published a book entitled *Against the Islamization of Our Society*, in which he made clear that he opposed the Muslim presence in Dutch society. It is also notable that El-Moumni's statements were also received quite differently to indigenous Dutch criticism of gay lifestyles. For example, on the occasion of the Gay Games in Amsterdam in 1998 (Mepschen et al 2010: 968), such 'provocations' received neither the extent of coverage devoted to El-Moumni nor the generalisation to an entire imagined community.

The incident represents a case of pro-active news-making; under pressure in a ratings war, the *Nova* journalist opportunistically asked extra questions on a controversial topic and circulated previews via social media so that the websites of several gay organisations carried the story before the actual broadcast, apparently deliberately to generate controversy and hence ratings (Cherribi 2010: 146). It thus illustrates the powerful role that mass media, in this case amplified by social media, can play in framing an event for public consumption, exerting a decisive influence on subsequent discussion, while the media's role in manufacturing the event is forgotten. In this case, it also coincided with another powerful media-driven phenomenon, the personalisation of politics, because it helped set the stage for the launch of Fortuyn's political career (Kleinnijenhuis et al. 2002; Cherribi 2010: 150).

3.2 Mediatised government

While some studies of media influence have tended to emphasise its effects on the least politically engaged, most easily manipulated audience segments (Kleinnijenhuis et al. 2002), Uitermark and Gielen's study (2010) of the Amsterdam locality of De Baarsjes, following the murder of Dutch film maker Theo van Gogh (2004), shows media influence on the most politically astute, e. g., those responsible for local policies. De Baarsjes had been the site of previous disturbances involving Moroccan youth – though, notably, there is no evidence of Islamic radicalisation – so local policy makers were keen to avoid further incidents in the wake of van Gogh's death. They therefore initiated a 'Contract with Society' which local mosques would be invited to sign to show their support for integration and to generate publicity to show local Muslims' support for this. In terms of media exposure the strategy was a success, producing high local and national visibility. But it proved less successful in building bridges with local Muslims; while the offer of media appearances appealed to some of the mosque leadership, only one leadership team was able to convince its committee to sign up, and even there tensions between the leadership and congregation were exacerbated. Most disturbingly, the whole strategy was formulated not in response to conditions on the ground, but rather in response to the calculated media impact on the majority of voters:

> The government acted against radicalism not because it observed radicalism in the neighbourhood, but because it sensed there was a demand amongst media audiences for images and narratives of the struggle against radicalism. (Uitermark and Gielen 2010: 1340)

In this case then, local politics became 'mediatised' in the strong sense that policy makers felt the need to respond to media audiences' demands, which overrode their assessment of local conditions, in particular in anticipation of impacts on precisely the groups the measure was ostensibly designed to protect.

Thus we have seen that mass media contribute to the 'othering' of Dutch Muslims in a range of ways. We have also seen social media playing an amplifying role in the circulation of negative representations, for example of pre-broadcast publicity in the El-Moumni affair. In the next section, we scrutinise its role more closely.

4 Social media, representation and resistance

Social media-based forms of activism may be grouped into three basic types. First, 'mass self-expression', that is the expression of opinion on publicly accessible social media sites, such as YouTube. Second, social media can function as a forum for discussion. Third, social media networks can be used to organise collective expressions of support or dissent, whether in the virtual or real world.

Research on Turkish and Moroccan minorities (two of the three largest Muslim populations) in the Netherlands suggests that these groups have similar levels of ICT skills and access as the majority but that there are some significant differences in contexts of access (which are more likely to be collective for minorities) and some 'very marked differences' in usage. Thus:

> Young people use ICT for a great variety of reasons. Thus the ICT usage of Moroccan and Turkish youths is more often well-targeted and aimed at information, for example, in actively participating in news groups, seeking information on religion, art and culture and keeping abreast of developments in their country of origin. Native youngsters look more often for entertainment, emailing and downloading files. (D'Haenens 2007: 296)

Further research has found that young Muslim women spend more time online than their male peers, and on activities with a stronger social dimension (Leurs et al. 2012: 160). Such evidence suggests that social media are likely to become an important arena for expression of alternative views, especially among groups (such as young Muslim women) whose voices have had limited representation in mainstream debate, and, as we shall see, some further evidence shows that this is already happening.

4.1 'Voice': social media as mass self-expression and sites for building solidarity

Critics have dismissed one-way communication by the posting of text or video online as 'civic narcissism' (Papacharissi 2009: 238), but others have argued that self-expression through social media provides the opportunity for articulation of identities by those marginalised in the mass media and is a legitimate and democratically useful response to problems of inequality of access to mainstream public spheres (Cottle 2006: 51). Further support comes from the concept of the 'public screen'. De Luca and Peeples (2002: 130) argue that thinking about the public sphere has been dominated by the idea of the face-to-face conversation as the ideal model of human communication and the belief that the conduct of politics should somehow approximate as closely as possible to it. Instead, they argue that political communication needs to be thought of not just as conversation but as dissemination, which opens up conceptual space for appreciation of non-verbal communication such as symbolic protest, visual practices and other performances as forms of cultural critique.

One example of self-expression as resistance might be the postings to *YouTube* of videos in response to Dutch MP Geert Wilders' anti-Islam compilation video, *Fitna*, in March 2008. Van Zoonen et al. (2011a) analysed 63 videos posted by women. They found contrasting voices to mainstream media commentators on *Fitna* in the Netherlands and the UK – mostly older, non-Muslim men (Scholten et al. 2008; Knott et al. 2010):

> [T]he YouTube videos give voice to women themselves who come from across the globe, are relatively young and often active Muslims. Second, they express different viewpoints in generically new ways, criticizing and ridiculing Wilders or producing serious and committed explanations of their own understanding of Islam. Third, although relatively few women appeared in the videos, those that did speak for themselves, not only take on Wilders, but also claim their right to speak within Islam. We propose to understand these videos as acts of citizenships through which women constitute themselves as global citizens. (van Zoonen et al. 2011a: 125)

Second, sites for minority ethnic groups provide 'hush harbours' (Leurs et al. 2012: 162) for discussion of issues affecting minority groups and may provide space for building solidarity and identity through sharing and debate. Researchers have found that on sites such as Marokko.nl, Maghreb.nl, Mahgrebonline.nl and Chaima.nl, 'a great deal of discussion on message boards is about the stereotypes and counter-positioning of Moroccan-Dutch youth in the Netherlands'. Their popularity suggests the importance of their social function: Marokko.nl is estimated to reach 70 – 75 % of Moroccan Dutch aged 15 – 35 (Leurs et al. 2012: 162).

4.2 Deliberation: social media as discussion forums

Van Zoonen et al. (2011b) also analysed viewer responses to the videos posted by a larger sample of female and male posters (n = 776) in order to assess 'how the video responses to *Fitna* were seen, listened to and reacted upon [sic] by others' (2011b: 1296). These responses provide an opportunity to assess the kind of debate generated by social media in response to mainstream mass media opinion. The videos attracted considerable attention, up to 3.6 million viewers, with an average [presumed median] of 24,000 (2011b: 1289), and generated about a quarter of a million comments. However, the interaction generated between them was limited – 'only some 13 % of posters engaged with each other through comments, subscriptions or "friendships"' (2011b: 1296) – and these connections were mostly 'limited to people with similar viewpoints' (2011b: 1290). Furthermore, where exchanges between posters of differing standpoints occurred, they tended to be antagonistic. The researchers therefore conclude that:

> [V]ideo practices that emerged in reaction to *Fitna* can thus be characterized as a set of online demonstrations against (and to a much lesser extent in favor of) *Fitna* that express both antagonistic and agonistic passions and views, but that are not particularly conducive to the emergence of dialogue or mutual understanding. (2011b: 1296 – 7)

Against this reading, it may be argued that, if viewed as a public screen for expression of dissent and solidarity, the number, viewing figures and volume of comment generated by videos suggest a significant phenomenon, particularly when the degree of co-ordination between some posts and concerted action organised through social media is considered, as below. Also, *YouTube* is not the best social media site for generating deliberative debate, although some constructive debate did take place, most notably around two videos posted by a group of Egyptian women activists (van Zoonen et al. 2011a: 123). Rather, researchers have argued that moderated forums provide better spaces for the development of deliberation (Stromer-Galley 2007), and those linked to major news sites in international languages, such the BBC World Service's *World Have Your Say* forums, may be best for generating participation from a broad range of contributors with diverse opinions (Herbert and Black, forthcoming).

4.3 Social media as resistance

Dutch new media lab *Mediamatic* organised a video protest against Wilders' video (van Zoonen et al. 2011: 1289). This encouraged participants to use the Fitna tag to post short video clips apologising for Wilders' video in an attempt to 'drown' references to Wilder's video in the sea of Internet information. As an organiser explains:

> Why? Well, we can't stop Wilders. He has a right to freedom of expression...We can compete for attention however. And we can produce disinformation. So we are going to make Movies called 'Fitna' in which we apologize for Geert Wilders' embarrassing behavior...So if you want to join in; just make your own Fitna movie and put it on line...Call it Fitna by Geert Wilders...If we work hard enough, no one will be able to find his crap among all the noise we produce. (in van Zoonen et al. 2011: 1289)

More than 200 such clips were uploaded (van Zoonen et al. 2011: 1289). Tagging has been condemned as anti-social online behaviour, causing 'content pollution' (Benevenuto et al. 2009); but as van Zoonen et al. argue, where one video and point of view is getting so much exposure, there may be an argument for this kind of tactic to demonstrate oppositional perspectives (van Zoonen et al. 2011: 1289).

Social media also provided the location for acts of resistance against another of Wilders' initiatives, the 'kopvoddentax' ('raghead' tax), a proposal that women wearing head coverings should pay an annual tax (policy announced 16th September 2009). For example, the Dutch social networking site Hyves hosted the community 'Wij Willen Geen Hoofddoek Verbod' ['We want no headscarf ban'], which attracted more than 15,000 members (Leurs et al. 2012: 152). As well as virtual solidarity being expressed, a series of local protests were organised (Leurs et al. 2012). Thus social media provided the space for the high levels of participation by Moroccan and Turkish young women, triply excluded from society by ascribed ethnicity, religion and gender roles, to translate into organization and off-line activism.

5 Conclusions

This account of the role of media factors in the spread of Islamophobia and attacks on institutional multiculturalism in Dutch society began by arguing that explanations which focus on multicultural policies themselves or the characteristics of Dutch Muslims fail for the same reason – most indicators show that differences, gaps and separation between the majority and Muslim minorities were diminishing between the mid-1990s and mid-2000s. Yet public discourse implied the opposite (Musterd and Ostendorf 2008: 89), already suggesting a significant role for media factors.

It was then argued that mass media impacts on the construction of Islamophobic attitudes amongst the Dutch public in a variety of ways. First, derogatory terms for Muslims and immigrant groups are common in Dutch news discourse and even in official discourse. Second, although Islamophobic politicians and leaders are also criticised, because this criticism tends to be directed at the integrity and competence of these politicians rather than at their Islamophobia, the effect is to feed narratives of victimisation by these politicians and their supporters rather than countering Islamophobia. Third, the effects of these discourses can be inferred from their presence amongst groups with limited direct experience of minorities (such as the 'critical liberals' in Sniderman and Hagendoorn's 2007 study). Fourth, the competitive media environment leads journalists to engage in practices such as 'pro-active newsmaking', in which media do not merely report but actively generate conflict in the search for ratings. Fifth, the trend towards the personalisation of politics and the culture of media celebrity arguably enabled Fortuyn to have a significant impact on national politics, without the need to build a traditional party political base. Sixth, in the mediatisation of politics, policy makers' public relations orientation actually led them to prioritise media audiences' perceived demand over local issues.

However, while mass and social media are deeply implicated in the process of 'othering' Dutch Muslims, the latter especially are also critical in the formation of minority voices and identities in response to and resistance of Islamophobia. While social media also play a role in the articulation of post-liberal Islamophobic voices – as Wilder's launch of *Fitna* illustrates – so media should not be dichotomised as mass media bad, social media good; social media's low access costs (in Europe) and horizontal communication properties provide opportunities for groups with limited social and political power to communicate and potentially organise and resist, as both *Mediamatic*'s anti-*Fitna* and the anti-*kopvoddentax* campaigns illustrate. Just as well, as another finding suggests that such resistance may become increasingly necessary. The experience of rapid secularisation (van der Veer 2006) and the cluster of Dutch social attitudes associated with individualism, hedonism and anti-authoritarianism found in the WVS data, which apparently makes this audience particularly receptive to negative representations of Islam as the archetypical collective, restrictive and authoritarian religion, also characterises younger white cohorts in other European countries (Norris and Inglehart 2011: 153), suggesting that these post-liberal Dutch culture wars may foreshadow developments elsewhere.

References

Bleich, E. 2010. "What Is Islamophobia and How Much Is There? Theorizing and Measuring an Emerging Comparative Concept." *American Behavioral Scientist* 55 (12): 1581–1600.

Boomkens, R. 2010. "Cultural citizenship and real politics: The Dutch case." *Citizenship Studies* 14 (3): 307–316.

Butler, J. 2008 "Sexual politics, torture, and secular time." *The British Journal of Sociology* (59) 1: 1–23

Castells, M. 1997. *The Information Age: Economy, Society, Culture. Vol. 2: The Power of Identity, III: End of Millennium.* Oxford: Blackwell.

Cherribi, S. 2010. *In the House of War: Dutch Islam Observed.* Oxford: Oxford University Press.

Cottle, S. 2006. *Mediatized Conflicts.* Maidenhead, Berkshire: Open University.

Danemark, Berth., Mats Ekstrom, Liselotte Jakobsen, and Jan ch. Karlsson. 1997. *Explaining Society: Critical Realism in the Social Sciences.* London: Routledge.

De Luca, K., and J. Peeples. 2002. "Public Sphere and Public Screen: Democracy, Activism and the 'Violence' of Seattle." *Critical Studies in Media Communication* 19 (2): 125–151.

D'Haenens, L., Joyce Koeman, and Frieda Saeys. 2007. "Digital citizenship among ethnic minority youths in the Netherlands and Flanders." *New Media and Society* 9 (2): 278–299.

Entman, R., and A. Rojecki. 2001. *The Black Image in the White Mind: Media and Race in America.* Chicago: Chicago University Press.

Entzinger, H. 2009. "Different Systems, Similar Problems: The French Urban Riots from a Dutch Perspective." *Journal of Ethnic and Migration Studies* 35 (5): 815–834.

European Commission Against Racism and Intolerance [ECRI]. 2008. *Third Report on the Netherlands.* Strasbourg: Council of Europe.

Eyerman, R. 2008. *The Assassination of Theo van Gogh: From Social Drama to Cultural Trauma.* Durham, NC: Duke University Press.

Fekete, L. 2009. *A Suitable Enemy: Racism, Migration and Islamophobia in Europe.* London: Pluto.

Fiske, J. 1996. *Media Matters: Race and Gender in US Politics.* Minneapolis: University of Minnesota Press.

France24. 2011. [citing AFP] "Sarkozy declares multiculturalism 'a failure'" http://www.france24.com/en/20110210-multiculturalism-failed-immigration-sarkozy-live-broadcast-tf1-france-public-questions. Accessed: 13 March 2012.

Graber, D. 2001. *Processing Politics: Learning from television in the internet age.* Chicago: Chicago University Press.

Gramberg, P., and G. Ledoux. 2005 "Bestrijden van schoolsegregatie: dringend nodig, zinloos of onhaalbaar?" ["Fighting against school segregation: urgently needed, meaningless or unattainable?"] In *Gescheiden of Gemengd. Een verkenning van etnische concentratie op school en in de wijk.* [Separate or Mixed. An exploration of ethnic concentration at school and in the neighbourhood], edited by P. Brasse and H. Krijnen, 17–31. Utrecht: Forum, Instituut voor Multiculturele Ontwikkeling.

Hekma, G. 2002. "Imams and Homosexuality. A Post-gay Debate in the Netherlands." *Sexualities* 5 (2): 237–48.

Herbert, D., and T. Black. Forthcoming. "What Kind of Global Conversation? Participation, Democratic Deepening and Public Diplomacy through BBCWS online forums: An examination of mediated global talk about religion, politics and society." In *Diasporas and Diplomacy: Cosmopolitan Contact Zones at the BBC World Service (1932–2012)*, edited by M. Gillespie and A. Webb, n.p. London: Routledge.

Hjarvard, Stig. 2008. "The mediatization of religion: A theory of the media as agents of religious change." *Northern Lights* 6 : 9–26.

Iqbal, Z. 2010. "Understanding Islamophobia: Conceptualizing and measuring the construct." *European Journal of Social Sciences* 13 (4): 574–590.

Joppke, C. 2004. "The Retreat of Multiculturalism in the Liberal State: Theory and Policy." *British Journal of Sociology* 55 (2): 238–257.

Karsten, S., C. Felix, G. Ledoux, W. Meijnen, J. Roeleveld, and E. van Schooten. 2006. "Choosing segregation or integration: The extent and effects of ethnic segregation in Dutch cities." *Education and Urban Society* 38 (2): 228–47.

Kleinnijenhuis, J., D. Oegema, J. de Ridder, A. van Hoof, and R. Vliegenthard. 2002. *De puinhopen in het nieuws: De rol van de media bij de Tweede-Kamerverkierzingen van 2002* [The ruins in the news: The role of the media in the Lower Chamber elections of 2002]. Alphen aan den Rijn: Kluwer.

Koopmans, R. 2010. "Trade-Offs between Equality and Difference: Immigrant Integration, Multiculturalism and the Welfare State in Cross-National Perspective." *Journal of Ethnic and Migration Studies* 36 (1): 1–26.

Leurs, K.H.A., E. Midden, and S. Ponzanesi. 2012. "Digital Multiculturalism in the Netherlands: Religious, Ethnic and Gender Positioning by Moroccan-Dutch Youth." *Religion and Gender* 2 (1): 150–175.

Margry, P. 2007. "Performative Memorials: Arenas of political resentment in Dutch society." In *Reframing Dutch Culture: Between Otherness and Authenticity*, edited by P. Margry and H. Roodenburg, 109–133. Aldershot: Ashgate.

Mazzoleni, G., J. Stewart, and B. Horsfield, eds. 2003. *The Media and Neo-Populism: A Contemporary Comparative Analysis.* Westport, CT: Praeger.

Mepschen, P., Jan Willem Duyvendak, and Evelien H. Tonkens. 2010. "Sexual Politics, Orientalism and Multicultural Citizenship in the Netherlands." *Sociology* 44: 962–979.

Meer, N., and T. Modood. 2009. "The Multicultural State We're In: Muslims, 'Multiculture' and the 'Civic Re-balancing' of British Multiculturalism." *Political Studies* 57: 473–497.

Musterd, S., and W. Ostendorf. 2008. "Integrated urban renewal in The Netherlands: A critical appraisal." *Urban Research and Practice* 1 (1): 78–92.

–. 2009. "Residential segregation and integration in the Netherlands." *Journal of Ethnic and Migration Studies* 35 (9): 1515–1532.

New Statesman. 2011. "David Cameron speech on radicalisation and Islamic extremism, Munich, 5 February 2011." Available at: http://www.newstatesman.com/blogs/the-staggers/2011/02/terrorism-islam-ideology. Accessed: 13 March 2012.

Norris, P., and R. Inglehart. 2006. *Sacred and Secular: Religion and Politics Worldwide.* Oxford: Oxford University Press.

Papacharissi, Z. 2009. "The virtual sphere 2.0: The internet, the public sphere and beyond." In. *Handbook of Internet Politics*, edited by A. Chadwick and P. Howard P, 230–245. London: Routledge.

Poole, E. 2002. *Reporting Islam: Media Representations of British Muslims.* London: I B Tauris.

Prins, B., and B. Saharso. 2008."In the spotlight: A blessing and a curse for immigrant women in the Netherlands." *Ethnicities* 8 (3): 365–384.

Rath, J., R. Penninx, K. Groenendijk, and A. Meyer. 1999. "The politics of recognizing religious diversity in Europe: Social reactions to the institutionalization of Islam in the Netherlands, Belgium and Great Britain." *The Netherlands Journal of Social Science* 35 (1): 53–68.

Reicher, S. 2004. "The Context of Social Identity: Domination, Resistance and Change." *Political Psychology* 25: 921–46.

Roes, T., ed. 2008. *Facts and Figures of the Netherlands.* Den Haag: The Netherlands Institute for Social Research.

Scholten, O., Nel Ruigrok, Martijn Krijt, Joep Schaper, and Hester Paanakker. 2008. "Fitna and the Media: An investigation of attention and role patterns." *Nederlandse Nieuwesmonitor.* Available at: http://www.nieuwsmonitor.net/publications/list Accessed: 06 March 2012.

Shadid, Wasif A. 2006. "Public Debates over Islam and the Awareness of Muslim Identity in the Netherlands." *European Education* 38 (2): 10–22.

Simpson, L. 2005. "On the Measurement and Meaning of Residential Segregation: A Reply to Johnston, Poulsen and Forrest." Urban Studies 42 (7): 1229–1230.

Sniderman, P., and L. Hagendoorn. 2007. *When ways of life collide: Multiculturalism and its discontents in the Netherlands.* Princeton, NJ: Princeton University Press.

Stromer-Galley, J. 2007. "Measuring deliberation's content: A coding scheme." *Journal of Public Deliberation* 3 (1): 1–37.

Uitermark, J. and A.J. Gielen. 2010. "Islam in the Spotlight: The Mediatisation of Politics in an Amsterdam Neighbourhood." *Urban Studies* 47 (6): 1325–1342.

van der Veer, P. 2006. "Pim Fortuyn, Theo van Gogh, and the Politics of Tolerance in the Netherlands." *Public Culture* 18 (1): 111–124.

van Zoonen, L., F. Vis, and S. Mihelj. 2011a. "YouTube interactions between agonism, antagonism and dialogue: Video responses to the anti-Islam film *Fitna*." *New Media and Society* 13 (8): 1283–1300.

– – –. 2011b. "Women responding to the anti-Islam film *Fitna:* Voices and acts of citizenship on YouTube." *Feminist Review* 97: 10–129.

Vasta, E. 2007. "From ethnic minorities to ethnic majority policy: Multiculturalism and the shift to assimilationism in the Netherlands." *Ethnic and Racial Studies* 30: 5, 713–740.

Vellenga, S. 2008. "The Dutch and British Public Debate on Islam: Responses to the Killing of Theo van Gogh and the London Bombings Compared." *Islam and Christian–Muslim Relations* 19 (4): 449–471.

Vertovec, S., and S. Wessendorf. 2010. "Introduction: Assessing the backlash against multiculturalism in Europe." In *The Multicultural Backlash: European discourses, policies and practices*, edited by S. Vertovec and S. Wessendorf, 1–22. London: Routledge.

Vink, M. 2007. "Dutch 'Multiculturalism' Beyond the Pillarisation Myth." *Political Studies Review* 5: 337–350

Vossen, K. 2010. "Populism in the Netherlands after Fortuyn: Rita Verdonk and Geert Wilders Compared." *Perspectives on European Politics and Society* 11 (1): 22–38.

Weaver, Mathew. 2010. "Angela Merkel: German multiculturalism has 'utterly failed.'" Available at: http://www.guardian.co.uk/world/2010/oct/17/angela-merkel-german-multiculturalism-failed.

WVS. 2009. World Values Survey 2006–9 wave. Available at: www.worldvaluessurvey.org/. Data downloaded: 22 February 2011.

Rebecca Haughey and Heidi A. Campbell

6 Modern-day Martyrs: Fans' Online Reconstruction of Celebrities as Divine

The infiltration of the celebrity phenomenon in contemporary popular culture is glaringly apparent in the flashy headlines of magazines and tabloids and the very existence of a 24-hour celebrity news cable channel, *E!*. Consumers' obsession with and supposed intimate connection to these distant yet famous strangers has been researched from a psychological standpoint as the manifestation of a pathological defect (Maltby et al 2004). However, a closer examination of individuals' extreme reverence and high regard for the select celebrity elite provokes further questions about the nature of so-called celebrity worship as just that – the authentic practice of implicit religion. While a review of the media's historical development reveals a definite connection between the creation of the celebrity and the mass media's promotion of select individuals, innovative online social media can be inferred to have further revolutionised fans' roles in the construction of celebrities and their unique public identities. Media professionals have been stripped of their exclusive narrative power as a multiplicity of individual fans have emerged, wielding the unprecedented ability to publish their own understandings of celebrities online through a wide variety of public venues, such as blogs, Facebook, Twitter and website forums. Deceased celebrities' personalities become particularly malleable, as fans reflect on these celebrities' public lives and resurrect such famed figures into martyr-like individuals, whose tragic deaths inspire reverence and heightened devotion. Through communally constructed narratives, fans can integrate a celebrity's 'martyrdom' into the greater context of a modern gospel, in which celebrities are viewed as higher beings unjustly persecuted by an unforgiving mass media and general public.

This chapter explores how fans' online actions can exhibit traits of implicit religion in the way they frame celebrities as religious entities. First, a literature review of the media's role in the creation of celebrities and fans' roles in the reconstruction of celebrities' identities is presented in order to understand how celebrity worship takes place and can be seen as a valid form of implicit religion. Next, a case study examination of Michael Jackson fans' creation of individualised online 'tributes' on memories.michaeljackson.com demonstrates the posthumous reconstruction of deceased celebrities as divine figures. Michael Jackson serves as a prime example of a celebrity who has been reconstructed by fans to be a modern-day martyr, an individual who defied many cultural, racial and gender expectations, but who ultimately is believed to serve as a sacrificial outcast.

Through their outpourings of praise, fans make sense of Jackson's unexpected death by framing it as a divinely ordained act for the greater good of humanity; in short, fans see Jackson as publicly victimised and finally free in death to spiritually watch over his family and devoted fandom. Finally, from these findings the central question of this study is addressed: How do fans' online actions reconstruct celebrities as religious figures, and how can these be interpreted as a form of implicit religion?

1 Defining implicit religion

Before we explore how fans construct celebrities as divine, a foundational definition of implicit religion must be established. Lord defines implicit religion as 'the mode of behaviour exhibited, rather than the goal towards which the behaviour is directed' (2006: 206). From this perspective, a fresh understanding of religion shatters notions of a 'sacred versus secular' dichotomy, such that implicit religion is not deemed authentic because of a link to the 'recognisably holy' but is noted instead in the 'observable actions carried out by a person, whether random, habitual, impulsive or rational' (2006: 206). Therefore, in relation to this understanding, in order for celebrity worship to be considered implicit religion, fans' actions in veneration of celebrities must be analysed.

For this discussion, it is important to note that implicit religion must be recognised as religion that is deinstitutionalised yet demonstrates what Bailey (cited in Lord 2006: 208) deemed 'the secular quest for meaning'. More so than simply meaningful behaviour, implicit religion has also been connected to the creation of sacred symbols from the secular world; as Chidester's study of Americans' reverence for Coca-Cola led him to conclude, 'religion is about sacred symbols and systems of sacred symbols that endow the world with meaning and value' (Chidester 2005: 214). In this sense, perhaps the public identity of an individual celebrity could be seen as a sacred symbol, providing meaning to devoted fans. This is illustrated by Campbell and La Pastina's study (2010) of the narrative framework used to reconstruct the iPhone as divine, in that fans adopted religious symbolism in order to spiritualise a secular icon and imbue it with seemingly miraculous capabilities, thus framing it as a form of implicit religion. From these examples we see how implicit religion can be characterised as practices – including both meaningful actions and language choices – that allow followers to make sense of the surrounding world by merging the secular with a sacred understanding. Therefore we argue that, for celebrity worship to be regarded as implicit religion, there must be significant evidence that fans apply their understanding of celebrities to their understandings of the greater world, and that their actions in reverence of celebrities create a religious experience, whether through meaning-infused rituals or through religiously charged language, thereby allowing fans to recast celebrities as new-age saints.

2 Understanding celebrity worship in relation to popular culture and implicit religion

Based on this understanding of implicit religion, we see that fans' use of online mass media can be interpreted as a practice by which they construct celebrities as divine figures to be worshipped, which exhibits an implicitly religious character and process of meaning-making. In order to provide support for this thesis, several issues must be explored. The first aspect we consider is how the mass media have historically created the very concept of the celebrity by providing constant public exposure to particular individuals, allowing them to accumulate attention and become firmly lodged in the public realm, regardless of actual talent or accomplishments. Secondly, we address the role that fans – those outside the official media profession – play in the reconstruction of celebrities' particular identities, especially with regard to the use of new social media. Lastly, we synthesise previous research surrounding the argument that practitioners of celebrity worship demonstrate the use of various characteristics indicative of an authentic form of implicit religion.

The mass media has led to the very development of the celebrity by promoting the constant public exposure of select individuals. For example, in Evans' (2005) reflection on the history of the celebrity, she explains that while fame is a value that has always had to be mediated, it was not until the 1920s and the advent of the film star – a product of mass media – that celebrities' private lives became nearly inextricable from their on-screen, performed personas. Boorstin (1961: xxviii) explains how the term 'celebrity' was coined to apply to a 'largely synthetic product', in constant need of public attention from the mass media and journalism venues in order to make the general population even aware of their continued existence and to draw veneration of their perceived attributes. Hollander (2010: 151) echoes these claims, deeming attention given to celebrities to be 'largely artificial', in that being a celebrity is not dependent on genuine talents, attractiveness or even the accumulation of wealth but is instead 'generated' by publicists, journalists and public relations firms. In this vein, Rothenbuhler (2005: 94) argues that we see an emergence of the 'Cult of the Church of the Individual', in which the individual emerges as a celebrated deity, with established celebrities at the top of the ranks. Importantly, he notes that this new church eschews physical or material bodies and instead is structured around the communication surrounding the individuals and is therefore ultimately dependent on discourse and text. Not only is mass communication necessary for the mere existence of celebrities, it is also through the mass media that public understandings of celebrities' personalities are manufactured and revered. For instance, Elvis is still loved because the version of him depicted in his movies is seen as solid evidence of his honesty, simplicity and other esteemed values (Rothenbuhler 2005: 98). Not only can the media present a biased interpretation of a celebrity in his or her contemporary life, it can also recreate them and perpetuate their fame after their deaths. A look into coverage of Michael Jackson's death by *People* magazine reveals an intentional avoidance of the negative traits that had plagued his reputation while living – his supposed paedophilia and his ambiguous sexual orientation, among others – 'ultimately purifying his private life after-the-fact' (Hollander 2010: 147). This understanding of the mass media's part in creating celebrities and defining their public personalities readily lends itself to an investigation of how fans, in turn, gather this information and reinterpret it for themselves.

Primary to fans' emotional investment and time commitments to the veneration of celebrities is the formation of parasocial interactions with these famous figures. Chia and Poo (2009: 25) described this process as being that through which fans experience the 'illusion' of intimate relations to distant celebrities through constant media exposure. Furthermore, as fans develop stronger parasocial relationships with beloved celebrities, they also demonstrate a tendency to emulate these celebrities, role-modelling select values they perceive the celebrity to exhibit (Chia and Poo 2009: 26). Fraser and Brown (2005: 183–206), for example, observed that Elvis fans developed an understanding of the deceased celebrity through his music, posters and other media products, consequently emphasising such prosocial behaviours as his perceived generosity and politeness. According to a constructionist view of the audience and celebrity, it is important to disregard the assumption that celebrities have a definite effect on an impressionable audience, but rather to acknowledge that the audience is varied in its reactions and that audiences can take up a variety of complex and competing discourses to reconstruct celebrities (Stevenson 2005: 160). In short, fans are an undeniable force in the manufacturing process of celebrities, and concern should not be about 'what celebrities do to us, but what we *do with* celebrities' (Stevenson 2005: 142, original emphasis).

Thus fans are involved in an active framing process by which they forge parasocial attachments to certain celebrity figures. In particular, fans tend to 'project onto the celebrity an interpersonal reality and a moral code, which they can then proceed to emulate' (Fraser and Brown 2005: 185). In this way, Fraser and

Brown noted in their study that the Elvis fans drew attention to the kind way it seems he treated his mother, for instance, while ignoring his drug abuse and other rumoured self-destructive behaviours. Hollander theorised that fans' attentive study of celebrity is a by-product of modern society's 'attention deficit', meaning that individuals fear they are not getting enough of the attention to which they feel inherently entitled, with celebrities epitomising individuals who are excessively praised and spotlighted, despite a lack of notable accomplishment or talent (Hollander 2010: 151). Celebrities' success is somewhat irrationally attributed to perceived positive personality traits, which allows them to emerge as role models with influence over fans' actions, and fans benefit from the ambiguous morality of distanced celebrities (Fraser and Brown 2005: 185). Furthermore, due to innovative social media technologies, the positive reconstruction of celebrities is no longer exclusively restricted to media professionals, as fans can create an original communal narrative with other individuals who share a parasocial attachment to the same celebrity figure (Sanderson and Cheong 2010: 329).

One means by which fans establish a universal interpretation of such celebrities is through application of explicitly religious metaphors. While journalists have already deemed Elvis to be '"like" a saint' (Porter 2009: 271) and trips to Graceland to be 'pilgrimage[s]' (Fraser and Brown 2005: 195), Sanderson and Cheong's study asserts that fans themselves construct and negotiate celebrities' identities using religiously charged language. In particular, religious discourse online aids fans in understanding difficult events, such as the passing of a beloved celebrity. The Internet allows fans to present preferred memories of celebrities and share these 'tributes' with others as a means to 'ameliorate the grieving process and [offer] a sympathetic domain wherein an individual's feelings about the deceased are both understood and valued' (Sanderson and Cheong 2010: 328). In both Sanderson and Cheong's work on Twitter use to express grief over Michael Jackson's death and Fraser and Brown's on fans' imitation of Elvis Presley, fans could exercise selectivity regarding which values they perceived to be exhibited in a celebrity's life and incorporate those preferred values into their own lives (Fraser and Brown 2005: 200). In this way, only positive aspects of Jackson's character are mentioned on memorial websites, such that he is 'transformed into a veritable saint and tragic figure' (Hollander 2010: 147). More so than the communal experience, these divine reconstructions of celebrities can provide higher meaning for individuals and '"resurrect" media celebrities into public consciousness', as fans 'mimicked behavior that one would expect from a disciple of an actual religious figure' (Sanderson and Cheong 2010: 328).

To summarise, online social media has furthered fans' feelings of personal connection to celebrities by dramatically increasing their sense of intimacy and allowing fans to personally construct the versions of celebrities they believe to be worthy of veneration and 'self-martyrdom' (Sanderson and Cheong 2010: 338). Fans' roles in reconstructing celebrities, particularly in reconstructing them as religious figures, contribute to an understanding of celebrity worship and fandom as implicit religion.

Overall, we argue that fans' veneration of celebrities can be viewed as a version of implicit religion. As Porter details, if an individual's actions mirror those of a traditionally religious person, it is unimportant that the framework for this mode of being originates from popular culture (Porter 2009: 279); in short, the authenticity of an implicit religion is not derived from its theological tenets – or lack thereof – but from the actions and associated emotions of its adherents. Porter draws support for her argument by providing a case study of *Star Trek* fans who incorporate certain values from the television series' storylines, including multiculturalism, tolerance and free will, into their own lives. It is not religious for fans to simply collect celebrity-related items or to admire celebrities; as Doss explains, these actions take on religious meaning only when they create a transcendent reality with the potential to influence human affairs (Doss 2005: 69). In particular, she investigates how Elvis fans' personal tributes and shrines to the entertainer after the star's death, such as those incorporating the famous 'velvet Elvis' image, can be interpreted as authentic devotional practices that provide comfort to grieving fans (Doss 2005: 79). In this way, fandom can be accepted as a meaningful understanding of the surrounding world, as individuals eschew conventional cultural standards of religion and negotiate new interpretations derived from popular culture.

Finally, these forms of celebrity worship reveal much more than modernity's mundane need for constant entertainment, but are rather indicative of a much greater human need that had been fulfilled in the past in other ways, hinting at a shift in society's constant pursuit of higher meaning (Hollander 2010: 150). Laderman similarly sees celebrity worship as implicitly religious, solidifying this by a comparison of modern-day saints, such as Princess Diana and Russell Crowe, to their more traditionally sanctified counterparts (Laderman 2009: 63–84). He states that new mythologies, ritualistic practices, personal transformations and the establishment of values develop from the 'spiritual-secular mixture' that is fans' devotion to celebrities (Laderman 2009: 84). Laderman particularly examines the frenzy following Rudolph Valentino's death in 1926 and how the fans and media collectively honoured his 'martyrdom' and effectively perpetuated his life through the creation of personal shrines to the deceased actor, filled with memorabilia, together with the authorship of extensive biographies to add to the Valentino mythology.

Taken together, all these studies indicate that celebrity worship can be viewed as a form of authentic implicit religion, where veneration of celebrities includes a selectivity – with the good raised up – and can then be seen as a source of higher meaning, whether this be guidance in life, the emergence of commonly shared mythologies and symbols or the creation of a religious experience.

This overview of previous studies suggests a sequential process can occur, by which arbitrary entertainers can be transformed into modern-day saints. First, the mass media generates the existence of the celebrity by presenting a certain public understanding of that individual through various mass communication venues. Next, these celebrities can then be interpreted and framed by individual fans in terms of particular perceived attributes, by which the fans form parasocial relations with these famed figures and even seek to emulate their prosocial traits. Then when fans' sense of intimacy with celebrities and their consequent acts of veneration for celebrities gain transcendent meaning, either through the creation of divine symbols, mythologies or experiences, celebrity worship becomes a form of implicit religion. These processes are more fully explored in the next section through a case study investigating fans' selective perceptions and religious language choices in relation to how Michael Jackson has been posthumously reconstructed as a divine figure and, in some ways, a martyr whose death is viewed by fans as preordained and motivated by undeserved persecution.

3 Case study: the construction of Michael Jackson as divine martyr

A greater understanding of how the mass media perpetuate the existence of the celebrity – even after death – and the part fans play in reconstructing that celebrity's identity, in alignment with the basic characteristics of implicit religion, can be found by examining fan practices and discourse surrounding the website memories.michaeljackson.com. This is an official site created by the Sony Music Entertainment Company, which holds the copyrights to Jackson's music. However, fans from all over the world are encouraged to share their personal 'tributes' to Michael Jackson by posting individualised messages on the webpage; fans are also able to promote the website via Twitter and Facebook.

Michael Jackson provides an interesting case study, not only because of his wildly devoted fan base and popularity, but because his unique public persona readily lends itself to an otherworldly interpretation, as he utilised his 'freakishness' – his childlike nature, seeming asexuality, ambiguous ethnicity, continually morphing facial appearance, etc. – to gain 'access into social spaces and identities typically denied to black male entertainers while [sidestepping] the pitfalls that tend to punish non-normative expressions of race and gender' (Gates 2003: 3). The huge attention given by the mass media to his death, memorial service and the posthumous release of the documentary *This Is It* led to an undeniable mourning period for fans; as stated in *People* magazine on the day of his death, 'the world seemed to pause together to measure this loss [...] Jackson's life, and now his death, profoundly affected his millions of fans in a way that is rarely seen' (quoted in Hollander 2010: 147). New social media venues allow for fans to 'invoke religious discourse as a comforting mechanism [drawing] solace from equating the celebrity with the divine' (Hollander 2010: 147), as Sanderson and Cheong (2010) also observed in their longitudinal study of fans' grief processes on Twitter, Facebook and TMZ.com. Their research found that not only did creating this communal narrative allow fans to find comfort in a 'resurrection' of a beloved celebrity but also provided the comfort of predictable rituals, such as 'Michael Mondays' on Twitter, on which fans would post favourite memories of Michael Jackson on a weekly basis. This provides a point of departure for examining memories.michaeljackson.com and the various means by which fans recreate Jackson as divine through their tributes on the site.

While there are hundreds of thousands of messages that have been posted on the site since its original launch, for this case study a strategic sampling of posts was collected from the hours of 12 a.m. to 3 a.m. on 29 August 2010. This date is significant in that it would have been Michael Jackson's 52nd birthday and is just 14 months after his death. This sample presented a total of 105 posts for analysis, although approximately half-a-dozen were identical 'repeat' posts, possibly caused by a technological error. Several of the posts were written in Spanish, Portuguese, Chinese and Russian; all were translated into English for this analysis using Google's online translator service.

In order to scrutinise these posts for evidence of implicitly religious traits, posts were read and flagged for certain explicitly religious terms, including 'angel', 'heaven' and 'God', as well as for other phrases that implied an understanding of the afterlife, such as 'God-like inspiration' or other less blatantly religious references. From these findings, it could be deduced that fans' implicitly religious responses to Michael Jackson's death could be roughly categorised into three slightly different understandings of Michael as a divine figure: Michael the angel, depicted by fans as called by God to join him in the afterlife; Michael the otherworldly messenger, believed by fans to have been sent to spread love and hope to the world; and Michael the immortal spirit, depicted by fans as being continually resurrected by their eternal adoration. Drawing from the research on the reconstruction of celebrities by fans and celebrity worship, as discussed above, the construction of each of these interpretations of Jackson will be examined through observation of religious terminology use (and the surrounding contexts) as well as the means by which fans selectively perceive Michael's personality traits and express the intimate connection they feel they have to him.

One of the most common reconstructions of Michael as divine is a general consensus that the entertainer is unquestionably in heaven now, as he is meant to be. While there is no discussion of Michael as Christian or faithful to any particular religion, fans reconstruct Jackson such that he seems to be redeemed by his own perceived goodness or preordained fate. Ten posts make explicit references to Jackson currently being an angel in heaven, if not considered a sort of guardian angel for his children or fans left on earth. Several of these posts directly connect the idea of Michael being an angel to the belief that God specifically called Michael from earth to serve a higher purpose. For instance, user 'Jen' (29 August 2010, 2:52 a.m.) comments, 'Heaven must have really needed an angel', and 'Talan' (29 August 2010, 1:30 a.m.) states that 'god was looking for his Angel' (*sic*). In both of these posts, Michael is directly referred to as an otherworldly figure, connected to the idea of a divine mission, whether on heaven or earth. One of the most vivid descriptions of Michael as an angel was posted by 'Lena' (29 August 2010, 2:39 a.m.); she envisions Michael in heaven with 'angelic wings, dancing, using the sky as [his] Stage and the Moonlight as [his] Spot Light' (*sic*). Like many of the other users who express belief in Michael's transcendent, eternal existence as perpetuated by his ever-loving fans – as will be discussed in depth later – 'Lena' expresses a personal belief that Jackson's entertaining power will continue forever, not merely symbolically, but literally in his afterlife.

In other posts, Michael himself is not considered to be an angel but to be among angels who either celebrate his greatness or provide comfort to him. These posts differ from others in that they hint at a more traditional notion of heaven as a place of refuge for the deceased. The aspect of divine experience emerges from fans' feelings of continued intimacy with Jackson – most strongly evident in the fact that the overwhelming majority of posts are addressed directly to the deceased Michael – and the sense of hope they derive from the belief that the 'King of Pop' is watching over them. User 'MJsprettybaby' (29 August 2010, 1:39 a.m.) posted, 'I hope that you are always smiling to us from heaven', and 'Nieves Lopez' (29 August 2010, 1:41 a.m.) posted, 'Someday we will see you in the KINGDOM OF GOD!' (*sic*). By creating a shared understanding of Michael as being in heaven, one who furthermore listens to fans' online pleas and awaits a reunion with his adoring audience, fans are able to make sense of Michael's sudden death. They can attribute it to a higher, although not fully understood, purpose (e. g., 'GOD doesn't make mistakes, and that he needed you to come home', *sic*, as stated by 'melliemel' at 2:01 a.m.) and therefore create a saint-like figure to whom they can feel justified in pouring forth praise.

The second reconstruction of Michael as divine is an interpretation of the celebrity as a supernatural messenger sent to unite people around the globe and spread his perceived message of hope and love. This particular interpretation of the celebrity stems from fans' heavily selective perception of the type of person Jackson is believed to have been. Despite the fury at antagonistic press coverage of Jackson's many puzzling antics – from his extensive rhinoplasty to his insistence on his children wearing masks in public – not one of Jackson's supposed vices is mentioned on the site. Instead, he is recreated as a nearly divine visionary, spreading goodness to all. While some fans are not specific in pinpointing Jackson's perceived gifts, offering ample praise such as 'You gave so much to this world' ('MJsprettybaby', 29 August 2010, 1:39 a.m.), others provide detailed lists. 'Bridget' (29 August 2010, 12:58 a.m.) lists Michael's 'smile, passion, spirituality, humility, genius talent and innocence which suffused the world with wonderment and joy, so much joy!' One user explicitly labels Michael to be 'MY Idol' (*sic*, 'SANDRA', 29 August 2010, 12:00 a.m.); two declare him to be their 'inspiration', and a few draw even stronger parallels to religious devotion, such as one stating avidly, 'i do believe in you. i know you are the truth' (*sic*, 'Alice Neverland', 29 August 2010, 12:00 a.m.).

Much more than simply describing Michael in highly praiseworthy terms, fans imply that a universal community has been forged through mutual love of Jackson. 'Bridget' (29 August 2010, 12:58 a.m.) says that '[Michael's] music harmonized the world with hope and communal reverence', and 'Lena' (29 August 2010, 2:39 a.m.) says, '[T]he power you evoke Michael, is almost God Like, it's Hypnotic, it draws people from world's away to become one' (*sic*). If the sprinkling of different languages present in this small sample has any further implications, Michael is a divine messenger who works to unify people, not only through his widely distributed music but also through the communally shared experience of his perceived love. A final Christ-like element of this reconstruction of Michael concerns fans' repeated assertions that he was falsely depicted or persecuted by the mass media, an active choice to ignore select aspects of the celebrity's life. 'Talan' (29 August 2010, 1:30 a.m.) bluntly states, 'F*** the press, Michael your the best' (*sic*), and 'Jovi Ramirez' (29 August 2010, 12:35 a.m.) pledges to Jackson, 'I love u with all my heart reguardless of wat people say' (*sic*). There are two other references in the postings to the 'lies' and 'doubts' surrounding what fans believe to be Michael's true character. While this is not explicitly religious language, it does provide a stronger framework for the interpretation of Michael as a persecuted martyr brought into the world with a higher purpose. Overall, Michael's life is recreated as a sort of new 'gospel', one for which fans confirm they will be faithful proselytisers, as 'all that were touched by [Jackson] continue to spread this wonderful message and live by it' ('Asha', 29 August 2010, 2:04 a.m.).

Additionally, Michael is seen as divine in a third sense by those fans who draw particular attention to his eternal nature, as perpetuated by belief in his continued existence via the mass media and fans' love. This is different from the first reconstruction of Michael the angel in that it does not draw from conventional faith in a heavenly afterlife, but rather provides fans with the hope that they can play a personal part in assuring Jackson's immortality. Sixteen posts make an explicit claim that Michael still lives; these posts were different from those stating that Michael had made a transition to a heavenly state, but rather imply that he, like an ethereal spirit, is one with humanity on earth for eternity. A few of these posts were straightforward acknowledgements of fans' belief in Michael's immortality, such as 'you will live forever' ('aditi varma', 29 August 2010, 1:16 a.m.) and 'R.I.P Michael Jackson [1958-INFINITE]' ('Eureka', 29 August 2010, 12:56 a.m.). Two posts contributed to the well-known 'Michael Jackson as Peter Pan' narrative by directly equating the star with the timeless, mythical character. Two other posts explicitly attributed Michael's perceived immortality to the continual devotion of his fans and their commitment to various Jackson-related media.

Another user ('susie oneal', 29 August 2010, 12:51 a.m.) connected belief in Jackson's eternal nature to fans' actions on the website by writing, '[Y]ou continue returning to life [...] every time we write on pages [... B]ecause we write THESE you will be more present than ever'. In two posts, fans expressed a ritualised aspect of their continued devotion to the King of Pop. The same user ('susie oneal', 29 August 2010, 12:51 a.m.) tells Michael, 'I listen to your music everyday wishing you could have been with us much longer' (*sic*). Due to the fact that this sample is limited, the degree to which belief in Michael as divine manifests itself in ritualistic behaviours is impossible to pinpoint without explicit reference to these practices by users, such as the aforementioned. However, the communicated belief in Jackson as a forever-present spirit is also expressed as an implicitly religious mechanism by which fans are able to cope with their grief and put faith in something greater than themselves. For example, 'niki' (29 August 2010, 2:50 a.m.) states, 'You are still here and you always will' (*sic*). In this reconstruction of Michael, fans' adoration provides the basis for a divine experience, as they are able to contribute to his God-like eternity and comfortingly believe in his continuous spiritual companionship.

Michael's death is also depicted as martyr-like by his fans, who piece together an all-encompassing narrative that casts the pop singer as a saintly figure who was unjustly killed despite the creed of love he promoted. This reconstruction is an accumulation of the previously described depictions of Michael as an angel, otherworldly messenger and eternal spirit, in that Michael the martyr is depicted by fans as chosen by God to fulfil a higher purpose – to spread his 'gospel' of love on earth – and he was then taken from the world after he suffered persecution by the media. Several posts on the website mention Michael's legacy of love and even describe themselves as 'witnesses' to his message. For example, 'Louise Costello' (29 August 2010, 1:31 a.m.) states that Michael 'Saved so many Lives and never wanted anything back in return except L.O.V.E' (*sic*), a description that parallels the stories of Christ. Similar to devotees of Christ or a martyred saint reflecting on such sacrificial deaths, 'Sayan Banerjee' (29 August 2010, 2:50 a.m.) asserts, 'The world stood perplexed for several minutes on hearing his untimely expiration. All should be thankful to him for showing us the ray of hope in this world of doom and despair'. 'Bridget of New Zealand' (29 August 2010, 12:58 a.m.) added that she felt 'so privileged that I was of a generation where I was able to witness it and be a part of it'. As a key element of a martyr is enduring suffering for a greater good, a number of posts reference the pain and prejudice inflicted upon Michael during his life, such as 'THE WORLD SHOULD OF APPRICIATED YOU MORE' (*sic*, 29 August 2010, 1:13 a.m.) and 'since you've passed away, your pain and suffering is no more' (29 August 2010, 12:56 a.m.). Finally, after Michael's believed ascension to heaven – 'GOD doesn't make mistakes [...] he needed you to come home' ('melliemel', 29 August 2010, 2:01 a.m.) – Michael's death continues to inspire his followers with his perceived prime value, namely, love for all. For instance, 'Asha' (29 August 2010, 2:04 a.m.) states that 'all that were touched by you continue to spread this wonderful message and live by it. Your fans worldwide will continue keeping your legacy alive no matter what'. While no individual post alone establishes a martyr narrative about Michael, together the fans' postings form a communal narrative by which different elements of a martyr or Christ-like story are asserted.

Throughout the posts, there is the notion of a clear division between supportive fans and an antagonistic general public. Jackson's talents are viewed as a gift to a suffering world in need, and through sacrificial death and the committed loyalty of his fans, Jackson's legacy is framed as otherworldly and never-ending. For example, 'Nieves Lopez' (29 August 2010, 1:41 a.m) dedicates his post to Michael for 'all these years you gave us, all your effort and dedication, your suffering, what they expected and never came, the injustice and lies [...]'. While Michael's global impact is frequently linked directly to his art, often Jackson himself is the sole object of reverence and a catalyst for change. For instance, 'Asha' (29 August 2010, 2:04 a.m.) affirms that 'our lives were enriched by your existence'. When compiled together, these different online voices tell the story of Michael the modern-day martyr, one who was willing to endure public suffering and even death but who would relentlessly continue to promote a message of overwhelming love.

In conclusion, a brief case study of fans' actions online at memories.michaeljackson.com demonstrates that, through the creation of shared narratives and symbols, a deceased celebrity can be collectively resurrected and reconstructed into a divine figure, one who provides a framework of meaning for fans struggling to accept Jackson's unforeseen death and make sense of the world. While the various words used to commemorate Jackson do not mean that the online users are rejecting more traditional religious beliefs – in fact, the described reconstructions of the celebrity draw heavily from Christian beliefs in heaven, the revolutionary love of Christ and the infiltration of the Holy Spirit ('Proshant', 29 August 2010, 2:24 a.m., writes '[W]e are not alone, he's still here with us') – the fans' created narrative does represent a merging of the sacred with the secular. Because there is no interaction between users on the website, all understandings of Jackson as divine must be drawn from individual fans' intentional language choices in their self-expression of who Michael was and still is to them. It is clear that fans exhibit discretion regarding which aspects of Michael Jackson's character they decide to focus on in the process of recreating Jackson as a divine figure, whether as a heavenly angel, an otherworldly messenger or an eternally present spirit. They choose to ignore any negative depictions of his character, reflecting instead on the positive force of his music and charity work. More so than mere symbols, these three different divine identities are infused with greater meaning, providing hope to faithful fans and a point of reference for what is deemed to be good and worthy in the world.

To summarise, fans' religiously-charged language and selective perceptions of Michael's identity readily mould the legendary and controversial entertainer into a venerable, divine figure. Through their praise and expressed perceptions of the meaning he infuses in their lives, Jackson is transformed into something much greater than a mere popular cultural icon. The many negative rumours and child molestation allegations that plagued his life are forgotten as fans draw attention to and celebrate his life, his message, his virtues and his legacy, and thence crown Jackson with saintly titles. Consequently, he emerges as a genuine religious idol, a shining symbol of hope, love, guardianship, destiny and eternity to those who perceive him as such.

4 Reflections on celebrity, divinity and martyrdom

From the findings of this study, it can be concluded that fans can recreate celebrities as religious figures through the online construction of communal narratives and symbols that provide higher meaning to their lives. One significant aspect of these narratives that appeared to be a common thread throughout each of the examples was that, despite a loosely unified understanding of a celebrity as divine, each individual fan played a personal role in the selective process that went into recreating a celebrity's perceived identity, resulting in fragmented interpretations. This echoes Fraser and Brown's (2005) study of Elvis fans and their imitation of the icon, a practice that could be viewed as an implicitly religious ritual or fan-generated posthumous 'resurrection' of the celebrity. They found that while few survey participants had ever actually met Elvis or seen him perform live, fans nevertheless readily formulated their own distinctive understandings of Elvis through creating personalised interpretations of his mediated personality, such as those lived out through their unique impersonations (Fraser and Brown 2005: 197). Similarly, Sanderson and Cheong's (2010) study of grieving Michael Jackson fans found that religious discourse was used to interpret Jackson's death in a multiplicity of ways. These included not only a mode of veneration and a coping mechanism for his passing but also condemnation of those who scorned his purportedly sinful nature. Here, celebrity worship represents a form of implicit religion, and thus multiple readings of a single celebrity's identity can be regarded as equally authentic religious interpretations.

This tendency is also seen in the case study of memories.michaeljackson.com. While many fans utilised religious language, this was used to create starkly different understandings of Michael. One example is the divergent groups who presented Michael as an angel in heaven and conversely as an ever-present spirit on earth. However, despite their differing manifestations, both of these interpretations serve as a framework for coping with loss, much like traditional religious beliefs. For instance, one user ('Steph Newton', 29 August 2010, 2:28 a.m.) recreates Michael as an angel and thus finds comfort that he would still be able to watch over his children, while another user ('paulasue', 29 August 2010, 12:00 a.m.) reconstructed Michael as more of a spiritual presence ('forever in our hearts'), but one who also provides comfort to his fans by manifesting himself in his legacy and resonating love for the world. Although there are recurrences of phrases and images used by fans to depict Michael as 'divine', it must be noted that the sheer subjectivity of personal interpretation is a critical aspect of celebrity worship as implicit religion, for it is not only in the fans' veneration of the individual but in the meaning *to* the fan that a religious experience is forged.

Predictably, fans take great liberties in terms of which aspects of a celebrity's perceived personality traits they choose to celebrate – or ignore – as well as the traditional religious ideas from which they construct new mythologies in the process of recreating celebrities as modern-day 'saints'. From these varied interpretations, a variety of religious metaphors and narratives inevitably emerge.

More than simply producing heterogeneous understandings of celebrities as divine, another important conclusion is that this mode of implicit religion is also highly dependent upon the existence of public discourse and communication. This might seem to be an overly fundamental observation, but it is nonetheless critical. It is through fans' explicitly religious choice of words that they create a communal narrative – however varied – that serves as a framework of implicitly religious meaning and the foundation for the genesis of a religious experience. As Rothenbuhler argues, culture has promoted 'the self [as] the holy object of the society carried by the medium of the individual'; as the self can only be fully expressed through communication, the Church of the Cult of the Individual 'can only exist in communicative interaction' (Rothenbuhler 2005: 99). It therefore seems no coincidence that celebrities, whose very public personas are dependent upon their mediated personalities, would promote a sort of worship that is heavily dependent upon a communicated religious experience or narrative.

Fraser and Brown (2005: 185) argue that celebrities' 'relation to reality and morality is ambiguous', for they are ultimately 'images without bottoms' (Ewen 1988: 13). With the blank slate for a public persona, fans are free to transform a celebrity into a divine figure, but to do so fans must use religious discourse. As Sanderson and Cheong's study (2010: 338) finds, 'religious discourse is a "common language" that [people] can use to communicate both their affection and contempt for celebrities'. Because of this flexibility and fluidity of implicit religion, deliberate choices must be made by fans in invoking religious language in a way that frames celebrities in a highly positive or reverential sense. For example, in the case study, online users' explicit use of religiously charged words, such as 'angel', 'heaven', 'God' and 'blessing', were necessary to convey an understanding of Michael Jackson as divine. Fans' word choices could even transform Jackson's commonly known nickname, 'the King of Pop', into a title reminiscent of Christ as the 'the King of Kings', e. g., 'the true King, the King of human hearts' ('YuliyaVV', 29 August 2010, 12:41 a.m.) and 'Dear and beloved King' ('Avik', 29 August 2010, 12:41 a.m.). Thus, it is ultimately through fans' deliberate word choices, words that evoke the idea of Michael as immortal and praiseworthy, that the celebrity is created as divine.

This study also shows how deceased celebrities who are framed as divine may also be seen as martyrs by their fans. Celebrities, especially popular musicians, have often been framed in terms of martyrdom in order to justify their deaths or self-destruction as a sacrificial gift by the iconic identity they symbol-ised to an undeserving world, e. g., discussion of the deaths of Kurt Cobain (Kahn 1999: 83–96) and Janis Joplin (Bradshaw 2008: 69–87), or to frame the sharing of their music or talents in terms of self-sacrifice and martyrdom for their fans. Hollander (2010) argues, for example, that Jackson (throughout his career) framed himself and the loss of his childhood, due to his musical career, in terms of self-martyrdom. Johnson (2009) likened Jackson to a martyr, similar to Princess Diana, immediately following Michael's death. In an op-ed article, Johnson wrote that while Diana evoked 'an astonishing response' because she spoke to women around the world, Jackson 'spoke to the billions of people the world over who feel that they do not conform in some way to the Hollywood stereotype of good looks [... I]n a world dominated by a demoralising canon of physical perfection, [Jackson] was the patron saint of dysmorphia'.

Throughout the posts on memories.michaeljackson.com, this concept of oth-erness plays a key role, as fans assert that, while Jackson was undeniably differ-ent, he was unique in a way that both made him somehow superior to the mass-es and yet unquestionably accepting of all. Here the frame of celebrity martyrdom presents the object of devotion in a spiritual light, highlighting char-acteristics of selflessness and willingness to give up their lives for their fans – together with the messages of love, peace, hope and justice that their music is seen to represent. In this investigation, we see that Michael Jackson's fans view his death as martyrdom in that, collectively, they reframe his death as the product of a hostile world unwilling to accept his legacy of the lyrical mes-sages of acceptance and charity.

Beyond the mere creation of religious narratives about celebrities, fans' di-vine experiences are derived from the meaning these communal mythologies provide to their lives. For '[i]t is in the impact of the text on its audiences that the religious import is to be found' (Porter 2009, 275) and it is through such texts that celebrities fully shine in an unexpectedly 'holy' light. It is through fans' selective reconstructions of celebrities as divine, via their communicated re-ligious narratives and fans' consequent transcendent experiences, that celebrity worship evades traditional notions of idolatry. Instead, it presents itself as a fully valid form of implicit religion, with celebrities 'mov[ing] people to action as well as contemplation [...], their personal stories becom[ing] public morality tales in-structing larger communities about right and wrong, success and failure, fulfil-ment and tragedy' (Laderman 2009: 73). This chapter argues that the actions of the fans are not so unlike certain aspects of traditional religions and shows how popular culture and the social affordances of new media may function as a form of implicit religion for many individuals.

References

Bradshaw, Melissa. 2008. "Devouring the diva: martyrdom as feminist backlash." *The Rose. Camera Obscura* 23: 69–87.

Boorstin, Daniel J. 1961. *The Image: A Guide to Pseudo-Events in America.* New York: Harper and Row.

Campbell, Heidi, and A. La Pastina. 2010. "How the iPhone became divine: New media, religion and the intertextual circulation of meaning." *New Media and Society* 12 (7): 1191–1207.

Chia, Stella C., and Y.L. Poo. "Media, celebrities, and fans: An examination of adolescents' media usage and involvement with entertainment celebrities". *Journalism and Mass Communication Quarterly* 86 (1): 23–44.

Chidester, David. 2005. "The church of baseball, the fetish of Coca-Cola, and the potlatch of rock and roll." In *Religion and Popular Culture in America*, edited by G. Forbes and J. Mahan, 213–232. Berkley, CA: University of California Press.

Doss, Erika. 2005. "Elvis forever." In *Afterlife as Afterimage: Understanding Posthumous Fame*, edited by S. Jones and J. Jensen, 61–80. New York: Peter Lang Publishing.

Evans, Jessica. 2005. "Audiences and Celebrity." In *Understanding Media: Inside Celebrity*, edited by J. Evans and D. Hesmondhalgh, 135–172. New York: Open University Press.

Ewen, Stuart. 1988. *All Consuming Images.* New York: Basic Books.

Fraser, Benson, and W. Brown. 2005. "Media, celebrities, and social influences: Identification with Elvis Presley." *Mass Communication and Society* 5: 183–206.

Gates, Racquel J. 2010. "Reclaiming the freak: Michael Jackson and the spectacle of identity." *The Velvet Light Trap* 65: 3–4.

Hollander, Paul. 2010. "Michael Jackson, the Celebrity Cult, and Popular Culture." *Society* 47: 147–152.

Johnson, Boris. 2009. "Michael Jackson: It would be wrong to sneer at this outpouring of public grief." *The Telegraph* June 29. Available at: http://www.telegraph.co.uk/culture/music/michael-jackson/5681132/Michael-Jackson-It-would-be-wrong-to-sneer-at-this-outpouring-of-public-grief.html.

Kahn, Seth. 1999. "Kurt Cobain, Martyrdom, and the problem of agency." *Studies in Popular Culture* 22: 83–96.

Laderman, Gary. 2009. "Celebrity." In *Sacred Matters: Celebrity Worship, Sexual Ecstasies, the Living Dead, and Other Signs of Religious Life in the United States*, edited by Gary Laderman, 63–84. New York: The New Press.

Lord, Karen. 2006. "Implicit religion: Definition and application." *Implicit Religion* 9: 205–219.

Maltby, John., L. Day, L.E. McCutcheon, R. Gillet, J. Houran, and D.D. Ashe. 2004. "Personality and coping: A context for examining celebrity worship and mental health." *British Journal of Psychology* 95: 411–428.

Porter, Jennifer. 2009. "Implicit religion in popular culture: The religious dimensions of fan communities." *Implicit Religion* 12: 271–280.

Rothenbuhler, Eric. 2005. "The church of the cult of the individual." In *Media Anthropology*, edited by Eric Rothenbuhler and Mihai Coman, 91–100. Thousand Oaks: Sage Publications.

Sanderson, Jimmy, and P.H. Cheong. 2010. "Tweeting prayers and communicating grief over Michael Jackson online." *Bulletin of Science Technology and Society* 30: 328–340.

Sony Music Entertainment. 2010. *Remembering Michael Jackson. Share Your Tribute.* Available at: http://memories.michaeljackson.com/.

Stevenson, Nick. 2005. "Audiences and celebrity." In *Understanding Media: Inside Celebrity*, edited by J. Evans and D. Hesmondhalgh, 135–172. New York: Open University Press.

Arjen Nauta
7 Radical Islam, Globalisation and Social Media: Martyrdom Videos on the Internet[1]

What does a martyr do? His function is not confined to resisting the enemy and, in the process, either giving him a blow or receiving a blow from him. Had that been the case, we could say that when his blood is shed it goes [to] waste. But at no time is a martyr's blood wasted. It does not flow on the ground. Every drop of it is turned into hundreds and thousands of drops, nay, into tons of blood and is transfused into the body of his society [...] Martyrdom means transfusion of blood into a particular human society, especially a society suffering from anaemia, so to speak, of the true faith. It is the martyr who infuses such fresh blood into the veins of such a society. (Ayatollah Murtaza Mutahhari 1980: 63)

1 Introduction

'A martyr! How strangely that word has been distorted from its original sense of a common witness', Edward Gibbon remarks as he mentions that Sigismund of Burgundy has become a saint and martyr (1963: 176). Gibbon seems somewhat short-sighted in his assessment of the ancient Greek word 'mártyr' (μάρτυρ)' however; witness or testimony is a very powerful form of advertisement because it communicates personal experience and credibility with an event to an audience – also to the ancient Greeks. In human history, many religious movements and organisations have taken this further and resorted to 'witnesses' for promotional purposes. What could be a more powerful testimony than a person who chooses suffering or death over life in order to testify to his or her absolute commitment to a religious cause? Especially if a belief system is not in a culturally or politically dominant situation, or under attack from an outsider, the sacrifice of the martyr is very helpful in defining the value of the cause s/he dies for. Martyrdom serves (1) as a boundary marker in which the borders between religious systems are sharpened; (2) it furthermore creates an example, a standard of conduct, which should be followed by fellow members of the religious community; and, (3) by creating boundaries and examples, the martyr provides

---

1 I would like to thank David Herbert and Anita Greenhill for their valuable comments to preliminary versions of this chapter. They corrected many flaws, for which I am very grateful.

a new sense of cohesion to a community, defining more sharply why a cause is worth dying for (Cook 2007: 1–2).

The martyr also needs witnesses, however, the spectators who witness the sacrifice to a certain cause and testify it to others so that it becomes part of the collective memory. In ancient times, Christian martyrs were often executed in public – quite regularly in the theatre. The Romans thus provided the necessary stage for the martyr, enabling the audience to witness it (Potter 1993). This might have been a deterrent to most spectators, as the Romans intended, but it enabled other Christians to witness the martyr's sacrifice as an example which should be followed, or at least praised. It was only through these public demonstrations and subsequently produced written records – which spread through the Christian communities in the empire and were eventually collected by Eusebius in the 4th century – that martyrs and martyrdom as such could gain a prominent position in Catholic Christianity (Brown 1981).

This is as true nowadays as it was during ancient times, except that the development of mass communications and media has conceptually extended the theatre. The theatre where the martyrs perform their sacrifice, witnessed by the audience, now extends to virtually anyone with access to the Internet. In the contemporary world, radical Muslims make frequent use of the instrument of martyrdom. Mass media and the Internet now serve as the means to spread these martyrdom stories, often in the form of suicide attacks, in carefully crafted hagiographies of martyrs, often produced on video. The current Eusebiuses are the many radical Islamic sites featuring martyrologies, written as well as filmed. This paper seeks to investigate these videos on the Internet: where they can be found, who makes them, how they are spread, and what they actually consist of. Most important, however, are the questions about how they function and for what purposes they have been produced.

This investigation attempts to form a contribution to the current study of radical Islam and terrorism. Although many facets have been extensively studied, the role of radical Islam on the Internet has so far had insufficient light shed on it. This essay seeks to show that martyrdom videos form an important part of radical Islamic propaganda and therefore need to be investigated more closely. In order to further clearly demarcate the breadth of my field of investigation, I will focus on martyrdom videos from suicide bombers. It is unnecessary to remind the reader of the major role which the discourse of radical Islam plays in contemporary Western societies. Within this discourse I include the many (often overlapping) currents that are usually associated with radical Islam – such as fundamentalism, Salafism, jihadism, and Islamism. Likewise, radical Islamic organizations have been labelled (whether by others or themselves) fundamentalist, terrorist, Salafist, jihadist or have simply been subsumed under the name of al Qaeda. When I refer to the organisations behind the individual suicide bombers in this essay, I will use the term 'jihadist movement'. Although the discursive use of *'jihad'* is contested in the Arab world itself, as well as in Western academia, I regard *jihad* as the religiously-driven struggle for Islamic orthodoxy and purity (in these cases turning violent). The jihadist movement is a loose collective term for the plethora of Islamic movements that regard themselves as part of that struggle (or war) and choose to engage in it. I am fully aware that this to a certain extent involves certain generalisations and reifications, but this is not detrimental for the purposes of this chapter.

2 Martyrdom videos on the Internet

Although the use of high-tech devices and instruments such as the Internet may appear to contradict their often fundamentalist ideals, radical Islamic organisations have recognised the use of the Internet as a multipurpose tool and weapon. Connections to the Internet have spread around the world in recent decades, making it easily accessible for radical Muslims. Even in the most remote parts of the Hindu Kush, the Internet is now readily available, and cybercafés have sprung out of the ground like mushrooms. This offers another advantage for the Muslim radical: the ability to remain anonymous (see Eickelman 1992; Sageman 2004; Linjakumpu 2008).[2] While with personal computers the danger remains that intelligence services may track the IP address, the emergence of cybercafés poses an excellent alternative in order to avoid tracing. Adding to the accessibility of the Internet are the relatively low prices, not only for using it but also for, e. g., creating a website, thus making it not just available for the wealthier classes. Moreover, the Internet forms an excellent source for information but, more importantly in this matter, also for sharing information (Anderson 2003a: 48 – 52 and 2003b: 887– 897). The use of the Internet as a means for global communication has been pivotal for the development and actions of radical Islamic organisations (see Devji 2005).[3]

Some of the means for which radical Muslims have actually used the Internet include the following: (1) They have used it as a vehicle for fundraising and financial transactions between involved groups and persons. Although the latter

---

2 Although academics have discussed the availability of the Internet to radical Muslims, I think we should nowadays assume that Internet access will somehow be available – for the reasons mentioned above.
3 Osama bin Laden himself affirmed the pivotal role of mass media and the Internet in the spread of Al Qaeda's messages (Devji 2005).

has declined in recent years, as increased monitoring has made it too risky, some transactions still occur through new 'pay-as-you-go' credit cards (see especially Atwan 2008). The use of the Internet as a vehicle for fundraising has become more popular though, as have efforts to sell merchandise (see Nacos 2007). (2) Radical Muslims have also used the Internet as a tool for the recruitment of new members. Personal contacts have traditionally been the most important means of winning new recruits, but with its global spread the Internet has proved instrumental in this respect (see e. g., Sageman 2004; Husayn 2007).[4] It also served consequently (3) as a virtual classroom for training recruits in radical Islamic thought and also in bomb and explosive making. The investigation of computers left behind by Al Qaeda members in Afghanistan has also shown that they were extensively used (4) for gathering information, such as maps and news. More important is the outlining of the Internet (5) as a virtual battle-field on which the enemy can be digitally attacked, e. g., by hacking into web-sites, e-mail, etc. This is the so-called 'Cyber Jihad' (Atwan 2008) or 'E-Jihad'(-Bunt 2003). Equally important, however, is its use in (6) logistics, the facilitating and planning of operations. The Hamburg-based perpetrators of the 9/11 attacks, for example, Mohammed Atta, Ziad Jarrah, Ramzi bin al-Shibh and Marwan al-Shehhi, communicated with Al Qaeda's operational boss, Khaled Sheikh Mohamed, via the Internet (Sageman 2004: 105–8).

Most important for the purpose of this chapter, however, is the use of the Internet (7) as a means of propaganda, narrowly related to though not entirely overlapping with the Internet as a tool for recruitment. One can find many sites on the Internet which roughly fit within the discourse of radical Islam, whether called Jihad, Salafist, Islamist or fundamentalist. The unprecedented possibilities of the Internet for marketing have been fully appreciated by the makers of many sites, seen in the plethora of interactive options, flashy banners and the amount of audio-visual material used for their purposes. Many of these sites are designed to rapidly disseminate their messages and often have graph-ical interfaces as well as familiar logos and symbols. Religious messages often contain Qur'anic quotes and are packed in attractive messages, coupled with ex-tensive use of religious symbolism (Bunt 2009: 177–80). On these sites hagiogra-phies for the martyrs – from here on referred to as martyrologies – can often be found, either written in biographical form or in video clips.

---

4 Sageman (2004) clearly states that integration in radical networks always happens through personal contacts, not through 'light communities' such as the Internet. An excellent example for this argument is given by Ed Husayn (2007). More recent investigations have demonstrated, however, that through its rapid global spread, the Internet has become an instrument for re-cruitment as well.

Many academics have so far undertaken research on radical Islamic sites, although the number and location of sites fluctuates considerably and thus only allows a snapshot of the situation at the time of investigation.[5] Government agencies (such as intelligence services), Internet providers and private organisations[6] regularly attack/hack these sites to get them offline, even though the servers often operate from countries such as China and Pakistan. The results of these attempts vary because the webmasters of these sites are very resilient, as I will show in the next section.

One of the first and most influential sites was azzam.com, named after Abdullah Yusuf Azzam.[7] It served during the 1990s as an influential source of information on the activities of jihadists throughout the world (although especially in Chechnya and Afghanistan). After its forced closure shortly after 9/11, IslamicAwakening.com continued to publish the Azzam news bulletins on its website. In its forum, as well as in many other forums and chatboxes on radical Islamic sites, one can find many hyperlinks connecting to martyrdom videos (Bunt 2009).[8] IslamicAwakening is moreover active on social media sites.

A Facebook presence was only comparatively recently established (in February 2011) and therefore relatively few posts have been made so far. Most of these are seemingly quite innocent and call for the release of prisoners or the ousting of a London-based Imam who has not followed the Islamic creed strictly enough, according to the appeal. One dates from March 31, 2011 and invites its users for a 'question-and-answer' session with a certain Tarek Mehanna on the forum IslamicAwakening.com (Facebook 2011). Although this seems harmless, Mehanna was arrested in October 2009 by US authorities in Boston because he allegedly conspired to attack civilians at a shopping mall, American soldiers abroad and two members of the executive branch of the federal government (*New York Times* 2009). Mehanna has not so far answered the many questions posted on IslamicAwakening.com – where most asked for his advice and spiritual guidance (islamicawakening.com n.d.). An apparently innocent link to a QandA session on Facebook is thus put in another light. On December 20, 2011 he was found guilty

---

5 The University of Arizona has developed a highly specialized search tool for jihad-related topics on the Internet, which enables them to carry out regular and more systematic research. An extensive list of radical Islamic sites can be found in Bunt (2009: 223 – 226).

6 Examples include Internet Haganah, run by computer programmer Aaron Weisburd, and the online activist Jonathan R. Galt (a pseudonym), who is credited by Azzam.com as the individual behind the removal of their website.

7 Azzam was a theologian and key figure in militant radical Islam until his assassination in Peshawar in 1989. He was the mentor of Osama bin Laden.

8 See especially the forum on 'Politics, Contemporary Issues and Jihad', which received by far the most hits and posts.

by the Boston US District Court on seven charges, including conspiring to kill in a foreign country, providing material and logistical support to terrorists and lying to authorities in a terrorism investigation (Valencia 2011). He was subsequently sentenced on April 12, 2012 and faces over 17 years in prison (Sweet 2012).

The contents on Twitter, which IslamicAwakening also only recently joined, are roughly the same as on Facebook as of the date of investigation (Islamic Awakening n.d.). Links to martyrdom videos cannot, however, be found on the Facebook and Twitter pages of this organisation, although many can be found in the forums of IslamicAwakening.com. This site forms an excellent example of the increasing insight gained concerning the potential of the Internet and the recent appearance of social media.

Another famous landmark in the world of social media is YouTube, where users can upload and share their own videos. Many martyrdom videos can be found on the website (as well as on a similar video-sharing website LiveLeak.com), mainly from Afghanistan, Iraq and Chechnya, the areas where most suicide attacks have occurred.[9] Simple search terms such as 'jihad', 'al qaeda' and 'martyrdom' lead to movies featuring the stories of suicide attacks. Apparently these are not forbidden by the guidelines set forth by the site for the contents of their videos; the YouTube guidelines state:

- Graphic or gratuitous violence is not allowed. If your video shows someone getting hurt, attacked or humiliated, don't post it.
- YouTube is not a shock site. Don't post disgusting videos of accidents, dead bodies and similar things.
- We encourage free speech and defend everyone's right to express unpopular points of view. But we do not permit hate speech (speech which attacks or demeans a group based on race or ethnic origin, religion, disability, gender, age, veteran status and sexual orientation/gender identity).[10]

Violent images are certainly present in martyrdom videos but are usually not very explicit. The main aim of these videos is not violence in itself, and the images usually originate from wars or other armed conflicts. Although the victims

---

9 In May 2008, US Senator Joe Lieberman, Al Gore's running mate during the 2000 Presidential Election, wrote to Google officials to urge them to remove videos on YouTube produced by Al Qaeda and other groups considered terrorist. YouTube removed some videos but left others, since they did not violate the guidelines of the website. See CNN (2008) 'Lieberman to YouTube: Remove al Qaeda videos'.

10 I have only mentioned the relevant guidelines in this article; for a full survey see YouTube (2010).

are sometimes visible, the images are not more shocking than those regularly appearing on public television. People are not being tortured or executed in these videos, which therefore more or less comply with the guidelines. The execution video of Daniel Pearl, for example, cannot be found on YouTube (or LiveLeak) but can be found on the Chinese video sharing website Wretch (n.d.). That the guidelines are not always observed and might be considered hazy can be illustrated with a video called 'a martyr or what????', which shows uninterrupted images of a wounded man who is dying, apparently fighting for the Chechens and wounded by the Russians (YouTube 2004). One hears Qur'anic recitations in the background, while the supposed martyr is slowly passing away.

Martyrdom videos are widely present on the Internet, although it might sometimes be hard to find them – if not on social media websites – as they are mainly traceable through links posted in chatboxes and forums on sites such as IslamicAwakening.com. These sites are often protected and one needs to register as well as enter a password in order to access files. They play a pivotal role in the distribution of the videos from the makers to the public. The next section will focus on the question of who actually makes these videos, how they are made and how they are spread over the Internet.

3 The production and spread of martyrdom videos

The extensive use of martyrdom videos started during the First Chechen War (1994–1996), in which especially Ibn al Khattab pioneered producing video footage of operations.[11] During the Second Chechen War (1999–2009), this trend developed towards the production of videos of martyrs, killed either by Russian forces or in suicide attacks. The radical Muslims who took many hostages in the Dubrovka theatre in Moscow in 2002 had also made a video in advance, which was broadcast inside the theatre during the crisis and in which they proclaimed themselves martyrs for Allah (Speckhard and Akhmedova 2006: 441). They produced the videos themselves, but the production process has become professionalised in recent years. Azzam Publications, a London-based production house which was behind Azzam.com, launched the website Qoqaz.net. On this Caucasus-focused radical Islamic site, they posted many high-quality martyrdom videos, most of them sophisticatedly produced by 'Sawt al-Qawqaz' (Voice of the Caucasus). A video of Ibn al Khattab himself – which can be

---

11 For an historical overview of suicide bombing in general, see Reuter (2004), Kippenberg (2008) and Pape (2010).

found on YouTube – was made when he was killed, allegedly by a poisoned letter sent to him by Russian Spetsnaz forces.[12]

Another important source of martyrdom videos was the Second Intifadah, during which many radical Muslims committed suicide attacks against Israeli targets. The videos were often made the night before the missions and are often home-made and of crude quality. They can be found anywhere in the Gaza strip and on the West Bank, where they are clandestinely circulated through radical Palestinian circles as well as on the Internet (Oliver and Steinberg 2005).[13] As these videos were readily available, Muslims in other places were also moved by their humiliation (by Russian and Israeli forces respectively), effectively lifting the impact of a local conflict to a grander scale (Khosrokhavar 2004: 70, 109).

The Iraq War was also the cause of a considerable increase in the production of martyrdom videos, although these were often of poor quality. Research has indicated that many of these videos were home-made and moreover filmed from cars (Hafez 2007). Other movies circulating around the Internet often featured coalition soldiers caught in a trap or shot by insurgent snipers. In the years after the invasion some media organisations were established, such as the straightforwardly called 'Jihad Media Battalion', the offspring of 'Dawlat al-Iraq al-Islamiyyah' (The Islamic State of Iraq), an umbrella organisation of radical Islamic insurgency groups in Iraq. Their videos often featured martyrs in addition to broadcasts from high-ranking officials but were often only of slightly better quality than those produced at home. Other groups, such as the 'Ansar al-Sunna' (Followers of the Sunna), also produced videos of suicide bombings for which they were responsible. However, in another video they claimed to have shot down a US spy plane near Latafiyah. The 'spy plane' actually transpired to be a Taiwan-made model airplane. The plane was most probably owned by an Iraqi child who was left wondering about the whereabouts of his favourite toy (Shackleford n.d.).

Much more professional than these clips, however, are those produced by 'Al Sahab' (The Clouds), Al Qaeda's audiovisual production house. Al Sahab was founded in 2001 under the leadership of Abdul Rahman al Maghrebi (Moghadam 2008: 204). Little is known about this secretive organisation. Some specialists have contended that their main centre of operations is located somewhere in

---

12 YouTube, "The Story of Commander Khattab" in 11 parts (accessed 10 March 2011). In Russian, Spetsnaz means special purpose forces.
13 Oliver and Steinberg have collected many of these Palestinian martyrdom videos in order to investigate the phenomenon of suicide bombing and the place which these martyrs occupy in the collective memory.

the Pakistani hills or valleys near the Afghan border, which are out of govern-ment control. The establishment of a secure base in this region, these specialists argue, should be linked to an enormous increase in video productions (Whitlock 2007). In 2007 Al Sahab produced 97 videos, a six-fold increase compared to 2005. Thus a new propaganda video was launched every 3–4 days, featuring one of Al Qaeda's commanders (Moss and Mekhennet 2008). Even though the producers of Al Sahab have to evade Pakistani as well as American forces, they manage to produce high-quality videos. These are released as documenta-ries, but also in formats suitable for iPods and cellphones.

According to US counterterrorism officials, when a high-ranking Al Qaeda of-ficial wants to make a public statement, a trusted cameraman is summoned to a safe house somewhere in Pakistan where he records the message. The video file is then edited by Al Sahab members who are equipped with high-quality mate-rial – such as ultra-light laptops and top-end video cameras – after which the file is taken by courier to an Internet café where it is uploaded to a passport-protect-ed website, only available to a small range of trusted Al Qaeda members.[14] These files are encrypted with very advanced software and are nearly impossible to crack or even detect. Because of the secrecy and encryption with which the video files are uploaded to a secure website, nothing can be said about the lo-cation where the videos are produced. Although theoretically videos could ap-pear on the Internet within a week of their recording, it usually takes longer be-fore they are released. According to Diaa Rashwan, an analyst at Al Ahram Centre for Political and Strategic Studies in Cairo, 'It is clear that [the producers – AN] are under no real pressure. [...] They take plenty of time to go to their film archives and edit their productions' (cited in Whitlock 2008). They work very carefully and circumspectly in order to avoid exposure to the attention of their enemies – so far with considerable success.[15]

For a few years the videos have been spread through a newly designed logis-tical distribution network, Al Fajr Media Center, which links thousands of web-masters throughout the world. The main method is probably the snowball-meth-

---

14 These have not included such people as Osama bin Laden (died May 2, 2011) and Ayman al Zawahiri, as they stopped using electronic communicational devices altogether in order to avoid tracking by hostile forces. All communications go through trusted couriers.
15 Intelligence services have so far been unable to trace the videos to their origins, although Abu Musab al Zarqawi was killed in a US airstrike only 2 months after he first appeared in a video message. The interrelatedness of these events can, however, not be firmly established. In recent years some Al Qaeda communication officials have been arrested, such as the London-based Younis Tsouli, originating from Morocco. Investigation of his computer gave intelligence services greater insight into al Qaeda's online modes of operation.

od, in which one webmaster distributes a production to several others in the chain, who spread it again to others, etc. Little is actually known about Al Fajr and its organisation, although it likely resembles Al Qaeda structures; the organisation is heavily decentralised and different branches (or webmasters) are generally unaware of one another's true identity. They often add subtitles to video productions in order to make them more readily available for the non-Arabic speaking public – and sometimes even dub them.[16] According to US intelligence analysts, Al Fajr has separate divisions devoted to cyber jihad, cyber security, distribution and multimedia (Whitlock 2008). After a few intermediate branches, announcements and videos are then posted on popular radical Islamic web forums such as AlFarouq.com, which are also often password-protected and highly regulated (Bunt 2009). Often only a few moderators are allowed to post material, thus ensuring that all material comes from an authentic source. Members are encouraged to download the video material and redistribute it on other sites – such as the above-mentioned IslamicAwakening.com. Thus the videos ultimately end up on the Web, available for all interested parties, after passing many intermediate stages for security reasons. The initial distribution takes place within a small network of core members, who communicate with each other solely through tightly secured websites.

4 The contents of martyrdom videos

Many videos released by Al Sahab are of excellent quality; not only have they been filmed and edited professionally, they also feature flashy banners, Qur'an recitations and 3D animations. Al Sahab has released dozens of martyrdom videos in recent years, often of considerable length (around 45 minutes) and featuring suicide bombers from different regions and organizations. Some videos focus on several martyrs at once, such as the 'Winds of Paradise' series, which is celebrated as one of Al Sahab's best productions so far in radical Islamic circles (Nanninga: forthcoming). This section will focus on two paradigmatic martyrdom videos produced by Al Sahab, called 'Jihad and Martyrdom' (YouTube n.d.), about the martyr Abu al Hassan, and 'The word is the word of the sword', featuring Abu Ghareeb al-Makki (YouTube 2009). Further attention will be paid to Iraqi martyrdom videos – mostly acquired from secondary sources.

---

16 Some videos are, however, primarily recorded by fluent speakers of English or French, such as American-born Adam Gadahn. The movie 'Jihad and martyrdom', for example, has been dubbed into Urdu, while one can find 'The word is the word of the sword' with German subtitles.

This section will present and enunciate the several stages and acts into which these videos can generally be divided. The subsequent section is devoted to the identification and analysis of the grand narratives in which the makers seek to embed the martyrs' sacrifice and how it is put to use.

The videos always open with the announcement of the contents, the name of the martyrs and a flashy animation featuring the logo of the production company, which often means the name of the production house written in complex Arabic calligraphy. Al Sahab's logo is quite similar to Al Jazeera's, although there is no connection whatsoever between the two (Al Jazeera used to broadcast Al Qaeda video clips featuring Osama bin Laden and Ayman Al Zawahiri but has not done so since 2005). These announcements usually take 10 to 20 seconds, and one often hears Qur'anic recitations.

In the second part of the video, the introduction to the testament of the martyr, a narrator takes about two-and-a-half minutes to justify martyrdom by placing it into a larger context of the struggle between the so-called 'Zio-Crusader forces' and the 'treacherous rulers of the Arab world' on the one side and the 'Muslim Ummah and its Mujahid vanguard' on the other. This is an unequal fight, according to the narrator, 'because the discrepancy in material strength between us and our enemy is so huge' and leads many to despair over the usefulness of the confrontation. With video footage of air raids, falling bombs, destroyed buildings and injured people, they illustrate the discrepancy in strength. The 'Zio-Crusader forces' merely have to press a button to create havoc and destruction, killing innocent civilians and destroying houses, hospitals and mosques in the name of the 'war on terror', while their troops remain safe and sound.

It is the job of the Mujahideen to demolish these 'imagined fortresses', according to the narrator, in order for the enemy to become vulnerable to physical attack in the field, in order to balance the scale on which this conflict is fought and to repel the assault. The means of carrying out martyrdom operations/suicide attacks (accompanied by video footage of the planes crashing into the World Trade Center on 9/11) is given, and the narrator subsequently implies that the martyr's dedication to death in the 'Path of Allah' empowers the *Ummah* (the imagined global community of all Muslims) and its militant vanguard to secure victory and restore the Ummah's dignity:

> The Mujahid Muslim vanguard must lead its Ummah in the two most critical fronts threatening its destiny: the front of the Jewish-Crusader assault and the front of the treasonous rulers. The Mujahid Muslim vanguard must spread the call for the defeat of the Crusaders and Jews and their expulsion from our countries and for the removal of the treasonous rulers and setting up of the Mujahid Muslim government until this call becomes an all-pervasive spirit flowing through the Ummah. But it will only accomplish that by providing the

role model and paying the price in terms of the noblest and dearest of blood until it breaks
the barrier of fear which stands between the Ummah and victory and establishment.

Thus the suicide bomber – who through his sacrifice is called a martyr – is portrayed as a soldier serving in the vanguard of the Islamic community, who strives
to restore lost dignity, defiled and tarnished by the Zio-Crusader forces (who
should be expelled from Muslim lands) and the treacherous Arab rulers.

This elaboration on the broader context of the martyrdom operation (or suicide attack) is followed by a third part, which comprises a biography of the martyr of a lengthy 30 minutes, as described by the narrator, Abu al Hassan, and
several other Al Qaeda leaders. Pieter Nanninga lucidly shows how this part
of the video is used to convey the message of Al Qaeda; the life of the martyr
and the movement Al Qaeda take a remarkably parallel course in the video,
thus providing many opportunities to dwell on the organisation's activities, motivations and ideologies. The editors, Nanninga (Forthcoming) reveals, have fully
grasped these opportunities; Al Qaeda's history is sophisticatedly integrated
through the biography of the martyr.

The video ends with the animation of the attack and Abu al Hassan's last
words, in which he smiles shyly, asks for forgiveness and prays to God to accept
him as a martyr. This last minute powerfully rounds off the narrative and seeks
to show the viewers that the martyr is just an ordinary Muslim, like most of
them. The difference from most Muslims, which the producers seek to emphasise, is that the martyr does not belong to the passive majority but to the
small vanguard willing to struggle for the cause of Islam. This theme – whether
implicitly or explicitly – recurs in every video, as exemplified by the next paradigmatic production, called 'The word is the word of the sword'.

This video was released by Al Sahab in 2008. The 50-minute documentary
features Abu Ghareeb al Makki, a muezzin (one who calls for prayer) who
blew himself up in his car in front of the Danish embassy in Islamabad in
2008. The reason for this attack was the publication of cartoons ridiculing the
prophet Mohammed in the Danish newspaper *Jyllandsposten*. The first 30 minutes of this documentary are dedicated to an extensive argument justifying
the use of violence against Denmark and others who defile Islam. The crisis is
thereby placed in a conflict of a much larger scale, in which the paradigmatic
narrative of global jihad is the underlying message. The then Danish PM Anders
Fogh Rasmussen, former British PM Tony Blair and King Abdullah of Saudi Arabia all feature in this sophisticated and extensive presentation of arguments. The
video does not attempt to ridicule them but seeks to show the hypocrisy of Western involvement and interference in Arab countries – aided by the 'Zionists' of
Israel and the Arab dictators who are financially backed by Western countries:

As for the second aspect of these double standards, it is apparent in their accusing the Mujahideen of targeting the innocents, although they are the ones who for decades haven't stopped targeting weak and defenceless women, children and elderly men. The latest of their crimes was the recent campaign targeting defenceless civilians in Afghanistan, in which they killed more than 50 women and children attending a wedding reception in the province of Nangahar, in addition to dozens of others they killed in other provinces. [...] Despite the ugliness of these atrocious crimes, they don't hesitate to justify it, at times claiming that the smart bombs missed their target and at other times claiming that the target was valuable and hence what's the problem if dozens of [the] defenceless and weak are killed in order to get at this target.

These allegations are accompanied by video footage and pictures of bombings and other atrocities claimed to have been committed by Western powers. The makers subsequently feature a US Air Force colonel, who states that innocent casualties are sometimes allowed in order to get to an important target, and Mark Galasco, former chief of high-value targeting at the Pentagon. According to Galasco, at the beginning of the Second Gulf War he was allowed to kill 30 civilians around each high-value target. If more lives were to be risked, either the Secretary of Defence, Donald Rumsfeld, or President Bush had to be consulted.

Subsequently, several Al Qaeda-related persons – such as Abdul Rahman Saleem (in the movie as Sheikh Abu Yahya) – severely criticize not only Western misdeeds but also many fellow Arabs, who they consider as infidels because they have neglected the obligation of their religious duty of jihad. It is then stated that it is not only the 'apostate rulers' but also the passive majority that 'prefer submission, cowardice and sitting behind in the name of the medial [*moderate*] nature of Islam'. The martyr, however, Saleem asserts, belongs to the small vanguard minority, after which they turn to Abu Ghareeb himself.

In the following scenes, the martyr reads his testament, alternating with recitations of passages from the Qur'an and short messages from the narrator, who places the individual martyrdom story into a global context. The last recording of Abu Ghareeb is made while he stands behind the door of a white Toyota Corolla, which he claims is filled with bombs. He chants a militant song, affirms his longing for paradise by renouncing the value of life in this world and enters the car. Then we see an animation of the suicide attack: a car approaches a building carrying the Danish flag and explodes just in front of the entrance. This part is repeated twice, accompanied by a jihadist song, after which Sheikh Mustafa Abu Al Yazeed announces that more attacks against infidels will follow in the name of the defence of the dignity of Islam. The film is concluded with the *azan* (call to prayer) given by the martyr, with the Ka'bah in Mecca featuring in the background and the narrator praising the 'suicide bomber turned martyr' and expressing his wish that he will receive Allah's grace.

Iraqi martyrdom movies generally show the same pattern and recurring themes, as Hafez (2007) expounds in his informative work *Suicide Bombers in Iraq*. These movies often start with footage from the Iraqi invasion in 2003, with horrifying pictures of dead and injured women and children, American soldiers desecrating a mosque and shooting people inside and soldiers storming and vandalizing houses. Images from the notorious Abu Ghraib prison in Baghdad also regularly feature. These pictures are then combined with footage from other regions, such as Palestine. The tanks and other high-tech weapons are presented in sharp contrast with stone-throwing Palestinian kids or other seemingly innocent and harmless civilians. World and regional leaders also feature in these movies – the most commonly used image, however, is a handshake between President Bush and former Israeli PM Ariel Sharon in the White House during the Al Aqsa Intifada, suggesting US support for the harsh crackdown against Palestinian insurgents. Then the remedy for national salvation is presented: martyrdom operations. Subsequently, the use of martyrdom is defended and legitimised, and the suicide bomber testifies to the sincerity and conviction of his faith. He reads his final will and seems eager to perform his 'religious duty'. The Iraqi martyrdom videos thus seem not particularly different from others, except that their outlook seems to be more explicitly focused on the situation in Iraq and less on the intrinsic global jihad, as portrayed in most Al Sahab productions.

Based on this investigation of different martyrdom movies, we can identify certain patterns and themes recurring in the majority of martyrdom videos: (1) Videos begin with an introduction in which a narrator describes how Muslims are repressed and embattled everywhere. He postulates a narrative in which the global Muslim *Ummah* is under attack by inimical forces searching to destroy it – accompanied by gruesome pictures or video material. Another theme is (2) a justification of martyrdom operations as the sole means to battle the forces of the enemy, thereby presenting the suicide bomber as a soldier in the vanguard – comprising the jihadist movement – of the *Ummah*. Sometimes the narrator presents this, but videos often feature radical sheiks who legitimate the use of martyrdom in the struggle and attest to the sincere religious motivations of the martyr. Then (3) the martyr reads his testament, interspersed with Qur'anic recitations. The movie concludes with (4) an animated video of the execution of the martyrdom operation and (5) some final remarks regarding the results of the attack and a laudation of the martyr, concluded with a prayer.

5 Analysing the narrative

These martyrdom videos are professionally structured and their messages sophisticatedly disguised in the choice of pictures and the narrative presented. The increasing professionalisation of the production of these videos – as stated above – is manifest in recent releases. After having described and analysed the content of martyrdom videos, this section will now focus more specifically on the implicit content and seek to interpret the aims of the videos.

According to Robert A. Pape (2005: 3–4), as a kind of warfare, suicide attacks have been used to repel enemies from the soil that the suicide attackers consider theirs. An excellent example of a successful operation is Al Qaeda's Madrid attack in 2004. The attacks influenced the parliamentary elections three days later, which eventually resulted in a leftist coalition led by José Zapatero (Chari 2008), who almost instantly decided to withdraw Spanish troops from Iraq and Afghanistan.[17] Moreover, the organisation is composed of national liberation movements (see Roy 2004).[18] The meaning of these attacks is not only militarily strategic but also serves several other instrumental and expressive functions, within and outside the jihadist movement (see also Bloom 2004; Atwan 2008).

The introductions to these videos explicitly pose a global dichotomy between the Muslim *Ummah* and the 'West'. The 'West' in these videos supports Israel and the Arab dictators and attacks Muslim countries (such as Afghanistan and Iraq). The Muslim *Ummah* is presented as an explicitly global community, transcending ethnicity and national borders – a huge conceptual entity preserved by its members. Western or Israeli attacks on Arab soil are presented as attacks on all Muslims in the world.[19] Thus formulated, the makers of the movie pull local conflicts out of their specific context to reinstate them into a global narrative, seeking to affect and engage those Muslims who are susceptible to it – whether living in Saudi Arabia, Malaysia or the UK (see Hoffman and McCormick 2004).[20] Moreover, Al Qaeda itself has no permanently fixed base any-

---

17 One week before the election, on March 8, 2004, Rajoy's ruling People's Party still enjoyed a five-point lead over Zapatero's SSWP (Spanish Socialist Workers' Party). On March 14, the SSWP defeated the PP with almost a 5-point lead (Chari 2008).
18 Roy (2004: 298–303). These include franchise movements such as Al Qaeda in the Islamic Maghreb (AQIM) and the Libyan Islamic Fighting Group (LIFG), although the latter recently merged with Al Qaeda. Other organisations are loosely affiliated with Al Qaeda, such as the Southeast Asian Jema'ah Islamiyyah.
19 For an analysis of this narrative, see Kippenberg (2010: 666–670) and Wright (2009: 17–26).
20 They function as a 'signalling game' in which organisations convey their ideology, activities and convictions to particular audiences (Hoffman and McCormick 2004: 245).

more; after being based in Saudi Arabia, Sudan and Afghanistan, the organisation now temporarily settles in unregulated areas which are out of government control, such as the Afghani-Pakistani border area, Somalia or the Yemeni mountains. We can thus detect a development of globalisation and deterritorialisation, reflected through the videos in the methods, tools, audience, followers and targets of the jihadist movement as well as in the movement itself (Roy 2004).

Despite this on-going globalisation, most targets of suicide bombers are still in the Islamic world itself, often directed within the framework of the nation-state. Many attacks seek to discredit and delegitimise secular national governments, which have often initiated crackdowns against radical Islamic movements. The mostly secular and autocratic rulers are depicted in the videos as enemies fraternising with their Western allies. Severe criticism is especially directed towards the Royal House of Saudi Arabia, which admitted armed foreigners in the first Gulf War and is referred to as a defilement of the 'land of the two cities'. A certain ambiguity thus seems present in the elaboration of the goals of the jihadist movement in these disseminated videos produced by the movement: on the one hand, they attempt to lift jihad to a global level, employing a global discourse and attacking the forces of the enemy on their own soil (such as the attacks in the US, Spain and the UK); on the other, their focus necessarily remains framed within the boundaries of the nation-state, because the main power interests are concentrated on this level. Also, regarding sources of potential supporters, the jihadist movement is in certain ways restricted to certain territories within the framework of global power interests (Bonnefoy 2009: 339). The makers of the videos seldom use the names of Islamic nation-states but always refer to them as one single entity – the global Muslim *Ummah* (see Al Rasheed 2009: 301–20; Roy 2004: 321).

Martyrdom is the only means to battle the forces of the enemy, many videos contend, and the suicide bomber must be regarded as a soldier fighting in the vanguard of the *Ummah*. Radical sheiks selectively use Qur'anic *suras* and the writings of influential theorists to religiously legitimise the means of martyrdom in the struggle. The same theorists repeatedly recur in this context, such as Ibn Taymiyya (1263–1328), Sayyid Qutb (1906–1966) and Abu Alaa Al-Mawdudi (1903–1979), who all professed a very strict – or radical – observance of religious duty and whose writings are utterly applicable to the jihadist movement. Furthermore, sheiks frequently refer to the initial period of Islam. Reasoning by analogy, they seek to legitimise martyrdom according to tradition, referring to comparable events in the times of the Prophet Muhammad. Contrary to Shia Islam or Catholic Christianity, however, martyrdom has never formed an important facet of religion in Sunni history (see Seidensticker 2004: 107–16). This 'tradition' of martyrdom which the radical sheiks seek to establish can therefore only be considered an invented tradition, 'a set of practices, normally governed by overtly or tacitly accepted rules and of a ritual or symbolic nature, which seeks to inculcate certain values and norms of behaviour by repetition, which automatically implies continuity with the past' (Hobsbawm 1963: 1; see also Cook 2007: 144 and 164). But if conveyed repeatedly, over and over, one could embrace this invention as a genuine tradition. As Eric Hobsbawm and Terence Ranger (1963) aptly show in their volume, it would certainly not be the first successfully implemented invented tradition.

6 Conclusion

Together with the subsequent parts – the reading of the martyr's testament, the animation recapitulating the suicide attack and the concluding remarks and prayers praising the martyr – this narrative forms a powerful compilation, one which seeks to psychologically and emotionally affect its viewers (Hafez 2007: 226). Thus, every section in the video is devoted to that purpose; an illustrative example forms the Hollywood-like scene in which the martyr Abu Harith al Dosari dramatically bids his wife farewell (Devji 2005: 95).

The producers have sophisticatedly construed and structured these movies in order to convey their message to their followers all over the world. They not only seek to capitalise on the religious convictions of the viewers but also on their feelings of morality and justice – regarding the accompanying pictures in the videos featuring wounded women and children and the attempts to show the hypocrisy of Western leaders and their Arab counterparts. By means of these videos, the jihadist movement seeks to disseminate a message to recontextualise suicide attacks to empower the Muslim *Ummah* to stand up against their infidel tyrants and the West, to establish an Islamic state and eventually to unite the world under the banner of Islam.

The crux of the whole video is the sacrifice of the martyr and his clearly stated willingness to die for these abstract yet powerful imaginings. His sacrifice might easily be the most powerful testimony for the intrinsic value of the message the video seeks to convey (for such reasoning see Stark 1996:186–8; Duby 1985: 151–2). Thus these videos sought to empower the members of the *Ummah*, testifying to the intrinsic value of religion and appealing to their sense of morality and justice, and they have succeeded in this – as we have seen above on websites and social media – with at least one group of Muslims (see Devji 2005: 95–6; and Nacos 2007: 132–4). The violence enacted by martyrdom operations can be experienced as dehumiliating and liberating and seeks to give the *Ummah* a sense of empowerment. These are acts of 'performance violence', since they are real as well as symbolic dramas designed to have an impact on the several audiences that they target (see Juergensmeyer 2003).

The continual spread of mass communications throughout the world, as well as the ever expanding availability of the Internet, form a crucial step in the ability to spread the deeds of suicide bombers in carefully constructed martyrdom videos. While Marcus Aurelius still had Christian martyrs executed in theatres throughout the Roman Empire, the theatre has now expanded globally through the mass media. The audience which can be reached and affected has grown exponentially through these developments. Those witnessing the violence – in the theatre in ancient times, but nowadays through mass media and the Internet as well – are part of and affected by what occurs.

The Internet has revealed itself as an invaluable tool in spreading the jihadists' message, and therein the social media form an advantageous and increasingly tapped tool, considering their longstanding utilisation of YouTube and LiveLeak and recent engagements with Facebook and Twitter. Even more than the rise of mass communications and media, the Internet has presented the jihadist movement with an unprecedented toolkit, not only to spread their propaganda uncensored but also as a means of targeted communication. Suicide operations recorded and contextualised in martyrdom videos retain a shocking effect; in that sense, martyrdom operations are still theatre (El Affendi 2009: 65).

In recent decades, a globalising and deterritorialising trend has been identified within radical Islamic movements, which is also visible in martyrdom videos. Together with an increasing professionalisation, the producers of these videos have increasingly sought to reconstruct their chosen events in a decontextualised global narrative, complying with the goals and ideology of the cause. The videos are immanently expressive in character, seeking to awe, inspire and motivate the audience and to give them a sense of belonging to the global *Ummah* (Atwan 2008: 140). Whether imagined and/or digital, these videos empower the idea of the *Ummah* as a global community, within which (disembedded) Muslims can regard themselves as members (Nacos 2007: 127; Sageman 2004: 161). And although many instruments are carefully and aptly used for that purpose, the message – as I have shown – remains highly ambiguous in certain ways.

References

Al Rasheed, Madawi. 2009. "The local and the global in Saudi Salafi discourse." In *Global Salafism: Islam's New Religious Movement*, edited by Roel Meijer, 301–320. New York: Columbia University Press.

Anderson, Benedict. 2006. *Imagined Communities*. London and New York: Verso.

Anderson, Jon W. 2003a. "The Internet and Islam's new interpreters." In *News Media in the Muslim World: The Emerging Public Sphere*, edited by Dale F. Eickelman and Jon W. Anderson, 41–55. Bloomington: Indiana University Press.

–. 2003b. "New media, new publics: Reconfiguring the public sphere of Islam." *Social Research* 70 (3): 887–907.

Atwan, Abdel Bari. 2008. *The Secret History of Al Qaeda*. Berkeley: University of California Press.

Bloom, Mia M. 2005. *Dying to Kill: The Allure of Suicide Terror*. New York: Columbia University Press.

–. 2004. "Palestinian suicide bombing: Public support, market share and outbidding." *Political Science Quarterly* 119: 61–88.

Bonnefoy, Laurent. 2009. "How transnational is Salafism in Yemen?" In *Global Salafism: Islam's New Religious Movement*, edited by Roel Meijer, 321–341. New York: Columbia University Press.

Brown, Peter. 1981. *The Cult of the Saints: Its Rise and Function in Latin Christianity*. Chicago: University of Chicago Press.

Bunt, Gary R. 2009. *iMuslims: Rewiring the House of Islam*. Chapel Hill: University of North Carolina Press.

–. 2003. *Islam in the Digital Age: e-Jihad, Online Fatwas and Cyber Islamic Environments*. London and Sterling: Pluto Press.

Chari, Raj S. 2004. "The 2004 Spanish election: Terrorism as a catalyst for change?" *West European Politics* 27 (5): 954–63.

CNN. 2008. "Lieberman to YouTube: Remove al Qaeda videos." Available at: http://edition.cnn.com/2008/POLITICS/05/20/youtube.lieberman/ Accessed: 4 July 2010.

Cook, David. 2007. *Martyrdom in Islam*. Cambridge and New York: Cambridge University Press.

Devji, Faisal. 2005. *Landscapes of the Jihad: Militancy, Morality, Modernity*. Ithaca: Cornell University Press.

Duby, Georges. 1985. "Ideologies in social history." In *Constructing the Past: Essays in Historical Methodology*, edited by Jacques Le Goff and Pierre Nora, 151–165. Cambridge: Cambridge University Press.

El Affendi, Abdelwahab. 2009. "The terror of belief and the belief in terror: On violently serving God and the nation." In *Dying for Faith: Religiously Motivated Violence in the Contemporary World*, edited by Madawi Al Rasheed and Marat Shterin, 59–78. London: I.B. Tauris.

Eickelman, Dale F. 1992. "Mass higher education and the religious imagination in contemporary Arab societies." *American Ethnologist* 19 (4): 643–655.

Facebook. n.d. "Islamic Awakening." Available at: http://www.facebook.com/pages/Islamic-Awakening/194445767239890

Free Tarek. 2012. Available at: www.freetarek.com. Accessed: 4 May 2012.

Gibbon, Edward. 1963 [1776–1788]. *The Decline and Fall of the Roman Empire.* Harmondsworth: Penguin. Chapter 38.

Goodnough, Abby, and L. Robbins. 2011. "Mass[achusetts] man arrested in terrorism case." *New York Times.* Available at: http://www.nytimes.com/2009/10/22/us/22terror.html. Accessed: 4 April 2011.

Hafez, Mohammed M. 2007a. *Suicide Bombers in Iraq: The Strategy and Ideology of Martyrdom.* Washington: The United States Institute of Peace.

–. 2007b "Martyrdom mythology in Iraq: How Jihadists frame suicide terrorism in videos and biographies." *Terrorism and Political Violence* 19: 95–115.

Hobsbawm, Eric. 1983. "Introduction: Inventing traditions." In *The Invention of Tradition,* edited by Eric Hobsbawm and Terence Ranger, 1–14. Cambridge: Cambridge University Press.

Hoffman, Bruce, and G.H. McCormick. 2004. "Terrorism, signalling, and suicide attack." *Studies in Conflict and Terrorism* 27: 243–281.

Husayn, Ed. 2007. *The Islamist.* London: Penguin

Islamicawakening. n.d. Available on Twitter: http://forums.islamicawakening.com/f47/i-want-to-know-[your-chance-to-ask-tarek-34806/index9.html#post453128. Accessed: 6 April 2011.

Juergensmeyer, Mark. 2003. *Terror in the Mind of God: The Global Rise of Religious Violence.* Berkeley: University of California Press.

Kepel, Gilles. 2003. *Jihad: The Trail of Political Islam.* London: I.B. Tauris.

Khosrokhavar, Farhad. 2005. *Suicide Bombers: Allah's New Martyrs.* London and Ann Arbor: Pluto Press.

Kippenberg, Hans G. 2008. *Gewalt als Gottesdienst: Religionskriege im Zeitalter der Globalisierung* [Violence as Religion: Religious Wars in the Age of Globalisation]. Munich: C.H. Beck Verlag.

–. 2010. "For the sake of the community: Two scripts of martyrdom operations among Muslims." In *Myths, Martyrs, and Modernity: Studies in the History of Religions in Honour of Jan N. Bremmer,* edited by Jitse Dijkstra, Justin Kroesen and Yme Kuiper, 651–670. Leiden and Boston: Brill.

Linjakumpu, Anja. 2008. *Political Islam in the Global World.* Reading: Ithaca Press.

Moghadam, Assaf. 2008. *The Globalization of Martyrdom.* Baltimore: Johns Hopkins University Press.

Moss, Michael, and S. Mekhennet. 2008. "Rising leader for next phase of al Qaeda's war." *New York Times* 4 April. Available at: http://www.nytimes.com/2008/04/04/world/asia/0 4qaeda.html?_r=1andoref=slogin. Accessed: 12 March 2011.

Mutahhari, Murtaza. 1980. *The Martyr* [transl. M.A. Ansari]. Karachi: Islamic Seminary Pakistan.

Nacos, Brigitte L. 2007. *Mass-Mediated Terrorism: The Central Role of the Media in Terrorism and Counterterrorism.* New York: Rowman and Littlefield Publishers.

Nanninga, Pieter. Forthcoming. "The words of the martyr." In *Words: Situating Religion in Language,* edited by Ernst van den Hemel, n.p. New York: Fordham University Press.

N.d. "The word is the word of the sword," in 5 parts. Available at: http://www.youtube.com/ watch?v=APRUrknhezs. Accessed: 14 March 2011.

Oliver, Anne Marie, and P. Steinberg. 2005. *The Road to Martyrs' Square: A Journey into the World of the Suicide Bomber.* Oxford and New York: Oxford University Press.

Pape, Robert A. 2010. *Cutting the Fuse: The Explosion of Global Suicide Terrorism and How to Stop It*. Chicago and London: University of Chicago Press.

–. 2005. *Dying to Win: The Strategic Logic of Suicide Terrorism*. New York: Random House.

Potter, David. 1993. "Martyrdom as spectacle." In *Theater and Society in the Classical World*, edited by Ruth Scodel, 53–88. Ann Arbor: University of Michigan Press.

Reuter, Christoph. 2004. *My Life is a Weapon: A Modern History of Suicide Bombing*. Princeton and Oxford: Princeton University Press.

Roy, Olivier. 2004. *Globalized Islam: The Search for a New Ummah*. London: Hurst.

Sageman, Marc. 2004. *Understanding Terror Networks*. Philadelphia: University of Pennsylvania Press.

Seidensticker, Tilman. 2004. "Der religiöse und historische Hintergrund des Selbstmordattentats im Islam" [The religious and historical background of suicide bombing in Islam]. In *Terror im Dienste Gottes: die 'geistliche Anleitung' der Attentäter des 11. September 2001* [Terror in the Service of God: The 'Spiritual Guide' of the 9–11 Bombers], edited by Hans G. Kippenberg and Tilman Seidensticker, 107–116. Frankfurt: Campus Verlag.

Shackleford, Rusty. n.d. "Terrorists shoot down US plane in Iraq." Available at: http://mypetjawa.mu.nu/archives/185447.php. Accessed: 15 March 2011.

Speckhard, Anne, and K. Akhmedova. 2006. "The making of a martyr: Chechen suicide terrorism." *Studies in Conflict and Terrorism* 29: 429–492.

Stark, Rodney. 1996. *The Rise of Christianity: A Sociologist Reconsiders History*. Princeton: Princeton University Press.

Sweet, Laurel J. 2012. "Sudbury terror sympathizer Mehanna sentenced to 17 years." *Boston Herald* April 12. Available at: http://bostonherald.com/news/regional/view/20220412sudbury_terror_sympathizer_mehanna_its_because_of_america_that_i_am_who_i_am/. Accessed: 14 April 2012.

Twitter (nd.) 'Islamic Awakening'. www.twitter.com.

YouTube. 2007. "A martyr or what???" Available at: http://www.youtube.com/watch?v=KLgIwLSL_eQandoref=http%3 A%2F%2Fwww.youtube.com%2Fresults%3Fsearch_query%3Da%2Bmartyr%2Bor%2Bwhat%26aq%3Dfandhas_verified=1 Accessed: 25 March 2010.

–. 2009. "Sheikh Ayman Al-Zawarhiri on the Bali bombers and the Interfaith initiative by King Abdullah." Uploaded 25 March 2009 by 'MHBrayman'. Produced by *unjustmedia.com*. Accessed: 14 April 2012.

–. 2010. "Community Guidelines." Available at: http://www.youtube.com/t/community_guidelines. Accessed: 10 June 2010.

–. N.d. "Jihad and Martyrdom," in 4 parts. http://www.youtube.com/watch?v=DS_XC8_IdSI Accessed: 21 April 2010. [Unavailable at date of publication].

–. N.d. "The story of Commander Khattab," in 11 parts. Accessed: 10 March 2011.

–. N.d. "The word is the word of the sword," in 5 parts. Available at: http://www.youtube.com/watch?v=APRUrknhezs. Accessed: 14 March 2011.

Valencia, Milton J. 2011. "Tarek Mehanna guilty of terror charges." *Boston Globe* 20 December. Available at: http://www.bostonglobe.com/metro/2011/12/20/tarek-mehanna-guilty-terror-charges/chpbwimRMbvdNMOladJ08 J/story.html. Accessed: 9 April 2012.

Whitlock, Craig. 2008. "Al-Qaeda's growing online offensive." *Washington Post* 24 June.
    Available at: http://www.washingtonpost.com/wp-dyn/content/article/2008/06/23/AR20
    08062302135.html. Accessed: 12 March 2011.
–. 2007. "The new al Qaeda central." *Washington Post* 9 September. Available at:
    http://www.washingtonpost.com/wp-dyn/content/article/2007/09/08/AR20
    07090801845.html. Accessed: 12 March 2011.
Wright, Stuart. 2009. "Martyrs and martial imagery: Exploring the volatile link between
    warfare frames and religious violence." In *Dying for Faith: Religiously Motivated Violence
    in the Contemporary World*, edited by Madawi Al Rasheed and Marat Shterin, 17–26.
    London: I.B. Tauris.
Wretch. N.d. "Taliban. Daniel Pearl execution video." Available at:
    http://www.wretch.cc/video/f0806449kandfunc=singleandvid=5836976. Accessed: 14
    October 2010.

Nathan Abrams, Sally Baker and B. J. Brown

8   Grassroots Religion: Facebook and Offline Post-Denominational Judaism

1 Introduction

Young peoples' Judaism online is thriving, yet little is known of the contribution that this makes to contemporary Jewish self-definition, practices, beliefs, values, behaviours and rituals, particularly in a post-denominational environment. Much scholarship so far regarding religion and the media tends to explore media activity that is consciously driven by religious organisations (Meyer and Moors 2006) rather than 'bottom up', self-generated activity by individuals. This chapter therefore aims to contribute to current debates about the role of new interactive electronic media in contemporary religious and spiritual life. It will address this via an examination of how the construction of Jewish identity is accomplished in one new media/online environment, Facebook, which has played a key role in enabling users to explore and define notions of meaning and being amongst young people in this area. It builds on the writing so far on young people engaging with religion using interactive technology (Brasher 2001; Beckerlegge 2002; Dawson and Cowan 2004; Hojsgaard and Warburg 2005; Karaflogka 2006) to address the curious lack of writing on how young people engage with Judaism online.

Social networking sites, such as Facebook, perhaps offer the ideal opportunity in twenty-first century Jewish life to explore and experiment with religious self-definition, meaning, congregation and even being itself, insofar as in Facebook one's being can be literally reinvented in ways without 'stifling' religiosity by forcing it to conform. We propose to investigate how religiously identified Jews are able to explore their Judaism in both the virtual and real worlds, using electronic means, to contribute to debates regarding religious self-definition in the context of increasing post-denominationalism. In particular, we will focus on the role of the Internet as a vehicle for helping to create and maintain congregations who meet also in an offline setting. As well as their own websites, many groups make use of third-party social networking facilities such as Facebook. Facebook's 150 million users indicate the substantial possibilities for global congregational formation. There are no precise figures for the number of Jewish users, although this project will examine the extent and nature of their participation.

By far the most research in the area of Judaism and the Internet, as Campbell (2011) notes, has been conducted in terms of the Orthodox engagement with it. This has overwhelmingly focussed on the Israeli and US contexts. As a consequence, to date, the use of the Internet by non-Orthodox diasporas, beyond these two poles of Jewry, has been largely ignored. This chapter hopes to rectify this gap by examining one representative European case study, the United Kingdom.

There are many emerging research questions, such as how web-based facilities and social networking contribute to the construction of post-denominational identities among young Jews. To what extent is Facebook used to address feelings of alienation or disenfranchisement amongst Jews who are dissatisfied with the existing denominational infrastructure? How is offline Judaism constructed and practised as a result of the online world? While data here will be exclusively drawn from the UK context, this chapter also aims to open up the possibility of the mobility of Jewish self-definition across geographical boundaries by virtue of utilisation of virtual networks. Participants are globally connected via the Internet and can be part of a global, post-national as well as post-denominational Jewish congregation. It is hoped that the chapter will not only interest students of Judaism, but will also provide a model for the study of other transnational diasporic and religious media in a world that is increasingly globalised and ethnically fragmented.

2 Research context

Existing scholarship on Judaism and the Internet has tended to focus on what happens *online*, exploring such issues as Judaism and Second Life (Voloj 2008; Shandler 2009). Surprisingly, social networking sites such as Facebook have not yet attracted significant academic attention in this area. The substantial, still burgeoning body of research exploring social networking sites has often focussed on students and reveals much interest in issues of trust, privacy, disclosure and security. Comparative studies involving different social networking sites have been conducted, but most research into social networks has concentrated specifically and particularly on Facebook.

There has been a substantial amount of work investigating the motivations and reasons for using social networking sites and work exploring the psychological parameters of the users of these sites. The effectiveness of using social networking sites for the purposes of formal education or educational purposes (such as educating patients about management of medical conditions) has attracted the interest of researchers. Other major interests for researchers of social networking sites have been identity construction, identity presentation and identity management of users, either as individuals or as members of wider cohorts, and social capital possessed by users of social networks. Boyd and Ellison (2008) provide an excellent overview of the definition, history and scholarship of social network sites.

Although there is a social networking site specifically aimed at members of Christian congregations (www.MyChurch.org), there is an evident dearth of research into religion/spirituality on such sites (Nyland and Near 2007), and at the time of writing we have found none at all specifically exploring Judaism on Facebook. Studies have begun to explore 'social networking' sites such as Facebook (Niezen 2005; Ellison, Steinfield and Lampe 2007) to show how 'friending' online differs from offline friendship (boyd 2006; Zhao, Grasmuch and Martin 2008) and also is dependent on user anonymity, but how this functions in a Judaic environment is less clear. While Young, Dutta and Dommety (2009) explored whether users' decisions to disclose their religious affiliation on Facebook may suggest their desire for seeking romantic partners of the same religious affiliation, their largely quantitative data was not limited to Jewish users, the sample size of which was small, meaning it too is of only limited use here. Boyd and Ellison (2008: 224) observe that 'vast, unchartered waters still remain to be explored' and note the lack of experimental or longitudinal studies as well as the limited understanding of the use of social network sites outside of the United States. They also suggest that large-scale quantitative and qualitative research would be fruitful and that 'richer, ethnographic research on populations more difficult to access' would further aid the understanding of the long-term implications of social networking sites (boyd and Ellison 2008).

Despite a great deal of work on young people and their sense of identity, there are significant gaps in our knowledge (Buckingham 2007). We still look at this from the outside rather than using peoples' own mechanisms for communication. In Jewish terms this is a new area. While research into online Judaism has been growing, it is restricted both geographically and denominationally in that it is largely confined to the United States and Israel and Orthodoxy, as suggested above. While there have been fairly recent studies of Internet use within Jewish religious communities in Israel, these are limited by their specific focus on *haredi*[1] denominations (Livio and Tenenboim 2004; Barzilai and Barzilai-

---

1 *Haredi* (plural: *haredim*) literally means 'one who trembles', derived from Isaiah 66:5, in which the prophet admonishes his people to 'Hear the word of the Lord, you who tremble [*haredim*] at His word'. It is often confused with the much more common term (in American English at least) Hasidic. *Haredi* is generally translated as 'ultra-Orthodox', a definition that

Nahon 2005). Since *haredim* have a fraught relationship with new technologies such as the Internet and mobile phones (Campbell 2010), their use in generalising overall patterns to fit non-*haredi* Jews' relationship to such media is limited. Furthermore, contributions such as Brasher (2001) and Voloj (2008) do not always benefit from a cross-disciplinary perspective. Where the latter solely concentrated on Second Life, the former argues that the Internet enables new forms of traditional religious expression, highlighting such examples as a cyber-Seder or virtual Passover as a way of helping people reconnect with their Judaism. There is little cross-cultural comparative work and even less work which examines and compares Jewish self-definition globally. The European/UK environment is virtually ignored. Following the model provided by Bunt (2009), which explored Islam, new media allows us to study the way in which British Jewish participants interact globally to develop their sense of religious self-identity in order to provide a non-*haredi*, non-US and non-Israeli case study in this area.

This chapter addresses these concerns by investigating the way new media and communication technologies are used in the construction of ethno-religious identities, communities and outlooks. It will examine how construction of Jewish identity is accomplished in one new media/online environment now widely used by young people, namely the social networking site Facebook. In this way, it hopes to build upon the recent move toward more theoretical work in studies of Judaism and the Internet. Such work explores in greater detail 'the offline implications of online religious activities and how the Internet may serve as a microcosm for studying shifts of behaviour and belief in offline religious culture' (Campbell 2011: 375). It seeks to address the challenge posed by Campbell that 'future research should explore in more detail the relationship and effect of online religious activities and groups on offline religious communities and institutions' (2011: 378). It takes as its starting point Campbell's observation that 'the Internet becomes a portal for the initiation and enculturation of Jews into a larger religious community and thus has interesting implications for the Jewish Diaspora' (Campbell 2011: 375). To quote Campbell further, and at length:

> New media raise age-old questions of how Jewish religious identity is constructed, what constitutes the boundaries of community life, how the sacred should be mitigated and lived out in contemporary society, and what constraints faith should place on engagement outside the Jewish world. These issues underlie the question of what it means to be Jewish in a new media world. (2011: 377)

---

does not do justice to an extensive and nuanced term, which covers a range of Jews who fall into this category, not all of whom are 'Orthodox' in the strictest definition of that term.

3 Defining Jewish identity

Definitions of Jewishness are complex and contested. They can be divided into ethno-cultural-historical and religious categories. There are two ways of being Jewish according to *Halacha* (Hebrew: Jewish law), that is, normative rabbinic Judaism: being born to a Jewish mother or conversion by a recognised rabbinic authority. *Halachic* (Hebrew: according to Jewish law) Judaism can further be subdivided into Masorti (Hebrew: traditional), modern Orthodox and *haredi*. Normative rabbinic Judaism, however, is under challenge, as the primacy of matrilineal descent is being undermined by the recognition of patrilineality by the Reform, Liberal and Progressive movements within contemporary Judaism. Cross-cutting these denominational divisions are those based on origin, including Sephardi (North African, southern European, Asian subcontinent), Mizrahi (Middle Eastern), Ashkenazi (eastern and central European) and Beta Israel (Ethiopian) traditions. Furthermore, although one can become Jewish 'by choice', i.e., through a process of rabbinic conversion, this is also subject to contestation by different groups within Judaism, which refuse to recognise and sanction certain conversions.[2] As a consequence, there is no single, common European Jewish identity (Graham 2004). Indeed, it has been argued that the only genuinely common Jewish characteristic is the propensity for a 'Jewish' person to self-identify as such, that is, 'what makes a person a Jew is saying they are one' (Konrád 1998). Following the model provided by the EC-funded DIALREL project (http://www.dialrel.eu/), which interviewed 'self declared Jewish participants', as well as the 'Identity à la carte' project (JDC-ICCD 2011), whereby the respondent and his/her relatives, grandparents, parents, partner and children were identified to be Jewish if s/he her/himself did so, we define Jewishness in the broadest possible fashion to include anyone who self-identifies as Jewish, regardless of their *halachic* or legal status (Dencik 2011). No conditions are placed on this criterion for classification. This challenges essentialist notions of Jewishness and uses a processual notion of identity formation.

However, as contemporary theories of identity argue (Bourdieu 1991; Calhoun 1994; Modood and Werbner 1997; Brubaker and Cooper 2000; Jenkins 2008), identity is always a construct; its construction is largely determined by situational, interactional, contextual and other changing factors. It may occur that Jews who in certain contexts opt for a strong 'Jewish' identity, incline to de-

---

2 Witness the recent controversy over the JFS School, a Jewish school in Brent, London, which was subject to a court ruling that its admissions policy breached the UK's Race Relations Act in 2009/10 (see UKSC 2009).

fine themselves by other identity categories in other contexts, for example, as members of a religious group, as citizens of the country where they live, as members of a national minority or simply as Europeans. We understand identity neither as entirely fluid, fragmented and contingent nor as solid and given once-for-all. It is rather an ongoing process of everyday, inter-subjective construction and reconstruction. It is also a category of everyday experience and everyday practices used by individuals to make sense of themselves in relation to the world they live in and in relation to others, who may be defined as 'similar' or 'different', 'us' or 'them'. Identities also function as cognitive schemata – internally stored information and meanings, which serve as frameworks for interpreting experiences. Since identity for us is a process rather than having a defined end, we ask not only what it is but also how it becomes, how it has been formed, maintained and transformed in the course of various life experiences and what are the mechanisms crucial for identity development.

4 Post-denominationalism

Recent research in the United States has indicated a sense of alienation from Jewish communal organizations and experiences among 20 – 30 year-olds who perceive them to be boring and uninviting (Kelman and Schonberg 2008). The result has been a general decline in synagogue membership and financial contributions (Cohen and Kelman 2007b) as well as in denominational affiliation, as greater numbers of younger Jews identify as 'just Jewish' rather than Reform, Conservative or Reconstructionist than in the past (Cohen et al. 2007). Cohen and Kelman (2007a) noted, 'As institutions experiment with ways to understand and engage the next generation, many younger American Jews have begun creating their own opportunities for Jewish engagement that are relatively independent of existing communal organizations and institutions'. Many among the Jewish-educated leaders of the next generation are choosing to pursue Jewish life outside of institutional structures (Cohen and Kelman 2006; Cohen et al. 2007; Bleyer 2007). 'Rather than following their parents into the halls of synagogues and federations, a significant segment of younger Jews are seeking to create new avenues of, and opportunities for, Jewish involvement that do not replicate older patterns of Jewish communal participation' (Kelman and Schonberg 2008: 12).

Commentators have defined this experience as that of the 'post-denominational Jew'. The post-denominational Jew 'refuses to be labelled or categorized in a religion that thrives on stereotypes. He [sic] has seen what the institutional branches of Judaism have to offer and believes that a better Judaism can be created' (Rosenthal 2006: 20). Rather than reject Judaism wholesale or 'engage in community structures they find alienating or bland' (Kelman and Schonberg 2008: 12), post-denominational Jews use their creativity and commitment to organise independently, to build meaningful Jewish experiences and to create ritual on their own terms outside of community institutions but within their own organic community of friends and family. They resist labelling by existing religious institutions and reject existing branches of Judaism to create something more fluid. These Jews tend to be, but are not exclusively, under thirty, and they often feel excluded from religious life. As Lurie put it, 'Justifiably so: the suburban mausoleum that is the liberal synagogue was, at best, built for a sociological reality decades out of date' (2011: 25). This has become known as 'Do-it-Yourself (DIY)' (Kelman and Schonberg 2008: 12) or 'empowered' Judaism (Kaunfer 2010).

Graham has drawn attention to 'an ongoing process of identity development' in Europe (2004: 22), what Webber has termed 'a reconstruction of identity', especially by the young (1994: 22). Dencik uses the term 'ethno-cultural smorgasbord' (2003a: 54). As early as 1977, Stein and Hill coined the term 'dime store ethnicity', in which individuals pick and choose from a variety of ethnic identities (cited in Graham 2004: 22). Using these observations, Graham uses a more generalised term, namely 'pick 'n' mix Judaism', reflecting an environment in which European Jewry now finds itself that is 'open and welcoming and encourages choice and personal preference above rules and dictates – Pick 'n' mix Judaism is European Jewry's adaptive response to this new environment' (2004: 22).

5 Pick 'n' Mix DIY Judaism in the UK

The last few years in the UK have witnessed the growth of a number of grassroots, bottom-up, young-people-generated activity, reflecting the rejection of institutional structures and an expression of the values of diversity and inclusiveness already witnessed in the United States in an offline setting. The most prominent of these are 'Wandering Jews', 'Carlebach Minyan Belsize Park', 'Jewdas' and 'MoHoLo'. Wandering Jews describes itself as:

> [...] a self organising collective that has been celebrating Jewish stuff in London since 2005. We meet once or twice a month in North, West, East and South London and occasionally further afield to eat and pray and drink and be. We are hosted by a new person every time and aim to 'never go to the same house twice'. We also hold firm to the ideal, 'your

house, your rules'. A little bit Fight Club, a little bit minyan,[3] almost 100 % good. We look forward to welcoming you soon. You and your veggie food, your vegan liquor and your beautiful *neshamas*.[4] (Wandering Jews. N.d.).

Wandering Jews meets regularly to *daven* (Yiddish: pray) and eat in different homes. This arrangement is achieved through email and social networking sites. Each host determines the *minhag* (Hebrew: tradition), doing it according to their style of Judaism. No leaders control the agenda; instead 'custodians' care for the group's continued existence as long as there is demand. It is open to 'all Jews and the people who love them'. And they are 'post-philanthropic', eschewing funding because 'asking for funding is akin to asking for permission to exist' (Boyd 2009).

Carlebach Minyan Belsize Park (CMBP n.d.) operates in a similar fashion to Wandering Jews. Carlebach Minyan runs Friday night services in members' homes or in more exotic locations such as Whitstable Beach, a Suffolk vineyard and even Tuscany. The services run in the style of the eponymous 'singing Rabbi' Shlomo Carlebach, and the emphasis is on song followed by a communal meal to which everyone is asked to contribute. A 'secret' Facebook group, to which new members can only be invited by existing ones, facilitates it. In this way it theoretically maintains exclusivity, but in reality more people attend than are members of the Facebook group.

Jewdas, on the other hand, does not provide religious or spiritual experiences *per se*, although some of its events are modelled on points in the Jewish calendar, such as East London Sukkah,[5] Nitl Nakht,[6] Rootless Cosmopolitan Yeshiva,[7] Night of Ritual Slaughter, Treifspotting,[8] Elephants of the Protocols of Zion and Punkpurim. It is a self-styled subversive organisation, led by a group of individuals all calling themselves 'Geoffrey Cohen'. Its tagline is 'radical voices for the alternative diaspora'.

---

3 A Minyan is the minimum number of ten Jewish males over the age of thirteen required for a *Halachic* communal religious service. Some non-Orthodox denominations include women in the count.
4 Hebrew: souls.
5 A temporary booth, hut or shelter, erected during the Jewish festival of *Sukkot* (Tabernacles), symbolising the wandering in the wilderness.
6 Christmas Eve in Yiddish, when some Jews would take a break from studying the Torah and enjoy themselves, though this is not for Orthodox Jews.
7 An educational institution that focuses on the study of traditional religious texts, primarily the Talmud and Torah.
8 *Treif* is non-kosher food.

Finally, MoHoLo is the shorter title for the Moishe House, London. Founded in October 2007, it is a subsidised home for six young Jews who are also tasked with holding a certain number of events in return for their subsidy, which means that they pay much lower rent than the market rate. They describe themselves thus:

> From our own home, we bring [an] exciting, creative, non-denominational Jewish community to London, also welcoming and supporting our local community. From Friday night dinners to film showings, impromptu concerts to study sessions, meditation to jam sessions to social action events – the possibilities are endless. Much of our programming is based around spirituality, the arts and social justice. We see ourselves as standing for experimental, creative and dynamic Judaism in the diaspora, and hope that our values will have a ripple effect on the Jewish and wider community. (MoHoLo n.d.)

It also runs an open-profile Facebook group which, at the time of writing, has 935 members. MoHoLo, unlike the others, is generously funded. It is part of an international organization, Moishe House (http://www.moishehouse.org/), which funds 36 houses in 14 countries worldwide, aiming to provide 'meaningful Jewish experiences to young adults in their twenties'. As its website states, 'Our innovative model trains, supports and sponsors young Jewish leaders as they create vibrant home-based communities for their peers'. Moishe House provides a budget for programming, which the residents must facilitate, as well as opening up the house to guests. It also receives sponsorship from the Pears Foundation, a UK-based Jewish philanthropic body.

Taken together, these groups pride themselves on 'creating gatherings which are heartfelt, soul centered and intellectually inspiring'(CMBP n.d.). One participant/observer described a common 'vibrancy and vitality that I so often find lacking in more traditional community events for Jews of my ilk' (Russell 2009: 11). They are self-organising collectives characterised by their refusal to be labelled by the existing denominational tags; for example, three individuals, drawn from Reform, Liberal and Orthodoxy respectively, founded Wandering Jews. The philosophy and principles of these collectives are to create very different Jewish spaces from the synagogues and other communal organisations as well as to be egalitarian, democratic, peer-led, informal and inclusive. They are avowedly open, welcoming to non-Jews, organised and led by volunteers, have no paid clergy or denominational affiliation, meet at least once a month and are not linked directly with any of the mainstream communal organisations in the UK. In all of these ways, they perceive themselves to be different from the existing communal infrastructure. These groupings are, in some ways, descendants or heirs of the '*havurot*' (Hebrew: fellowships), participatory communities that sprang up in the 1960s and 1970s in the United States and were marked by a 'countercultural, anti-institutional, Do-It-Yourself aesthetic' (Lurie 2011: 25). What is different, however, is that each of these *offline* activities has been facilitated through extensive Facebook networking. Indeed, as mentioned above, Carlebach Minyan is an invite-only 'secret' group. Jonathan Boyd, one of the few thus far to pay serious attention to this development, has argued:

> These members of the 'Net Generation' who have grown up with the Internet, differ significantly from their forebears in Jewish outlook, expectations and notions of community. They have little faith in the 'authoritative' or 'authentic' view – they scrutinize information online, and decide what makes sense to them. They refuse to be passive consumers – they satisfy their desire for choice, convenience, customization and control by designing their own products. And they don't retreat into a lonely world behind their computers, they collaborate and network in the vast array of communities online. (Boyd 2009)

It should also be added here that they collaborate and network in the vast array of communities offline.

6 Grassroots Jews

Building upon these networks, in September 2009, individuals connected with these groups met to create, for the first time, independent High Holyday, namely Rosh Hashana (Jewish New Year) and Yom Kippur (Day of Atonement) services in North West London. This was not done within an existing synagogue, nor in partnership with one, but entirely autonomously. At no point was communal approval requested or sought. They described themselves thus: 'We are a group of friends with many different Jewish backgrounds and perspectives'. A website (grassrootsjews.org), a blog, (http://grassrootsjewishnewyearproject.wordpress.-com/2010/09/03/ellul-boot-camp/) and a Facebook group (http://www.facebook.com/groups/97599398526) were set up, a downloadable video (http://vimeo.com/5667190) was produced, promising 'the most exciting autonomous and non-hierarchical Judaism ever to surface', and a series of invitations were sent out via Facebook. A flat fee of £45 for the services was requested; however, the inability to pay was taken into consideration, and others paid what they could afford. As Schalit (2009: 1 Sept) observed in a blog post, Grassroots Jews are 'largely unwilling to buy into a model of community that implicitly, if not explicitly, demands that they sign-up for the whole synagogue package at considerable expense'. A second promotional video (http://vimeo.com/14154519) clearly symbolizes how Grassroots Jews feel about the existing options. Opening with shots of a traditional Reform service, after 44 seconds it cuts to a black screen emblazoned with the large white letters 'Bored of shul [Yiddish: synagogue]?'

as a reggae soundtrack blares over a montage sequence of traditional Jewish iconography, including *haredim* dancing the *hora*, synagogue interiors, the Torah, Hebrew lettering, praying and so on. Such imagery is then intercut with a series of statements: 'Looking for something new and fresh?', 'A new form of community' and 'Where do you belong?'. Thus, the group clearly positions itself as one which would appeal to those who are seeking both novelty and a sense of belonging (grassrootsjews.org n.d.).

The Grassroots Jews services took place along *Halachic*, that is, normative rabbinic lines, but with some distinct and non-traditional differences. Atypically, *three* discrete areas of seating were provided. There was a traditional segregated section in which men and women were divided by a *mechitza* (partition). There was also a mixed section along Reform/Liberal/Progressive/Masorti lines. Finally, there was an unallocated area, described as a 'free wheeling, open, free to come and go, chill out spaces, cushions, tents, friendly, space for mothers and babies' and 'space for breastfeeding'. Grassroots Jews presupposes some of 'the permanence of innovations made by Reform and Conservative movements in having women lead all parts of the services, men and women [can] sit together, and both [can] count in the prayer quorum' (Lurie 2011: 25), but at the same time, as the above arrangements demonstrate, they are flexible enough on these issues in order to accommodate those who are more to the right on the religious spectrum. At the same time, Grassroots Jews is united in its desire to provide an egalitarian experience, 'usually with the full liturgy, but with *feeling*' (Lurie 2011: 25). Thus, Grassroots Jews' innovations rely on older, canonical and traditional religious practices.

The aim was to be as avowedly religiously inclusive and non-hierarchical as possible: 'We want to be PARTICIPATORY AND FRIENDLY' (sic), and 'We want to be the kind of place where people say hello to people they don't know' (Grassroots Jews Community, n.d.). Women were called up to the Torah in accordance with *Halacha*, led the *davening* (Yiddish: praying) and sang the *haftorah* (Hebrew: a short reading from the Prophets following the reading of the Torah in synagogue). There were no age restrictions: 'This is for people of all ages[,] from children to grandparents'. A guest cantor and a teacher from Israel – a musician and a professor of medieval Jewish history at the University of Haifa – was flown in (Grassroots Jews Community, n.d.). The initial venues were a marquee in the back garden of a private home and a classical music concert hall, both in Hampstead. In their second year of operation, they relocated to the premises of the Moishe House in London.

Grassroots Jews attempts to blend the traditional with the innovative. Its preference for Hebrew prayer and traditional liturgy is one indicator, but this also most likely stems from the upbringing of a sizeable number of attendees from the United Synagogue – the British variant of mainstream Orthodoxy. Drawing upon the Jewish exegetical tradition, they state, 'exploring, questioning and challenging is important'. At the same time, however, they investigated alternatives to tradition not typically found in mainstream religious infrastructures in the United Kingdom, such as 'parallel sessions with less structure and more spontaneity', including 'experimental approaches to prayer, meditation and yoga'. In this way, they 'intend to bring this spirit of joy and Jewish exploration to our services' (Grassroots Jews Community, n.d.).

It is clear then that Grassroots Jews feel that inclusiveness, experimentation, exploration and a spirit of joy are missing from the typical UK fare and that such fare is the antithesis of 'heartfelt, soul centred and intellectually inspiring', in comparison to what one blogger described as 'the Judaism they find elsewhere in the community [that] is rather dull, meaningless and stuffy' (Schalit 2009: 1 Sept). Have 'you ever sat in Shul and thought "there must be more to it than this?"', they ask. Thus, if mainstream Jewish religious organisations are not willing or are not able to provide this outlet, Grassroots Jews will; not by challenging the mainstream organisations to change from within, but by providing their own alternatives. Reflecting the US experience, as Lurie has commented:

> Without a doubt, core minyan-goers have a more serious commitment to community and to prayer than does the average synagogue member, who can rely on institutional staff to look after logistics and lead prayers. There are, however, ragged edges to these commitments. Most minyanim (plural of minyan) that stress prayer over other forms of Jewish communal life do not meet weekly. (2011: 27)

This group feels their agency is denied within mainstream British Judaism, that their voices are not heard. But, rather than get angry with the old denominations, they are just saying no to them, and 'we can find what we like or create what we like'. Consequently, using the Internet in general and Facebook in particular, this group set about producing its own alternative in which, as Schalit (2009: 1 Sept) pointed out, 'most of all, they want to do it their way, on their terms, and with their people'. The group's very name encapsulates their aspirations: to build something completely new and from the bottom up, not to rely on existing alternatives. Significantly, the organisers and participants are not marginalised Jews. They are what Cohen described as 'groomed, not bloomed Jews' (Neroulias 2008). What this means is that '[t]heir renegade independence from the denominational label has been made possible by years of communal education, involvement, and training in denominational institutions', training for which the established movements have reaped little reward (Lurie 2011: 28). Most of them are in the late-twenties to early-forties age band, are well known for their communal activism and are individuals who cut their teeth in such mainstream organisations as the Union of Jewish Students, Bnei Akiva,[9] Noam,[10] RSY-Netzer[11] and Limmud[12] as well as the new initiatives mentioned above. Some of them are even the children of well-known rabbis. In short, as one commentator pointed out, they are 'people you would think the community would be bending over backwards to include within existing frameworks' (Schalit 2009: 1 Sept).

To take one example, in an interview in the *Jewish Chronicle*, thirty-year-old Zoe Jankel, a member of the Grassroots Jews organising committee, explained the motivations for her involvement (Kasriel 2009: 62). She initially described herself as 'barely religious and rarely interested in matters of the spirit'. Her non-Jewish friends identify her as a 'cultural Jew', and she 'mainly avoids synagogue', but on the 'rare occasions' she attends, she will sit, hiding her paperback inside a prayer book, 'studiously ignoring the prayers' around her and hence 'not an obvious contender for involvement in something such as Grassroots Jews'. At the same time, however, for the past ten years or so she has participated

> both actively and passively in a number of informal Jewish organisations, most of which concentrate on the evolution of Judaism into a practice relevant to our lives today. For me this is not just a cultural affiliation – it is definitely a connection to the religious practice – one that is not synagogue-based but is fluid and changing and more in line with the world outside the walls of prayer (Kasriel 2009: 62).

Like many young Jews, Zoe enjoys the experience of Rosh Hashanah and Yom Kippur with her family but is turned off by the synagogue service, which she finds very passive ('It used to be quite a lot of looking at my watch [...] quite dry and boring') and which denies her agency ('Last year I was a little bit annoyed with myself because I thought I could have just stayed at home'). That is one of the key reasons she became involved with Grassroots Jews, as it allowed her a sense of ownership and action in constructing the sort of services *she* would like to attend ('We're all involved in creating this for the first time'), but at the same time, as many of her friends were involved, an important social aspect was also provided. Clearly she was dissatisfied with the existing religious infrastructure: 'I think Grassroots Jews is a commentary on today's synagogues. It's a way to move forward and to engage in what is going on in the Jewish community'. Informally she admitted that, without Facebook, Grassroots Jews would not have happened (Kasriel 2009: 62).

---

9 The UK's largest Orthodox Jewish youth movement.
10 Zionist youth movement of the Assembly of Masorti (traditional) Synagogues.
11 Zionist youth movement for Reform Judaism.
12 A cross-communal Jewish learning organisation.

Feedback from participants posted on the Facebook site between 20 September 2009 and 14 October 2010 was overwhelmingly positive. 'It's mid-October, and I'm still feeling the effects of the incredible High Holy Days experience. I resolved to be more grateful this year, so Thank You to everyone who made it so special, and continue to grow our lovely community'; 'thank you so much for an amazing rosh hashana and yom kipur. I'll never forget the magic *neilah* with everyone coming together'; 'THANK YOU ALL FOR THE WONDERFUL CELEBRATIONS!' (sic); 'Thankyou GRJ, AMAZINGGGGGG. sending out love and thanks to everyone who made it happen. It was a spiritual sensation. Still can not believe how you all made it happen. U r all stars. Put me down for next year!!! love you all' (sic); and 'Thank you so much to the whole team who have organised GRJ. it has been a truly amazing and special experience thus far [...]' (sic). Clearly, Grassroots Jews fulfilled a need that was missing for some. However, given that the number of posters is tiny in terms of the number of attendees, it is difficult to ascertain just how representative this is without further in-depth research.

7 Future work: biographical narrative analysis

The information above was primarily drawn from online and printed sources, blended with ethnographic research.[13] Further clarity about the role of online resources in the lives of the new post-denominational Jewish communities would be enabled through more intensive biographic examination of a small number of individuals currently resident in the UK who maintain a strong presence in Jewish congregations on Facebook. Interviewees could also be identified according to their degree of 'presence', with preference given to people who contribute a great deal to online and offline Jewish congregations in terms of participation and leadership. Peer nomination could also identify key individuals. A biographical narrative method would illuminate the points during an interviewee's life trajectory as well as the processes by which the interviewees became involved with online fora and the reasons why. With such a biographically oriented approach, it would be possible to explore when and how these people met others with different perspectives, where they found places in which they could not say hello to people that they did not know and how they went off to find something more palatable to them.

---

13 This took place over two years from 2008 – 2010, including attendance at many of these groups' events as well as the Grassroots Jews services.

Biographical approaches of this kind were developed originally at Otto Van Guericke University in Magdeburg by Fritz Schütze (2008). They focus on two aspects of the life story: its actual biographical content and its specific chronological and spatial structure. The narrator's free choice to tell his or her life story in a specific way and the form in which the story is told provides valuable insights into biographical processes. This kind of reflexivity emerges at a point in life at which the individual faces real-life dilemmas, when s/he is expected to make her/his own decisions and deal with the consequences. These two elements – the scope of experiences and the ability to reflexively assess them – would enable future researchers to reconnoitre the history of participants' involvement with online worlds, the pleasures, satisfactions and frustrations of doing so, the relationship of their online involvement to their faith and self-definition in corporeal life and the differences between online and virtual experiences. Participants' views of their online communities could also be examined, particularly in terms of their understanding of why people engage in this kind of activity and what are the gains and the gratifications.

Biographical analysis will reveal the events in people's lives, their backgrounds in terms of family experiences, societal position and religious involvement as well as their educational backgrounds and career aspirations, and so on, that led them to their involvement in on- and off-line religious communities. The information gleaned so far provides a clear indication of *how* these people feel and what they are trying to achieve – but biographical analyses will reveal the unfolding of their lives and which life experiences may have led them to feeling and doing the things that they are now feeling and doing. In addition, there is a strong case for a longitudinal element to the kind of study we are advocating. Further biographical narrative analysis carried out in a few years hence will also allow us to reveal what occurred over the passage of time. As the nucleus of these Jewish users is predominantly single, unmarried or recently-married young adults in their twenties and thirties, if not exclusively so, it will be poignant to chart what happens once they settle down and start families, require a Hebrew school and bar/bat mitzvah training, and whether they continue with such Internet-provided activities or integrate into more mainstream communities. Will they be happy to continue with these more ad hoc (although becoming increasingly regularised and familiar) activities, or will they eventually succumb to what Schalit (2009: 1 Sept) calls 'the more concrete and stable versions of community that one typically finds within an existing synagogue framework'? Will collectives such as Grassroots Jews enable what has been variously labelled in the United States as 'the long-extended enabled adolescence', 'post-college, pre-whatever' (Kaunfer quoted in Shapiro 2010), 'emerging adulthood' (Arnett

2004) or 'the odyssey years' (Brooks 2007)? According to Lurie, in the US (and therefore using it as a model for the UK),

> [o]n the ground, what this looks like is upper middle class Americans spending the ten to fifteen years after college messing around and 'figuring out their lives' while postponing marriage, children, and responsibilities. One way or another, the bill for this eclectic adventurousness is footed by parents, or, for the best and brightest, by various institutions and sinecures. Certainly, in opting out of synagogue life, most young Jews become unaccustomed to supporting Jewish institutions financially. We can feel connected to a particular religious community without attending, paying money, or even living in the city where the community is located (2011: 26).

Indeed, Kaunfer (2010) found that such Jews reported an average of five different community affiliations. Certainly, it has been suggested that such groups do not require the hard work, commitment, loyalty or steadfastness of a traditional congregation, i.e., an 'if I don't like it, I'll leave it and find something better' attitude. At the same time, Kaunfer discovered in the United States that independent *minyanim* do not age *per se*, as a revolving-door effect means that as those who are past their mid-thirties leave the community, they are simply replaced by a new crop of university graduates who move in. The institution becomes quite stable because it caters to a demographic that is constantly replenishing itself. It will also be interesting to see what type of internal dynamic these communities/congregations develop.

Furthermore, future biographical narrative analysis will also test the views of some within the communal mainstream who tend to adopt a rather *laissez faire* attitude to these and other similar endeavours, arguing that, as these young people settle down and start families, their passion for Judaism will almost inevitably ensure that they slot back into the existing infrastructure and the structure and stability it offers. Boyd (2009), for example, observed, 'These behaviours are not a passing fad; even if this generation later gravitates to established frameworks, it will do so with a set of assumptions that will necessitate significant communal change'. Perhaps initiatives like Grassroots Jews will slot into, or even become, the mainstream. At the same time, it will be interesting to watch the response of the communal and denominational leadership to the rise of these new initiatives. Will they adapt or sit back and watch complacently? Will Grassroots Jews impact on traditional religious authority in the UK? Boyd (2009) has suggested, 'Grassroots Jews is a fringe endeavour that, in 2009, barely registers on the communal Richter scale. But the principles and behaviours that underpin it may herald a raft of changes to Jewish life in the future. Grassroots Americans recently elected the first Afro-American president; who knows what Grassroots Jews might achieve?' Furthermore, as Campbell put it, 'It will be important to consider the relationship between religious new media users and innovators and the offline religious communities they identify with' (2010: 192). Overall, then, this will be an excellent case study by which, a few years into the future, it may be possible to assess more fully the impact of Facebook in a post-denominational offline setting.

8 Conclusion

New forms of social software such as Facebook are providing an 'architecture of participation', fostering collaboration and creativity by facilitating communication and the adapting of the technologies themselves, thus giving rise to new social practices, rituals, congregations and even beliefs across the Jewish spectrum. Social networking sites, here Facebook, have created discursive spaces where choices that were once private have become increasingly public and visible and where small, emergent and labile offline congregations can form. Facebook is clearly helping to address increasing feelings of alienation or disenfranchisement amongst post-denominational Jews who are dissatisfied with the existing communal and congregational infrastructure, providing greater opportunities for religious self-definition as well as a *qualitatively* different encounter with Judaism. It is seemingly allowing a new form of Judaism to emerge, unshackled from the constraints of denominational control, or at the very least reinventing and reviving earlier forms.

Yet there are many further questions still to be asked. Does Facebook really meet the needs for congregation formation at a time when increasing numbers of Jews are isolated and feeling disenfranchised or do not want to be affiliated? Since all of the groups explored above are based in London, providing for metropolitan Jews, what about the non-urban or non-London populations in the UK? Can religious questions be raised on Facebook that may not be asked in real life because it does not involve face-to-face conversation, thus providing a more welcoming encounter with religion? Does the Internet provide a greater access to core Judaic sacred texts and/or does it renegotiate the user's relationship with such texts? Are the Judaic meanings and beliefs derived from them qualitatively different from those that already exist? Is a new form of online/electronic Judaism emerging which may lead to the need to re-evaluate Judaism in the real world? What does it mean to be an online Jew? What can new electronic Judaism tell us about the Jewish religion today? What is the nature of the virtual-real relationship in Judaism? Is there any connection? How do electronic Judaic identities relate to questions of national context? And how have the institutional branches of Judaism reacted in terms of utilising Facebook? How does electronic culture address the nature of contemporary Judaism? How does it attempt to express Judaic positions within religious frameworks that are identified with the non-Jewish majority? Does it furnish an independent self-definition of Judaism, and how does this relate to wider and fluctuating notions of other identities? It is hoped that future research will answer some or all of these questions.

References

Arnett, Jeffrey J. 2004. *Emerging Adulthood: The Winding Road from Late Teens through the Twenties.* New York and Oxford: Oxford University Press.
Barzilai, Gad, and K. Barzilai-Nahon. 2005. "Cultured technology: Internet and religious fundamentalism." *The Information Society.* Available at: http://www.indiana.edu/~tisj/21/1/ab-barzilai.html. Accessed 20 July 2011.
Bourdieu, Pierre. 1991. *Language and Symbolic Power.* Cambridge, MA: Harvard University Press.
boyd, danah m. 2006. "Friends, friendsters, and top 8: Writing community into being on social network sites." *First Monday* 11: 12.
boyd, danah m., and N.B. Ellison. 2008. "Social network sites: Definition, history and scholarship." *Journal of Computer-mediated Communication* 13: 210–30. Available at: http://www.uic.edu/htbin/cgiwrap/bin/ojs/index.php/fm/article/view/1418/1336.
Boyd, J. 2009. "My way, the Sinatra style of Judaism." *The Jewish Chronicle* 27 August. Available at: http://www.thejc.com/comment/comment/my-way-sinatra-style-judaism. Accessed: 28 June 2013.
Brasher, Brenda. 2001. *Give Me That Online Religion.* San Francisco: Jossey-Bass.
Brooks, David. 2007. "The odyssey years". *The New York Times* 9 October. Availabe at: http://www.nytimes.com/2007/10/09/opinion/09brooks.html?_r=0. Accessed: 28 June 2013..
Brubaker, Rogers, and F. Cooper. 2000. "Beyond 'identity.'" *Theory and Society* 291: 1–47.
Buckingham, David. 2007. *Beyond Technology: Children's Learning in the Age of Digital Culture.* Cambridge and Malden, MA: Polity Press.
Bunt, Gary R. 2009. *iMuslims: Rewiring the House of Islam.* Chapel Hill: University of North Carolina Press.
Calhoun, Craig. 2003. "The democratic integration of Europe: Interests, identity, and the public sphere." In *Europe Without Borders: Re-Mapping Territory, Citizenship and Identity in a Transnational Age,* edited by M. Berezin and M. Schain, 243–274. Baltimore: Johns Hopkins University Press.
Campbell, Heidi A. 2010. *When Religion Meets New Media.* Oxford and New York: Routledge.
–. 2011. "Religion and the Internet in the Israeli Jewish context." *Israel Affairs* 17 (3): 364–383.
CMBP. N.d. "About our community." Available at: http://carlebachminyan.org/aboutus.html
Cohen, Steven M. 2005. "Engaging the next generation of American Jews: Distinguishing the in-married, inter-married, and non-married." *Journal of Jewish Communal Service* 81: 43–52.
Cohen, Steven M., E. Kaunfer, J.S. Landres, and M. Shain. 2007. *Emergent Jewish Communities and their Participants: Preliminary Findings from the 2007 National*

Spiritual Communities Study. Los Angeles and New York: Synagogue 3000 and Mechon Hadar.

Cohen, Steven M., and A.Y. Kelman. 2006. *Cultural Events and Jewish Identities: Young Adult Jews in New York*. New York: National Foundation for Jewish Culture.

–. 2007a. *The Continuity of Discontinuity*. Andrea and Charles Bronfman Philanthropies.

–. 2007b. *Beyond Distancing: Young Adult American Jews and Their Alienation from Israel*. Andrea and Charles Bronfman Philanthropies.

Dawson, Lorne, and D.E. Cowan. 2004. *Religion Online: Finding Faith on the Internet*. London and New York: Routledge.

Dencik, Lars. 2003. *Paideia Report. "Jewishness" in Postmodernity: The Case of Sweden*. The European Institute for Jewish Studies, Sweden.

–. 2011. "The dialectics of diaspora: On the art of being Jewish in the Swedish minority." In *A Road to Nowhere: Jewish Experiences in Unifying Europe*, edited by J.H. Schoeps, O. Glockner, and A. Kreinenbrink, 121–150. Leiden and Boston: Brill.

Ellison, Nicole., C. Steinfield, and C. Lampe. 2007. "The benefits of Facebook 'Friends': Social capital and college students' use of online social network sites." *Journal of Computer-Mediated Communication* 12: 4. Available at: http://jcmc.indiana.edu/vol12/issue4/ellison.html.

Graham, D. 2004. *European Jewish Identity at the Dawn of the 21st Century: A Working Paper*. A report for the American Jewish Joint Distribution Committee and Hanadiv Charitable Foundation presented to the European General Assembly of the European Council of Jewish Communities. Budapest, 20–23 May. Available at: http://www.jpr.org.uk/downloads/European_Jewish_Identity_in_21st_Century.pdf. Accessed: 31 August 2012.

Grassroots Jews Community. N.d. Available at: http://grassrootsjews.org/about-grassroots/.

Hojsgaard, Morton T., and M. Warburg. 2005. *Religion and Cyberspace*. Abingdon: Routledge.

Jewdas. N.d. Available at: http://www.jewdas.org/

JDC-ICCD. 2011. *Identity à la carte: Research on Jewish identities, participation and affiliation in five European countries*. Oxford: JDC-International Centre for Community Development.

Jenkins, Richard. 2008. *Social Identity*. London: Routledge.

Karaflogka, Anastasia. 2006. *E-Religion: A Critical Appraisal of Religious Discourse on the World Wide Web*. London: Equinox.

Kasriel, Alex. 2009. "Getting our spiritual fix." *The Jewish Chronicle* 17 September: 62.

Kaunfer, Elie. 2010. *Empowered Judaism: What Independent Minyanim Can Teach Us about Building Vibrant Jewish Communities*. Woodstock, VT: Jewish Lights Publishing.

Kelman, Ari Y., and E. Schonberg. 2008. *Legwork, Framework, Artwork: Engaging the Next Generation of Jews*. Denver, CO: Rose Community Foundation.

Konrád, G. 1998. "Aphorisms on the durability of the Jews." In Graham, D. 2004. *European Jewish Identity at the Dawn of the 21st Century: A Working Paper*. A report for the American Jewish Joint Distribution Committee and Hanadiv Charitable Foundation presented to the European General Assembly of the European Council of Jewish Communities. Budapest, 20–23 May. Available at: http://www.jpr.org.uk/downloads/European_Jewish_Identity_in_21st_Century.pdf. Accessed: 31 August 2012.

Livio, Oren, and K. Tenenboim. 2004. "Discursive legitimation of a controversial technology: Ultra-orthodox Jewish women in Israel and the Internet." Unpublished paper presented at AoIR 5.0. University of Sussex, England.

Lurie, Margot. 2011. "Minyan 2.0." *Jewish Review of Books* Winter: 25–8.

Meyer, Birgit, and A. Moors. 2006. *Religion, Media and the Public Sphere*. Bloomington: Indiana University Press.

Modood, Tariq, and P. Werbner, eds. 1997. *The Politics of Multiculturalism in the New Europe: Racism, Identity and Community*. London: Zed Books.

MoLoHo. N.d. "Moishe House: Our model." Available at: http://www.moishehouse.org/background.asp.

Neroulias, Nicole. 2008. "Study Finds More Conservative, Orthodox Jews Drawn to Prayer Groups." Available at http://blog.beliefnet.com/news/2008/11/study-finds-more-conservative.php#ixzz2XUlaNdhC. Accessed: 26 June 2013.

Niezen, Ronald. 2005. "Digital identity: The construction of virtual selfhood in the indigenous peoples' movement." *Society for the Comparative Study of Society and History* 45 (2): 532–551.

Nyland, Rob, and C. Near. 2007. "Jesus is my friend: Religiosity as a mediating factor in Internet social networking use." Paper Presented at AEJMC Midwinter Conference, Reno, NV.

Rosenthal, Rachel. 2006. "What's in a name? The future of post-denominational Judaism." *Kedma* 1: 20–32.

Russell, D. 2009. "Why cool communities are hot." *Jewish Renaissance* July: 9–11. Available at: http://www.natan.org/html/Jewish_Salons_Cool_Communities.pdf. Accessed: 31 August 2012.

Schalit, Joel. 2009. "Grassroots Jews." www.jewcy.com. 1 September. Available at: http://www.jewcy.com/post/grassroots_jews. Accessed: 20 July 2012.

Schütze, Fritz. 2008. "Biography analysis on the empirical base of autobiographical narratives: How to analyze autobiographical narrative interviews – parts one and two." *European Studies on Inequalities and Social Cohesion* 1/2, 3/4.

Shandler, Jeffrey. 2009. *Jews, God, and Videotape: Religion and Media in America*. New York: New York University Press.

Shapiro, Samantha M. 2010. "Minyan man." *Tablet* 19 February. Available at: http://www.tabletmag.com/life-and-religion/26047/minyin-man/. Accessed: 20 July 2012.

Stein, Howard F., and R.F. Hill. 1977. *The Ethnic Imperative: Examining the New White Ethnic Movement*. University Park, PA: Pennsylvania State University Press.

UKSC. 2009. "Judgment R on the application of E respondent v governing body of JFS and the admissions appeal panel of JFS appellants and others and R on the application of E respondent v governing body of JFS and the admissions appeal panel of JFS and others." Available at: http://www.supremecourt.gov.uk/docs/uksc_2009_0105_judgmentV2.pdf.

Voloj, Julian. 2008. "Virtual Jewish topography: The genesis of Jewish second life." In *Jewish Topographies: Visions of Space, Traditions of Place*, edited by J. Brauch, A. Lipphardt, and A. Nocke, 345–56. Farnham: Ashgate.

Wandering Jews. N.d. "Welcome to Wandering Jews." Available at: http://www.wanderingjews.co.uk/.

Webber, Jonathan, ed. 1994. *Jewish Identities in the New Europe*. London: Littman Library of Jewish Civilization.

Young, Sean., D. Dutta, and G. Dommety. 2009. "Extrapolating psychological insights from Facebook profiles: A study of religion and relationship status." *Cyberpsychology and Behavior* 123: 347–50.

Zhao, Shanyang, S. Grasmuck, and M. Jason. 2008. "Identity Construction on Facebook: Digital Empowerment in Anchored Relationships." *Computers in Human Behavior* 24: 1816–18.

Stephen Pihlaja

9   Truck Stops and Fashion Shows: A Case Study of the Discursive Performance of Evangelical Christian Group Affiliation on YouTube

In the last five years, use of the popular video-sharing site YouTube has grown enormously. On YouTube, Evangelical Christian video bloggers (vloggers) frequently discuss topics of religion amongst themselves and with other users from different religious backgrounds, but given the diverse viewpoints from which users come, developing clear distinctions between oneself and others who call themselves 'Christians', but with whom one may not particularly agree on controversial theological questions, is a difficult issue. As YouTube does not feature any 'group' function, as on other social networking sites, users must associate or disassociate with one another only through their talk. My previous research has investigated similar issues using longitudinal observation linked with metaphor-led discourse analysis (Cameron and Maslen 2010) to show how misunderstanding between atheists and Christians emerges (Pihlaja 2010: 2011a). This chapter will extend analysis of YouTube discourse by investigating the emergence of categories of Evangelical Christian users on YouTube in one video. Drawing on a longitudinal observation of a group of users over two years, analysis will focus on one video in which a user (*Yokeup*) aligns with and distances himself from other users and how users react in the video comments section to the categories *Yokeup* employs. Analysis will show that *Yokeup* employs traditional denominations as well as metaphorical categorisations to position himself and others, often drawing on a biblical text and his own exegesis of the text to accomplish this.

Since its founding in 2005, YouTube has become an important site of social interaction and media production. During 2006, YouTube quickly became the key site for video content on the web, allowing users to post content with only a limitation placed on how long a video could be. Coupled with the growth of personal blog publishing and the affordance of cheap video recording devices, the new technology allowed users to logically extend the conversational nature of the blog genre by posting videos of themselves talking directly to the YouTube audience. 'Video blogs' or 'vlogs' became the video equivalent of diary style blogs, with thoughts spoken directly to the camera rather than written down. Although the bounds on what is and is not a vlog are not always clear, Burgess and Green have suggested the very simple description of 'a talking head, a camera, and some editing' (2008: 6) and free expression of one's own opinions and experiences in an online, public space. YouTubers (YouTube users) can align or associate with other users through 'subscribing' to channels, but the real work of aligning with or distancing from other users occurs in discourse activity, both in videos and in text comments. In this chapter, I will analyse a single video, entitled 'I doubt JesusFreek is saved', in which the user *Yokeup* discusses whom he believes to be truly 'saved' and whom he believes is merely 'religious'. Using close textual analysis of the video and comments, I will seek to answer two questions: first, what are the criteria *Yokeup* employs to identify Christians he sees as 'saved' from those who are 'religious'; and second, were these criteria recognised and accepted by others in response, or were other criteria applied by different users?

1 Background and methods: YouTube in context

Since 2005, research into YouTube has also grown substantially and in diversity, with researchers having investigated copyright issues on YouTube (O'Brien and Fitzgerald 2006; Hilderbrand 2007), the prevalence of YouTube in the life of youth (Madden 2007), YouTube as a social-networking site (Lange 2007), the educational potential of YouTube (Snelson 2008), the effect of YouTube on the US political process (Burgess and Green 2009; Duman and Locher 2008), responses to anti-Muslim media (van Zoonen, Vis and Mihelj 2010) and antagonism in YouTube comments (Garcés-Conejos Blitvich 2010; Lorenzo-Dus, Garcés-Conejos Blitvich and Bou-Franch 2011). Maia, Almeida and Almeida (2008) have done quantitative analysis of YouTube networks to identify user behaviour, similar to the work of Benevenuto et al. (2008), who have also used statistical analysis to describe interactions on YouTube. O'Donnell et al. (2008) have used questionnaire data to investigate how the YouTube community is constructed and how reactions to videos differ based on the user group viewing the video. O'Donnell et al.'s research was particularly oriented towards use of language and how text comments related to videos, but videos analysed were not user-generated and analysis did not include video interactions between users.

Anthropologist Patricia Lange's studies of YouTube interaction and user experience (2007a, 2007b, 2007c) have perhaps been the most rigorous, in-depth analyses of the YouTube social experience to date. Adopting an ethnographic perspective, Lange has investigated user interpretations of YouTube interactions and limits on participation in the YouTube 'community' as well as the antagonistic nature of YouTube interaction. In particular, a unique form of antagonistic behaviour has developed on the site, referred to by YouTubers as 'drama', a phenomenon 'that emerge[s] when a flurry of video posts clusters around an internal "controversy" or antagonistic debate between one or more YouTubers' (Burgess and Green 2009: 98). Studies of YouTube antagonism and drama have been, unfortunately, incomplete in taking into account all elements of the video page as well as the dynamic nature of interactions on the site. Although the studies above have attempted to understand antagonism and drama, research into antagonistic YouTube discourse activity has continued to rely on analysis of comments and user reports of experience online rather than close analysis of videos. Lack of close discourse analysis tends to move research away from the actual YouTube video page and interactions between users and towards quantitative analysis of YouTube activity or reports of experiences on the site. In contrast, my analysis of YouTube video pages focuses on the dynamic interaction between users on the site, using only the discourse data.

The development of treatment of online communication not as a static, textual artefact to be extracted and analysed but rather as a dynamic system of interaction, using discourse analytic tools created and adapted from analysis of offline communication, has shown promise. In an attempt to bridge discourse analysis and online ethnography, Androutsopoulos has developed a discourse-centred online ethnography (DCOE) to describe and analyse online texts (Androutsopoulos 2008), treating online discourse as emergent rather than fossilised artefacts to be extracted and analysed. DCOE is influenced heavily by linguistic ethnography (LE), which seeks to contextualise language by integrating an applied linguistic perspective of language with ethnographic theories and methods. Ethnography investigates connections between individual communication instances and context, drawing in all relevant contextual elements to bear on analysis, with a particular emphasis on taking an emic rather than etic perspective. Inherently interdisciplinary, LE draws on linguistics, social theory and ethnographic methodology (Tusting and Maybin 2007). From this perspective, all tools available to situate the text should be employed in analysis of discourse (Wetherell 2007) as language data is one component embedded in a complex system full of components influencing any given talk or text.

In proposing DCOE, Androutsopoulos (2010) argues that researchers must engage online texts and environments as dynamic, using discourse analysis in longitudinal studies focused on discourse practices online. Androutsopoulos further proposes systematic observation and direct contact with participants, coupled with discourse analysis of user text, to provide the best perspective on online data. With longitudinal user observation, user accounts of their own action and discourse analysis, data can be compared and contrasted and analysts can move between local and global phenomena. Although the LE goal to 'get familiar' with speaker experience (Rampton et al. 2004: 12) through holistic descriptions of contextualised talk differs from my goal to explain category emergence in YouTube discourse, using LE methods to situate user talk is likely to help explain group emergence. Androutsopoulos (2010) then suggests that, within the observation of and contact with users, the analyst investigates user talk, employing an analytic framework for the talk contained on a given site. The form of discourse analysis can develop in a recursive process of observation and refining of research questions, leading the analyst to the most useful discourse analytic tools for a particular online environment. In an attempt to trace the dynamics of user talk about categorisation in the dataset (necessary to fully answer the research question), my analysis of the video page interaction will employ two forms of discourse analysis: membership categorisation analysis and discourse-led metaphor analysis.

Built on the early lectures of conversational analyst Harvey Sacks' analysis of calls made to suicide prevention lines in the 1960s (Sacks 1995), membership categorisation analysis (MCA) describes the 'procedures people employ to make sense of other people and their activities' (Leudar, Marsland and Nekvapil 2004: 244) and describes the process by which people use everyday knowledge to categorise the world around them (Sacks 1995; Lepper 2000). Sacks used an example taken from a child's story ('The baby cried, the mommy picked it up') to show how listeners were able to infer the relationship between the mother and child using rules of membership in categories and membership categorisation devices (MCDs) or 'collection[s of categories] plus rules of application [...]' (Lepper 2000: 17). Categories can be any way of grouping together people, actions or locations (Schegloff 2007) and can be grouped together into collections of categories. In the above example, Sacks argued the hearer understands the two categories (mommy and baby) in terms of the collection of 'family' and the category-bound activity of 'picking up'. MCDs provide the guide for placing members into categories and provide an accounting for the resources or common sense people take for granted when categorising others (Eglin and Hester 2003). Categories can be explicitly stated in talk or inferred from the context.

Although categorisation is a clear theme in the dataset, longitudinal observation and initial analysis of categorisation led me to include analysis of metaphor in the dataset as well. Drawing on previous work (Pihlaja 2010, 2011a, 2011b), dynamics of metaphor use (Cameron 2003, 2007; Cameron et al. 2009; Zanotto, Cameron and Cavalcanti 2008; Cameron and Maslen 2010) will also be employed to analyse metaphor use, complementing categorisation analysis. A discourse dynamics approach to metaphor studies begins with the notions of complex systems theory, in which metaphor is not 'a static, fixed mapping, but a temporary stability emerging from the activity of interconnecting systems of socially-situated language use and cognitive activity' (Cameron et al. 2009:

64). This approach is particularly appropriate for researchers interested in how language is organised in discourse, not in conscious, prescribed ways but as naturally occurring from the interactions of the speakers. In the context of asynchronous Internet text where videos exist in a dynamic environment with responses and comments being produced by different users, mapping the dynamic interactions particularly around categorisation is likely to show how metaphorical language emerges from use. Although the definition of metaphor has been debated, I understand metaphor in terms of transfer of meaning; metaphor is 'seeing something in terms of something else' (Burke 1945: 503). Metaphor begins with a 'focus term or vehicle' in the text, which is incongruous with the surrounding text and context and in which the incongruity can be understood by some 'transfer of meaning' between the vehicle and the topic (Cameron 2003: 60).

Based on these tools, I will now introduce the particular video analysed in this chapter by providing the necessary background and presenting the drama episode from which it came.

2 'I doubt Jezuzfreek is saved'

In contrast to the previous research, I am less interested in describing the typical YouTuber, but rather more interested in describing a particular subset of YouTubers: Evangelical Christians. Although categorisation of Christians is at the heart of this chapter, given the diverse meanings of 'Christian', it is necessary to describe in analytic terms the users in the dataset. Although the term 'Evangelical Christian' is not employed by the users, it provides a useful starting point to encompass a majority of users observed. Bebbington (1989: 19) describes an 'Evangelical Christian' as strongly agreeing that 'through the life, death and resurrection of Jesus, God provided a way for the forgiveness of my sins' (crucicentrism); strongly agreeing that 'the Bible is the inspired word of God' or agreeing to whatever degree that 'the Bible is God's word, and is to be taken literally, word for word' (biblicism); strongly agreeing that 'I have committed my life to Christ and consider myself to be a converted Christian' (conversionism); and agreeing or agreeing strongly that 'it is important to encourage non-Christians to become Christians' (activism). Although the Evangelical YouTubers in my dataset do not ever explicitly attest to a certain set of religious beliefs, it does seem that Bebbington's four descriptions apply generally to the group.

Observation of the Evangelical YouTubers in the dataset began in 2007, starting with observation of one atheist YouTuber who broadly criticised religion and religious users on the site. This is done through following connections to this user by observing who made video responses to his videos, who he discussed in his videos and commenters. Following this pattern of identifying potential connections, I was able to build a group of between 15–20 Christian and atheist users who frequently interacted with one another. The number of users fluctuated during the observation period, as certain YouTubers joined and left the site. In the course of the observation period I also began to identify potential 'drama episodes' for analysis, particularly episodes in which users took positions that aligned with or distanced themselves from other users. Inclusion of atheists in the dataset was necessary, as users frequently interacted with one another, and it would be impossible (as I will show in the data) to understand the interaction of the Evangelical Christians on the site without also considering their interaction with atheists, as this interaction is, especially in this dataset, a key source of disagreement. Although linguistic ethnography (LE) takes an explicitly emic perspective (often informed by user interviews and participant observation), attempts were made to contact users but this largely failed, and I was unable to elicit reports from users about their perceptions of interaction; therefore I relied only on reports from videos.

In early 2009, an episode of drama began when the Evangelical Christian YouTuber *Yokeup* used the term 'human garbage' in a subsequently removed video. In the video, *Yokeup* calls an atheist user *crosisborg* (CB) 'human garbage' in response to insulting comments CB had made in an earlier (also subsequently removed) video about *Yokeup*'s wife. In this video and others *Yokeup* produced during January 2009, *Yokeup* makes the claim that calling someone 'human garbage' is based on the biblical parable of the vinedresser and the branches (John 15: 1–24). The initial exchange between CB and *Yokeup* is marked by insults and strong disagreement and results in a long-term argument among *Yokeup*, atheists and other Christians over whether or not *Yokeup* should use this term. I attempted to identify videos which were both related to the drama episode and still posted on the site. Starting with a search of the term 'human garbage', potential videos related to the dramatic episode were identified as appearing in the search and/or from examining responses to these videos and/or videos made around the time the controversy was responded to by key users, but which did not appear in the search as the text 'human garbage' was not attached to the video. After 40 videos were identified as having some relation to the dramatic episode, I determined that there were 24 videos which related directly to this episode and were posted either near the time of the drama or re-posted later, but in obvious reference to the episode.

YouTube provides users two options when they post a video: they can keep the video private and only viewable to friends, or they can publish the video openly on the site, allowing for access by anyone at any time. Although the distinction between private and public space in social networks has been problematised, most notably by Lange (2007) in discussing how users present themselves in YouTube videos, in terms of the technical function of the site, YouTube is clear about the implications of posting videos publicly. Its user policy states explicitly: 'Any videos that you submit to the YouTube Sites may be redistributed through the Internet and other media channels, and may be viewed by the general public' (YouTube 2010). Because of this, informed consent to use the videos was not obtained.

Videos were transcribed and entered into the qualitative analysis software Atlas.TI, where I coded all categories and metaphors. I identified a category as any word or phrase used to describe a group of people (e. g., Christians, atheists, the religious) and metaphors using Cameron's vehicle identification procedure (Cameron 2003). Although the videos included responses from both atheists and Christians, this chapter will focus primarily on the response of Christians to the use of the term, particularly in one video in which *Yokeup* makes explicit issue of Evangelical Christian categorisation, wondering whether one user in particular, *jezuzfreek777*, is 'saved' or whether he is simply 'religious'. The video was made in April 2009, well into the drama episode, and addresses *Yokeup*'s sense that other Christian users have joined with atheists in denouncing his use of 'human garbage' in insulting *crosisborg*.

Figure 1 shows the key information about the video.

Figure 1: Video information: 'I doubt JezuzFreek is saved ...'

Description

'...but my opinion doesn't matter ... think about it, think about what Jesus Christ taught us, and then make your own choice as to how you want to respond to God ...'

YokeUp Ministries
http://www.yokeup.net

URL	http://www.youtube.com/watch?v=cAm5HUfSO4U		
Time	9:45 (mins:secs)	**Date**	25 April 2009
Views	2,331 [18 – 5-10]	**Comments**	93 [18 – 5-10]
Tags	YokeUp, Ministries, Salvation, Jesus, Christ	**Category**	People and Blogs

The description box text and tags were written by the user, *Yokeup*, and the number of views and comments were taken at the time of transcription on 18 May 2010. As the video is not still online, the number of views and comments may have continued to increase before its withdrawal, but, as with most videos on YouTube, there is generally a period of high traffic when the video is first posted, which can be assumed to have passed for this video. As new videos are made, both the number of comments and views tend to stabilise, as users watch and comment on new videos.

In another article (Pihlaja 2011b) I present a more in-depth textual analysis of the video, identifying all categories and their interaction with metaphorical language, but for this chapter I focus only on the development of two categories, 'saved' and 'religious', in both the video and the text comments.

3 Video analysis

The video (*YokedtoJesus* 2009) is recorded early in the morning and starts with a video bumper[1] that *Yokeup* has used on many of his videos, and this includes the man counting down from 5 and loud music playing. The image consists of *Yoke-up*, a middle-aged American man, standing in front of what appears to be his house as the sun is coming up behind him. *Yokeup* is wearing a t-shirt with cut-off sleeves, and the tattoos on both of his arms are clearly visible. As in many of his videos, *Yokeup* makes the video after returning from working out and is sweaty and energetic in his presentation. There are small edits made throughout the video, but *Yokeup* does not appear to have prepared the actual content of the video, although as a frequent vlogger his delivery is clear and relaxed throughout. At the beginning of the video, he greets the viewer loudly over the sound of the edited-in music, shouting 'Good morning!' while the music fades. He stops and listens quietly to the sound of birds singing in the background and says to the camera, 'Listen to that' and returns to listening to the birds. After several seconds, he comments, 'We serve an awesome God' and reminds the viewer that God has created all the animals before repeating, 'We serve an awesome God'.

After the opening of the video, *Yokeup* begins to address the main topic contained in the title 'I doubt JezuzFreek is saved'. Speaking directly to the camera, *Yokeup* says the following:

> But one interesting thing that that I've been thinking about: I wonder if jezuzfreek is saved. I wonder if he's had a salvation moment. I wonder if Paula's saved, if she's had a salvation moment. And you know, I, I [sic] wonder about a lot of people. A lot of people that claim to be Christians, and it seems to be a theme in the Baptist community, you know, are they re-

---

1 An element that acts as a transition, e. g., to or from commercial breaks, or, as in this case, at the start or end of a video clip (see http://en.wikipedia.org/wiki/List_of_broadcasting_terms, accessed 27.6.13).

ligious or are they saved? I mean, is the holy spirit, have they, have they [sic] had that moment when the holy spirit comes into their heart, and uh, the reason, uh, and you know, and in [the Christian user] hislivingsacrifice's, Paula's video, you know, she talked about church in one of her videos; she talked about church. And um, and she said, 'You know, it's more like a fashion show'. And, and it's kind of struck me, are you going to church to be seen? Are you going to church to hear the word of God? You know, we preach down at the truck stop every Sunday. Ain't no fashion show. It's people hungry to hear the word of God, and I, uh, and I thank God for that church. I thank God for, for putting us in the ministry of preaching at a truck stop, um, because when people show up, they're hungry for God. And I don't care if there's two in there or ten in there. I don't care, you know? I'd rather be talking to those folks who are hungry to hear the word of God, rather than to be seen and, you know, have it be a fashion show. (*YokedtoJesus* 2009).

In this extract, *Yokeup* employs two common descriptions of Christians: 'saved' and 'religious', but goes on to develop how other YouTubers can be placed into these two categories. First, *Yokeup* identifies two users for potential inclusion in the 'religious' category: Paula and *jezuzfreck777*. *Jezuzfreek777*, who the title of the video identifies as someone that *Yokeup* doubts is saved, is identified as potentially religious rather than saved because *Yokeup* wonders if he has had a 'salvation moment', suggesting that one key difference between the religious and the saved is 'a moment when the holy spirit comes into [one's] heart'. Although the term 'salvation moment' appears elsewhere in *Yokeup*'s discourse, here there is little description of what this moment might entail and how one might know if another has had one. Paula, another Evangelical Christian YouTuber who subsequently closed her account after the drama episode, is also singled out for 'religious' categorisation. *Yokeup* positions Paula and *jezuzfreek777* both as also not having had a salvation moment, but he presents Paula as engaging in an additional category-bound activity similar to that of *jezuzfreek777*: she is overly concerned with appearances rather than with 'hearing the word of God'.

Categorised with Paula and *jezuzfreek777* are several other groups that are also suspected of being 'religious' rather than 'saved'. First, *Yokeup* suggests that 'a lot of people' fall into the 'religious' category. Moreover, not only Paula but Paula's church, and not only her church but the 'Baptist community', are included in the potentially 'religious' category. Paula's church is included in this category based on *Yokeup*'s reporting of Paula's speech that the church treats meetings as 'fashion shows' rather than instances to 'hear the word of God'. Throughout the video, although *Yokeup* repeatedly talks about other groups of users, 'Baptist' is the only denomination of Evangelical Christian mentioned. *Yokeup* makes it clear in his description of the users that their actions are evidence of their placement in the 'religious' category, not their denominational affiliation. What they have or have not done is explicitly the issue for *Yokeup*, not what they believe or which church they attend.

The category of 'saved' by contrast appears implicitly in the section, namely as the inverse of the category-bound activities of the religious. The contrast, however, does not occur between *Yokeup* and Paula or *jezuzfreek777*, but rather between the institutions they are associated with. *Yokeup* doesn't present himself in contrast to Paula and her church; rather he says of the truck stop church, 'It ain't no fashion show'. Instead, he says, 'It's people hungry to hear the word of God'. Although *Yokeup* and his wife Caroline are put 'in the ministry' of the truck stop church, the description of the people attending is not a description of *Yokeup per se*, but of the other attendees of the church. In addition to not being a fashion show and being populated by people hungry to hear the word of God, *Yokeup* states that he doesn't care how many people attend, another statement that contrasts with *jezuzfreek777* who, as *Yokeup* goes on to describe him, is overly concerned with the number of people hearing his message, a 'subwhore'[2] who is more concerned about the popularity of his message than the content.

As the video progresses, *Yokeup* includes discussion of another set of users, including several atheists and Christians who *Yokeup* doesn't regard as 'saved', further expounding the difference between the 'saved' and the 'religious' Christians on YouTube. In particular, *Yokeup* criticises *jezuzfreek* for 'considering as a friend' and 'hanging out with' an atheist YouTuber, *tommyfromthebronx*, with whom *Yokeup* also occasionally had an adversarial relationship. In this instance, *Yokeup* contrasts *jezuzfreek*'s actions with those of Jesus, whom he describes as not caring about numbers and reaching out to the 'lost', but being 'adamant' about not being friends or buddies with those to whom he was reaching out.

Instead, *Yokeup* presents Jesus as preaching what he considers a 'hard' message to his disciples, saying, 'Look, this road's getting awfully hard, man. You know, if you ain't willin to sell everything and, and uh, you know, come and follow me, and give it all up, you know'.

In this presentation of Jesus's message (apparently a re-voicing of Luke 18:22), *Yokeup* presents the message of Jesus as aggressive and difficult, not intended to gain great numbers of followers and causing many people to leave him. Although *Yokeup* seems to accept that Jesus was at times popular, he casts Jesus as rejecting a popular message in favour of a hard message that drove people away from him.

---

2 Subscriber whore: apparently someone who is willing to do anything to increase the number of people subscribed to their channel.

In this extract, *jezuzfreek777* is cast in opposition not to other religious people but against Jesus, who is presented as the ideal. Again, *Yokeup* does not explicitly align himself with Jesus (*Yokeup* is also critical of *jezuzfreek777*'s apparent lack of humility), the re-voicing of scripture in the extract above appears to match the voice of *Yokeup*, in particular his marked use of the word 'ain't', which *Yokeup* doesn't consistently use. Although *Yokeup* doesn't describe himself as saved, by setting up the categories at the beginning of the video and following through a description of *jezuzfreek777* in opposition not only to Christians he sees as saved but to the ideal person, Jesus himself, *Yokeup* is able to implicitly align himself with Jesus and *jezuzfreek777* with the 'absolute evil' users on YouTube.

I will now turn to the text comments posted on the video to investigate how other users interact not only with *Yokeup*'s description of *jezuzfreek777* but also with the categories of 'religious' and 'saved', and to what extent categorisations are accepted by commenters.

3 Text comments

Before beginning analysis of the text comments, it is important to keep in mind that the video producer (in this case, the user *Yokeup* on the *yokedtojesus* channel) retains control of who may or may not comment on his or her video. In the case of *Yokeup*, his channel page features very clear rules for commenters, stating that he will delete comments that he feels to be inappropriate. To what extent comments are deleted is only known by the channel owner, but it does appear that *Yokeup* frequently deletes comments and blocks users. The absence, for example, of atheist commenters and antagonistic comments seems to be a function of *Yokeup*'s censorship of his channel, and the analyst must be aware, in looking at the comments, that all have been approved by *Yokeup*, with the strong possibility that others who may have hoped to comment were unable to. Moreover, users whom *Yokeup* had blocked in the past would also be unable to comment on the videos, which may explain why there are no comments from either *jezuzfreek777* or *hislivingsacrifice*, to whom the video is ostensibly addressed. At the time the data was accessed, 18 months after the video had been posted, there were 93 comments on the video and 2,426 views.

In the comments section, *Yokeup*'s 'saved' and 'religious' categories are both recognised and engaged by other users, particularly by those who appear to be Evangelical Christian users, but categorisation appears to be explicitly at issue. *Ele12957* writes:

Jeff,[3] saved people can become religious and religious people can get saved. I don't doubt Jesusfreek is truly saved, I may not agree with him on everything he says but I have listened to him enough to know he has a relationship with God and have heard him talk about his born again experience.[4]

In this comment, the question does not appear to concern whether or not the description of someone as 'religious' or 'saved' is in any way inappropriate, but that *Yokeup* has mislabelled *jezuzfreek777* as not being 'truly' saved (an addition to the category that is not present in *Yokeup*'s talk) because he appears to have a 'relationship with God'. Rather than describe the same category-bound activity that *Yokeup* has described, namely having a 'salvation moment', *ele12957* understands his perception of *jezuzfreek777*'s 'relationship with God' as being a sign of true salvation.

Yokeup engages with the commenter, stressing a new category-bound activity of the saved, namely that saved people, like Jesus, do not 'condone' sin or 'compromise with sinners'. *Yokeup* writes, '[A]bsolutely, and YOU NEVER compromise Christ for sin ... [Y]ou never take the side of sin against Christ[.] JF sides with the sinners, encourages their arguments, joins in on them, partakes with them, doesn't stand outside of the sin', adding, '[T]he lost need to know that many "posers" claiming to have Christ are flat out liars and deceivers, they need to know that the standards of Christ are not to be negotiated, or compromised ... EVER!' Here, the religious category is conflated with a new category, 'posers', which is extended to include 'liars' and 'deceivers'. The conflation of the categories implicates *jezuzfreek777* in much more serious negative behaviour, i.e., lying and deceiving, without making a clear statement about *jezuzfreek777* in particular. Rather than stating, '*jezuzfreek777* is a liar', *Yokeup* is able to imply that *jezuzfreek777* lies through a series of equivalency statements about categories and the category-bound activities members engage in.

Metaphor also plays a role in categorisation, as in the video *Yokeup* claims that jezuzfreek's decision to 'hang out with' the atheists was also wrong, as Jesus never 'hung out' with sinners. Attempting to clarify this activity, *MrTh1rteen* writes, 'He did continue to "hang out" (Don't think that's an accurate phrase, sry 4 using it) while they were in sin because they were Always in sin. He never once condoned any of their sins. The fact is Jesus preached to ALL, he didn't keep himself away from people who were demonic'. *MrTh1rteen* recognises the difficulty of employing a description of a user's actions as 'hanging out', be-

---

3 *Yokeup*'s real name.
4 Text comments often contain typographical errors. All comments in this chapter have been reproduced as they are found on the video page.

cause what does or does not constitute 'hanging out' is ultimately ambiguous. Although the metaphor is identified at this point, *Yokeup* and *MrTh1rteen* continue to employ it in their exchange, with *Yokeup* responding, 'Amen, and what did Jesus do when He hung out with them? care to share those details... did Jesus condone their sins, continue to hang out with them for years while they lived in sin? well, did HE?', and *MrTh1rteen* responding, 'Jesus hung out with tax collectors, who at that time were not highly thought of. When questioned he responded, "it's not the healthy that need a doctor He didn't hang out with the pharasis (sp?) in fact he criticized the "men of god" at the time'. Although the metaphor has been flagged by *MrTh1rteen* as being potentially too ambiguous to be useful, both continue to employ it, negotiating some shared, pragmatically applicable definition that appears to be mutually acceptable.

The text comments show that debate between users that *Yokeup* is happy to include on his page (rather than delete) includes categories from the video which users seem happy to accept, but that users are unhappy with *Yokeup*'s decision to categorise *jezuzfreek777* as religious rather than saved. To contest this rather than reject the categories, the users reject elements of *Yokeup*'s categorisation, often made possible by the ambiguity of the language that *Yokeup* has initially employed. Yokeup, in response, posits new categories and new categorisations, expanding on what is said in the video in some cases but also appealing to new ways of describing *jezuzfreek777*'s actions in others. In doing so, he is able to continue to hold his position that *jezuzfreek777*'s behaviour is unacceptable, regardless of the categorical label applied to it.

4 Discussion

Based on the analysis of the video and comments, I would like to draw together three main points of discussion to consider what *Yokeup*'s categorisation of *jezuzfreek777* might tell about how affiliation and opposition are performed on YouTube.

1) Unlike traditional church denominations, the categories and categorisations in the video and video comments were user-dependent.

Rather than employing categories that might be easily discussed in terms of what a user may or may not believe, in this video, *Yokeup* uses the categories 'saved' and 'religious' only in relation to how he perceives certain users behaving on the site rather than the particular beliefs they hold. In the dataset, users did not, in most cases, present their denominational affiliations. Although I have employed the term 'Evangelical', it is an analyst's term, as no user in this video, the video comments or the whole of the 24-video dataset uses the term

'Evangelical'. Rather, there seems to be a particular aversion to denominational labels for most of the Evangelicals, and when a denominational label does appear in this video (in *Yokeup*'s reference to the 'Baptist' community), it is used in a negative way. Although there is an aversion to using denominational labels, the term 'Christian' does not appear to be sufficient for the users on the site, requiring users like *Yokeup* to appeal to different descriptions of Christians that are not based on the particular beliefs that another user holds (especially when other users whom one perceives as different from oneself claim to hold identical beliefs), but rather on how *Yokeup* perceives their actions on the site aligning with his own.

Although one might expect users from different denominations to argue about doctrinal issues, this drama episode is less about issues of faith and more about the behaviours of individuals on the site. *Yokeup*'s argument against *jezuzfreek777* and Paula is ultimately a behavioural one, questioning whether or not they have become too close to atheists on the site and whether or not they are as eager as *Yokeup* to aggressively speak what *Yokeup* believes to be the truth to others on YouTube. Although *Yokeup* does not explicitly cast himself as the model Christian, his positioning in contrast to the religious suggests that he views not only his beliefs about God to be the best, but, perhaps more importantly, he views his behaviour to be appropriate and the ideal expression of Christianity, fighting evil and proclaiming the truth. His denominational affiliation is inconsequential in relation to this.

2) Categories seemed to be rooted in standardised Christian discourse, but the categorisations of users were dynamic and contextually dependent.

The notion of 'religious' and 'saved' Christians is not absent in offline Evangelical Christian discourse, and it seems, as evidenced in the comments on the video, that both categories are accepted by the viewers. In Evangelical discourse, 'saved' and 'religious' categorisation can be seen in discourse surrounding the notions of religious works rather than salvation by grace. From this Evangelical belief, as seen in Bebbington's definition given earlier, the only way one can be 'saved' is by believing 'through the life, death and resurrection of Jesus, God provided a way for the forgiveness of my sins'. The religious, on the other hand, are shown as believing that one must also do some amount of 'good works' to be saved. Evangelicals root this teaching in Jesus Christ's own teaching against the Pharisees throughout the New Testament and can be particularly critical of forms of Christianity (particularly Catholicism) which include some notion of 'good works' in addition to salvation by grace.

In the video, however, although *Yokeup* draws on this standard narrative in Evangelical Christianity, the two users he singles out are both also Evangelical Christians who appear to hold the same belief as *Yokeup* in regard to salvation by grace alone. The categories that he uses, 'religious' and 'saved', then carry with them not only the negative value he ascribes to them in his talk through the descriptions of the negative category-bound activities attributed to the category 'religious', but also fixed notions of 'religious' Christians that users may already have. By employing the category as well as his own description of category-bound activities, *Yokeup* is able to link what appears to already be a stabilised, negative evaluation of certain kinds of Christians by Evangelicals with his own mobilisation of the term, built on categorisations that are emergent in his talk. The result is a negative evaluation through a category that is both stabilised and remade in the context.

3) Metaphor provided the affordance of ambiguity, creating more flexible categorisation that did not include empirically verifiable descriptions.

What is particularly interesting about *Yokeup*'s use of the 'fashion show' metaphor in describing Paula and Paula's church is the inability to precisely identify when a church would be behaving in this way. Unlike statements of belief in which clear, canonised disagreements might be identified (particularly between denominations), it's unclear what empirical criteria might be applied to distinguish 'religious' churches and people from 'saved' people. The 'fashion show' church is contrasted with the 'truck stop' church. Although the church does meet in a truck stop, the description of it as a 'truck stop' church suggests a different environment than a fashion show, with different members from different class backgrounds. The difference between the two is both readily accessible in the metaphors used, provided the viewer has a basic knowledge of both the fashion show and the truck stop concepts, and fundamentally obscured, even as *Yokeup* goes on to describe the members of his own church. *Yokeup* says that attendees of his own church are 'hungry for the word of God', another metaphorical description that is also not explicitly described. Rather, the categorisations seem to be built on his impressions of both churches and groups of believers rather than observed doctrinal differences.

The difference, however, is performed by *Yokeup* as he stands in his front yard in a sleeveless t-shirt, having just returned from working out and with his heavily tattooed arms clearly displayed. By tying himself to the truck stop church and presenting himself as not caring about outward appearances, *Yokeup* is able to distance himself from the 'religious', both in his description of his own church and his appearance. In performing authenticity in this way and describing his religious experience in terms of 'listening to the word of God', he suggests that his interpretation of God's word is more accurate because it is more authentic, particularly as he hasn't done anything to present it or himself in a false way. He, in contrast to *jezuzfreek777* and in the same manner as Jesus, doesn't care about the perception of others, only about listening to the word of God. *Yokeup* performs his affiliation with Jesus further by embodying the voice of Jesus in his own voice and colloquial expressions, presenting himself as not only aligned with the teachings of Jesus but speaking in the same aggressive, simple way. Conversely, when speaking in the voice of *jezuzfreek777*, *Yokeup* presents an individual focused on popularity and numbers of viewers, a clear contrast to Jesus and *Yokeup*.

5 Conclusion

Membership categorisation and metaphor analysis reveal that *Yokeup* mobilised two recognised categories in Evangelical Christian discourse, 'saved' and 'religious', to position himself and other Christians in the drama episode, but that the criteria he employed to make these categorisations were dynamic and dependent on descriptions of other users rather than fixed descriptions of denominations or articles of belief. The subsequent comments revealed that *Yokeup*'s categories were recognised and accepted by others in response, but that there was disagreement over how *Yokeup* had categorised others. The analysis also showed that metaphor use in categorisation created ambiguity about precisely what activity was acceptable or not and allowed *Yokeup* to present the behaviour of others as inappropriate for 'saved' Christians without clear, specific boundaries for appropriate or inappropriate actions. The analysis suggests that, rather than belief or conventional denominational affiliations or particular theological positions, the extent to which *Yokeup* recognised the actions of others as similar to his own descriptions of proper behaviour dictated his categorisation of and, consequently, his affiliation with or opposition to other users.

Given the relatively small amount of data included in this analysis, precautions must be taken to applying any findings on a larger scale. Indeed, although the dramatic episode was part of a longitudinal observation period, the extent to which the findings apply to this group of users alone is unknown. More work is needed to investigate the extent to which dynamic categorisation plays a role in YouTube discourse more generally or whether other groups of users engage more readily with traditional denominational categories. Still, the findings seem to suggest that particular YouTube contexts provide challenges to traditional means of thinking about religious or denominational affiliation. If users in the dataset were less concerned with established means of identifying belief and more with descriptions of actions on the site, it seems that, at least in this small dataset, which belief statement one claims to adhere to is ultimately less important than how others perceive one's online activity. If this is indeed the case in a broader context, it requires a rethinking of the role of denominational affiliation online and new theories for describing how users of faith identify and affiliate with like-minded users in online fora like YouTube.

References

Androutsopoulos, Jannis. 2008. *Potentials and Limitations of Discourse-Centred Online Ethnography.* Available at: http://www.languageatinternet.org/articles/2008/1610.
–. 2010. "Localising the global on the participatory web." In *Handbook of Language and Globalization*, edited by N. Coupland, *203–222.* Oxford: Wiley-Blackwell.
Bebbington, David W. 1989. *Evangelicalism in Modern Britain: A History from the 1730s to the 1980s.* London: Routledge.
Benevenuto, Fabricio, F. Duarte, T. Rodrigues, V. Almeida, J. Almeida, and K. Ross. 2008. "Understanding video interactions in YouTube." Unpublished conference paper, 16th ACM International Conference on Multimedia, MM'08, October 26–31, 2008, Vancouver, British Columbia, Canada.
Burgess, Jean, and Joshua Green. 2008. "Agency and Controversy in the YouTube Community." Unpublished conference paper, Internet Research 9.0: Rethinking Community, Rethinking Place. 15–18 October: Copenhagen.
–. 2009. *YouTube: Online Video and Participatory Culture.* Cambridge: Polity Press.
Burke, Kenneth. 1945. *A Grammar of Motives.* New York: Prentice Hall.
Cameron, Lynne. 2003. *Metaphor in Educational Research.* London: Continuum.
–. 2007. "Patterns of metaphor use in reconciliation talk." *Discourse and Society* 18 (2): 197–222.
Cameron, Lynne, and Robert Maslen, eds. 2010. *Metaphor Analysis: Research Practice in Applied Linguistics, Social Sciences and the Humanities.* London: Equinox.
Cameron, Lynne, R. Maslen, Z. Todd, J. Maule, P. Stratton, and N. Stanley. 2009. "The discourse dynamics approach to metaphor and metaphor-led discourse analysis." *Metaphor and Symbol* 24 (2): 63–89.
Duman, Steve, and M. Locher. 2008. "'So let's talk. Let's chat. Let's start a dialog': An analysis of the conversation metaphor employed in Clinton's and Obama's YouTube campaign clips." *Multilingua – Journal of Cross-Cultural and Interlanguage Communication* 27 (3): 193–230.
Eglin, Peter, and S. Hester. 2003. *The Montreal Massacre: A Story of Membership Categorization Analysis.* Waterloo: Wilfrid Laurier University Press.
Garcés-Conejos Blitvich, Pilar. 2010. "The *YouTubification* of politics, impoliteness and polarization." In *Handbook of Research on Discourse Behaviour and Digital Communication: Language Structures and Social Interaction*, edited by T. Rotimi, 540–563. Hershey, PA: IGI Global.
Hilderbrand, Lucas. 2007. YouTube: Where cultural memory and copyright converge. *Film Quarterly* 61 (1): 48–57.
Lange, Patricia. 2007. "Publicly private and privately public: Social networking on YouTube." *Journal of Computer-Mediated Communication* 13 (1): 361–380.
Lepper, Georgia. 2000. *Categories in Text and Talk.* London: Sage.

Leudar, Ivan, V. Marsland, and J. Nekvapil. 2004. "On membership categorization: 'Us', 'them' and 'doing violence' in political discourse." *Discourse and Society* 15 (2/3): 243–266.

Lorenzo-Dus, Nuria, P. Garcés-Conejos Blitvich, and P. Bou-Franch. 2011. "On-line polylogues and impoliteness: The case of postings sent in response to the Obama Reggaeton YouTube video." *Journal of Pragmatics* 43 (10): 2578–2593.

Madden, Mary. 2007. "Online video: 57 % of internet users have watched videos online and most of them share what they find with others." *Pew Internet and American Life Project.* http://www.pewinternet.org/Reports/2007/Online-Video.aspx.

Maia, Marcelo, J. Almeida, and V. Almeida. 2008. "Identifying user behavior in online social networks." Unpublished conference paper, First Workshop on Social Network Systems. Glasgow, UK: April 1–4.

O'Brien, Damien., and Fitzgerald, B. 2006. "Digital copyright law in a YouTube world". *Internet Law Bulletin.* 9(6 /7): 71–74.

O'Donnell, Susan, K. Gibson, M. Milliken, and J. Singer. 2008. "Reacting to YouTube videos: Exploring differences among user groups." *Proceedings of the International Communication Association Annual Conference.* http://nparc.cisti-icist.nrc-cnrc.gc.ca/npsi/ctrl?action=rtdoc&an=8914081&article=0&lang=en.

Pihlaja, Stephen. 2010. "The pope of YouTube: Metaphor and misunderstanding in atheist-Christian YouTube dialogue." *The Journal of Inter-Religious Dialogue* 3: 25–35.

–. 2011a. "Cops, popes, kings, and garbagemen: A case study of dynamic metaphor use in asynchronous Internet communication." *Language@Internet* 1. Available at: http://www.languageatinternet.de/articles/2011/pihlaja.

–. 2011b. "'Are you religious or are you saved?': Defining membership categorisation rules in religious discussions on YouTube." *Fieldwork in Religion* 6 (1): 27–46.

Rampton, Ben, K. Tusting, J. Maybin, R. Barwell, A. Creese, and V. Lytra. 2004. *UK Linguistic Ethnography: A Discussion Paper.* Available at: http://www.lancs.ac.uk/fss/organisations/lingethn/documents/discussion_paper_-jan_05.pdf.

Sacks, Harvey. 1995. *Lectures on Conversation.* Oxford: Blackwell.

Schegloff, Emanuel A. 2007. "A tutorial on membership categorization." *Journal of Pragmatics* 39 (3): 462–482.

Snelson, Chareen. 2008. "YouTube and beyond: Integrating web-based video into online education." *Technology and Teacher Education Annual* 19 (2): 732–737.

Tusting, Karin, and J. Maybin. 2007. "Linguistic ethnography and interdisciplinarity: Opening the discussion." *Journal of Sociolinguistics* 11 (5): 575–583.

van Zoonen, Liesbet, F. Vis, and S. Mihelj. 2010. "Performing citizenship on YouTube: Activism, satire and online debate around the anti-Islam video Fitna." *Critical Discourse Studies* 7 (4): 249–262.

Wetherell, Margaret. 2007. "A step too far: Discursive psychology, linguistic ethnography and questions of identity." *Journal of Sociolinguistics* 11 (5): 661–81.

YokedtoJesus. 2009. *I Doubt JezuzFreek is Saved … .* Available at: http://www.youtube.com/watch?v=cAm5HUfSO4U. Accessed: 21 April 2010.

YouTube. 2010. *YouTube Community Guidelines.* Available at: http://www.youtube.com/t/community_guidelines. Accessed: 1 April 2010.

Zanotto, Mara Sophia, L. Cameron, and M.C. Cavalcanti, eds. 2008. *Confronting Metaphor in Use: An applied linguistic approach.* Amsterdam: John Benjamins.

Heidi A. Campbell and Drake Fulton

10 Bounded Religious Communities' Management of the Challenge of New Media: Baha'í Negotiation with the Internet

The negotiation of new forms of media by religious groups is a dynamic and complex process that involves decision-making engaging the history, tradition and beliefs of the community. This negotiation process is especially complex for bounded religious communities, which establish rigid social and value-laden boundaries allowing them to create and maintain a unique and separate cultural system. Observing how members of bounded religious communities interact with the Internet enables us to consider how some groups resist the fluidity of networked relations and instead use technology to maintain closed social structures and solidify their unique identities. This is clearly seen in the case of the Bahá'í faith, especially in the patterns of use and limits American Bahá'ís have developed to engage with the Internet. By using the Religious Social Shaping of Technology approach, developed by Campbell (2010), as a lens to explore the challenges and choices made by the Bahá'ís, this process of technological negotiation is unpacked.

1 Bounded religious community and new media

Bounded community is a term used to describe groups who live within a fixed geographic region and/or possess strict ideological boundaries limiting their engagement with outside groups. It has also been used to as a way to discuss tensions that arise between groups attempting to maintain tight identity structures in light of the increasingly permeable social boundaries of a networked society. Describing a group as a bounded community can be challenging. In one sense all communities are bounded, in that all communities possess certain boundaries related to their quintessential characteristics, such as membership, identity or locality. In the 1980s, identifying a group as a bounded community within the sociology of community studies became a way to distinguish traditional communities constrained by geography and familial small-scale relations with more contemporary notions of community as a network of social relations where boundaries are permeable (Wellman 1979; 1988). It also draws on the notion that all communities are symbolically constructed, and their identity formation and presentation is based on varying degrees of boundary maintenance in order to maintain the desired continuity of community (Cohen 1965). Bounded communities thus become a way to talk about certain normative inclinations of groups, such as constraints forming the basis for identity construction, organization and control of people, materials and territories (Linklater 1988: 133).

The notion of a bounded community is important when considering certain forms of religious community. It is useful as it denotes those religious groups which seek to live within a constrained social and cultural system that seeks to resist the forces and patterns of life within modern networked society. In this chapter the concept of the bounded community draws attention to the fact that some religious groups actively seek to mark out and protect their identities in a cultural milieu that encourages fluidity of identity and relations over static and controlled ones.

Researchers have found that the ambiguity and fluidity of postmodern culture encourages the creation of hybrid or blended cultural spaces among many groups that were traditionally tightly-knit groups, such as ethnic minorities (e. g., Waldinger 2007). This ambiguity is accentuated by the social affordances of digital technology that can make it difficult to retain a cohesive identity structure. Increasingly, religious community leaders struggle to monitor the practices and interactions of their members with external sources, as the Internet can make it easier for members to bypass traditional gatekeepers and channels of control (Livio and Teneboim 2007). This struggle raises provocative questions about how new media technologies such as the Internet are impacting community authority and power relations, especially conservative and fundamentalist groups' negotiation with the Internet (Howard 2000; Shandler 2009). In order to carefully consider how bounded communities negotiate new media usage we turn to the social shaping of technology, which we argue provides a clear frame for studying this phenomenon.

2 The social shaping of technology as a frame for understanding media appropriation

One way to approach how bounded communities negotiate their use of new media technologies is through the lens of the social shaping of technology. This approach frames technology as a product of the interplay between different technical and social factors in both design and use (MacKenzie and Wajcman 2001). Technology use and creation is seen as a social process. Social groups shape technologies towards their own ends rather than the character of a technology determining its use and outcomes. Scholars taking this approach examine how social processes within a particular group influence user negotiations with different technologies. It acknowledges that groups employ a given technology in distinctive ways, so a group's technology use is unique, and their appropriation reinforces valued patterns of community life or practice.

In order to understand how religious communities and individuals negotiate their choices related to new forms of media technology, it is necessary to study these groups' choices in relation to religious norms and social factors which guide their technological decision-making. This is referred to as the religious-social shaping of technology approach, which attempts to give an account of the specific conditions influencing a community of users' negotiations with a technology that can lead to changes in use or belief within a given social context. It also attempts to explain responses to new technology in socio-technological terms. In other words, the success, failure or redesign of a given technology by a specific group of users is based not simply on the innate qualities of the technology but on the ability of users to socially construct the technology in line with the moral economy of the user community or context. It recognises that individuals and groups of actors within particular social situations see their choices and options constrained by broader structural elements of their worldview and belief system.

3 The religious-social shaping of technology approach to media

Based on extensive online and offline ethnographic research regarding how various religious user communities engage media technology, it has been observed that religious communities typically do not reject new forms of technology outright, even if the communities they come from are highly bounded or controlled groupings. Rather, they undergo a sophisticated negotiation process to determine what effect technology may have on their community. If a religious community sees a new technology as valuable but notes its use may promote beliefs or behaviours that run counter to their community's values, the group must carefully consider what aspects of that technology must be resisted. This resistance often leads to the reconstruction of the technology regarding either how it is used or discussed within the community. It may even lead to innovation, where technical aspects or structures are modified so that they are more in line with the community's social and religious life. The religious-social shaping of technology approach is offered as a way to investigate and analyse the practical and ideological negotiation process these communities undergo. This approach is outlined in detail in the text *When Religion Meets New Media* (Campbell 2010) and involves scholars employing four levels of examination in relation to the specific group being studied: (1) the history and tradition of the community, (2) its core beliefs and patterns related to media, (3) the specific negotiation processes it undergoes with a new technology, and finally (4) the communal framing and discourses created by them, which are used to define and justify the extent of their technology use and the way they will or will not engage certain media. Together, these form the basis of the religious-social shaping of technology theoretical approach to the study of religious communities' use of media, which is described below.

As suggested, taking a religious-social shaping of technology approach begins with studying the *history and tradition* of a given religious community in relation to their media use. Here, researchers start by carefully considering the historical context of the specific religious community under study to see how a religious community's positions toward and use of different media have emerged over time and what decisions or events in the community history might have shaped these decisions. It is important to note that decisions made regarding texts, one of the earliest forms of media, often serve as a template for future negotiation with other media. In this phase of study, researchers should pay attention to how history and tradition form standards and a trajectory for future media negotiations.

This leads to investigating religious communities' *core beliefs and patterns*, where attention is paid to how these specific communities live out their core social values. It is important to note that while beliefs are often derived from a historically grounded tradition, they must always be contextualised and applied anew to the social, cultural and historic context in which a given community finds itself. Researchers should identify how a community's dominant social and religious values are integrated into patterns of contemporary life and how these might influence their interactions with contemporary technologies. In an age of digital technologies, close attention must be paid to how core beliefs guide communal decision-making processes related to media use and what patterns of use this encourages and discourages.

These two areas set the stage for the study of the *negotiation process* that religious communities undergo when faced with a new form of media. Religious communities must consider in what respect the new form of media mirrors past technologies so that old rules can be applied. If qualities, outcomes or social conditions created by the technology are problematic in any way for the group, the community must enter into a rigorous negotiation process to see what aspects of the technology can be accepted and which ones might need to be rejected or reconstructed.

Innovation takes place if a technology is viewed as valuable but possesses problematic qualities requiring it to be altered in order to be more in line with community beliefs and practices. Researchers consider how the previous phases inform a community's choices and responses to the new technology when considering the ways in which a new technology is accepted, rejected and/or reconstructed. Key to this stage is the community's positions towards authority roles and structures, which can indicate who has the right to govern media decision-making processes and involvement in innovation.

Finally, attention must be paid to *communal framing and discourse* resulting from the adoption of the new media form. This is a stage often overlooked in studies of the social-shaping of technology, yet it plays an important role for religious communities in their internal justification for their approach to new media. Researchers should consider how new technologies may require amendments to previous language about media or how official policies regarding technology are constructed and publicized. The negotiation and adoption of new technologies requires the religious group to create public and private discourses that validate their technology choices in light of established community boundaries, values and identities. The communal discourse can also serve as tool for reaffirming traditions and past standards as well as for setting a new trajectory for the future use or negotiation of technology. Thus, it is important for researchers to pay attention to the language used by a religious community to frame technology and prescribe communal use. Together, these four levels of inquiry make up the religious-social shaping of technology approach to show how multiple social and structural processes influence religious groups' responses to new media.

4 Negotiation between the Baha'i faith and the Internet

Investigating the American Bahá'í community shows the complex process religious groups undergo in their negotiations with new forms of media. This examination of their history, tradition, core beliefs and reactions to older forms of media provides a clear basis for understanding this religious group's current response to the Internet.

4.1 History and tradition

The negotiation of new forms of media by religious groups is a dynamic and complex process that begins with reflection on the religious history, tradition and beliefs of the group. In the case of the Bahá'í faith, it is important to consider how this history has directly affected the negotiation process that practicing Bahá'ís in America have with the Internet. The Bábí movement began in 1844 in the city of Shiraz, located in south-western Iran. In this year, Sayyid 'Ali Muhammad declared having had 'some sort of extraordinary relationship with the Hidden Imam' (Cole 1990: 3). The Hidden Imam, or Mahdi, is believed to be the redeemer or messiah by Shi'a Muslims and is believed to help restore order and peace to the world. Sayyid 'Ali Muhammad, also known as the Báb, was seen as a divine messenger (similar to Moses, Muhammad, Jesus, etc.) by his followers and remains the central figure of the Bahá'í faith. According to Cole, members of the Bábí movement believed the Báb was 'the return of the Imam Mahdi himself, and he asserted that divine inspiration led him to reveal a new holy book abrogating the Quran' (1990: 3). The belief that the Báb was the manifestation of the Hidden Imam to return and their 'abrogation' of the Qur'an were problematic to many practising Muslims and led to the persecution of the individuals associated with the Bábí movement in the nineteenth century. According Adam Berry (2004: 1), the Bábí movement was met with much resistance, as shown by the execution of the Báb in 1850. Further proof of persecution can be seen by the number of followers killed between 1849 and the mid-1850s. Around 5,000 followers were killed during that period, in which the adherents to the movement numbered 100,000 (Cole 1990: 3). After the death of the Báb, Mirza Husayn 'Ali, the successor of the Báb, adopted the Bahá'í name in an attempt to unify the members and survive persecution in Iran. Not only would this history of persecution affect the way Bahá'ís view media, it would also help shape the faith's core beliefs and where these beliefs would be practised.

In an attempt to escape the persecution prevalent in Iran, many Bahá'ís moved to new areas in an attempt to practise their religion peacefully. With the idea of the Bahá'í faith symbolising 'threatening aspects of modernity' in Iran, Bahá'ís looked to the western world for new opportunities (Cole 1990: 7). From the 1970s to the mid-1980s, around 12,000 Iranian Bahá'ís emigrated to the US to escape persecution, taking advantage of the religious freedom in America. With this migration of Iranian Bahá'ís, the US Bahá'í community grew from 10,000 to about 48,000 individuals with confirmed addresses, or 'sure members' (Cole 1998: 238). According to Juan Cole, this growth can be explained by 'the impact of the civil rights movements, the Vietnam War, the youth counterculture'

(Cole 1998: 236). Currently, there are around 60,000 practising Bahá'ís in the US,[1] and many rely on the Internet to stay connected to the faith. This idea will be explored in depth in the media use negotiation section.

It is also important to note that, as the Baha'i faith emerged out of Shi'a Islam in Iran, these roots and connections in some respects have informed the faith. Scholars have noted a connection between the Baha'i and the Shiite movements, in that both draw from esoteric and charismatic roots, have a defined hierarchical structure of gatekeepers and represent conservative traditions with a certain degree of secrecy in relation to religious knowledge (Warburg 1999). These tendencies can also be seen in their dealings with the spread of information, both inside and outside the community, and their position toward media, as discussed in the following sections. Before moving on to how members of the Bahá'í faith currently negotiate their relationship with the media, it is vital to address the core beliefs and the religion's relationship to authority. According to the official Bahá'í Website of the United States, the purpose of life is to 'worship God, to acquire virtues, and to promote the oneness of humankind' (2010). These beliefs directly influence the Bahá'ís' relationship with other religions which strive for religious universalism. Furthermore, Bahá'ís advocate for service to humanity while maintaining a peaceful and pacifist nature. In relation to social principles, Bahá'ís desire the equality of men and women, universal education and the abandonment of all forms of prejudice. The final factor that directs how the media is treated by practising Bahá'ís is seen in the administrative order of the Bahá'ís community. The formation of an individual order of adherence to a hierarchy occurred in 1921 after the death of Abbás Effendi, who was the son of the first successor to the Báb (Cole 1990: 3). Examples of how these structure the hierarchy of the Bahá'ís community and inform their view of media are explored in greater detail in the next section.

4.2 Media values and policies

Along with the history and tradition of the Bahá'í faith, the core values directly lead to more unified policies towards the uses of media. In order to achieve such beliefs as religious universalism and universal education, Bahá'ís thought it would be important to make the transition from an individual order to an admin-

---

1 According to the American Religious Identification Survey (ARIS 2004), there were an estimated 84,000 adult Bahá'í members. The difference between these figures may be accounted for in the word 'practising' as opposed to membership.

istrative order. An example of an administrative body in the Bahá'í faith is the Universal House of Justice. Established in 1963, the Universal House of Justice has guided and directed the activities of the global Bahá'í community for over 40 years. By educating followers on how to practise and live their faith, the Universal House of Justice determines which activities are permitted based on the laws of Mirza Husayn 'Ali (the first successor of the Báb and founder of the Bahá'í faith).

Even though the core values, beliefs and admiration of the Bahá'í faith are related to the creation of the Universal House of Justice, the preceding history and tradition of the Bahá'í faith have contributed to a strict media trajectory. As mentioned above, many practicing Bahá'ís in Iran experienced heavy persecution for their beliefs. Many viewed the western world as an opportunity to practice their religion in peace and to educate others about the Bahá'í faith. However, along with more rights and freedoms has come criticism of Bahá'í policies by Bahá'í followers in the western world. To counter these criticisms, the Universal House of Justice has increased restrictions of certain types of media usage. For example, through the use of National Spiritual Assemblies, which are located throughout the Bahá'í world, the Universal House of Justice has censored or restricted material published by Bahá'ís. Cole states that the 'National Spiritual Assembly claims the prerogative of telling private Bahá'í publishers what Bahá'í-related books they may or may not publish'. This shows the importance of the core Bahá'í belief of having 'conformity of views and behavior' and how it has been directly challenged by the freedoms shared in the western world (Cole 1998: 244).

In relation to this, the Universal House of Justice has not only produced strict policies on media content but also on individuals who produce media content that challenges existing Bahá'í policies. One of the mechanisms used by the Universal House of Justice to achieve unification and conformity is the threat of labelling someone a 'covenant-breaker'. Basically, a person accused of covenant-breaking has committed a form of heresy and is shunned by the practising community. One who even associates with a covenant-breaker can possibly be shunned and not recognised by the community. This has led to Bahá'ís 'informing' the House of Justice of individuals who undermine its policies. 'The House of Justice encourages Bahá'ís who hear something they think out of the ordinary to challenge the speaker to justify his or her statement with regard to the covenant' (cited in Cole 1998: 244). This directly affects what kind of content can be produced and expressed through the media because of the fear of being labelled a covenant-breaker.

The actions and policies created by the House of Justice reveal how the Bahá'í faith negotiates and teaches the Bahá'í how to use media. Due to the availability of freedoms in the western world, the House of Justice took strong stances against criticizing opinions expressed in the media. One mechanism addressed above was the use of labelling someone a covenant-breaker and how this has led to an 'informing' culture by practicing Bahá'ís. 'Although Baha'u'llah (or Mirza Husayn 'Ali) himself attempted to abolish the practices of shunning', the House of Justice enforces these policies to achieve the core belief of unification (Cole 1998: 243). The work of the House of Justice also sets standards for media engagement, which guide Bahá'ís' views about and uses of the Internet. This media negotiation is explored in more detail in the third area of investigation.

4.3 Media use negotiation

In order to understand how the history, tradition and core beliefs affect the media use negotiation by the Bahá'í faith, it is important to focus in on a specific community and media. Examining the Bahá'í faith community in America reveals how this specific branch of the Baha'i community negotiates its Internet usage and how this has been informed by the Universal House of Justice. In order to fully understand how the American Community of Bahá'ís use the Internet, it is imperative to examine the Bahá'í Internet Agency. This agency was established in 2004 by the Universal House of Justice, the legislative institution and the highest governing body of the Bahá'í faith, and is under the auspices of its International Teaching Centre. The Bahá'í Internet Agency (BIA) seeks to advise and direct members of the Bahá'í faith on how to properly use the Internet as well as offer assistance to the global community through technical support for Bahá'í institutions and to support community-related online initiatives. The BIA has also written a number of documents that provide members with specific guidance about appropriate Internet use, such as blogging, podcasting and social networking (see BIA n.d.).

Bahá'ís in the United States currently have 'official' pages on Facebook, Twitter, Beliefnet and PeaceNext where they post Bahá'í news as well as links to blogs from various bloggers who discuss Bahá'í themes. The US Bahá'í Office of Communications advocates the use of the Internet, yet this use is encouraged or framed within certain constraints. One key emphasis of this office is to encourage community members to engage with the Internet in ways that affirm the beliefs and structures of the movement. They strongly advocate that members seek information from web sites which are published and maintained by the official organization and engage in dialogue in these contexts:

> Baha'is are encouraged to participate in a wide range of Internet initiatives carried out in light of Bahá'í principles such as moderation, courtesy, probity, fairness, dignity, accuracy and wisdom. Promoting mutual understanding, fellowship and a spirit of cooperation among diverse individuals and groups is an essential characteristic of all Bahá'í activity. (US Bahá'í Office of Communications 2010)

A further examination of this agency reveals the restrictions Bahá'í faith members in the US face while using the Internet. The Internet is an essential part of any organisation in America due to the high number of users in this country. As of December 2011, according to the Internet World Statistics (2011), the United States has over 245,000,000 users (with a population penetration of 78.6 %), numerically second only to China (penetration of 38.4 %), with over half-a-billion users.

In order to understand how the Bahá'í Internet Agency has reconfigured the usage of the Internet, it is important to examine which aspects of the Internet are beneficial and which are problematic. One activity that seems to be deemed both beneficial and problematic by the Bahá'í community in the US is the use of blogging. According to the Bahá'í Internet Agency's white paper on 'Blogging and the Bahá'í faith: suggestions and possible approaches' (2006), blogging 'offers opportunities to explore Bahá'í teachings' and 'opens new avenues for sharing the message' of the Bahá'í faith. Furthermore, the Agency advocates that 'individual blogging' allows for a 'community of interest to the Revelation and to Bahá'í community activity'.

However, there are some aspects that the American Bahá'ís must reject with regard to blogging, as outlined by the Bahá'í Internet Agency. One of the aspects discouraged for practising Bahá'ís is the use of confrontational and negative discussion threads on the Internet. This includes any blog post that is seen to undermine or challenge Bahá'í policies or beliefs, which is to be ignored/deleted. If the blogger who makes negative claims happens to be a practising Bahá'í, he/she can be labelled as a covenant-breaker and shunned by the community. Cole explains that 'threats to use shunning' have increased with 'the rise of cyberspace' (1998: 243). The Internet allows some members to post confidentially so other practising Bahá'ís will not know who they are. In response to this, the Universal House of Justice has encouraged Bahá'ís to 'inform' them of members partaking in these restricted actions. Such moves show how the Universal House of Justice has reconfigured the Internet and encouraged certain actions to achieve the core belief of unification and adherence to the given structure.

Another problematic aspect for followers of the Bahá'í faith that has emerged on the Internet is the use of social networking sites in the US. Although many social networking sites, such as Facebook, attempt to connect people from around the world, there have been many concerns about the association of Bahá'ís with covenant-breakers. One specific example of this problematic activity is outlined on truebahai.com (Weinberg 2008). According to the website, the Bahá'í Internet Agency sent an e-mail out on 28 February 2008 to alert members to the current activities of a specific covenant-breaker who ran an unauthorized 'Orthodox Bahá'í page on Facebook', which was perceived to be threatening to the 'spiritual well-being' of practising Bahá'í youth members (Weinburg 2008). What is interesting is that simply accepting a friend request from this individual is seen as a community violation, as being in association with a covenant-breaker (see BIA n.d.). Through the Bahá'í Internet Agency, the meaning of a (cyber) friendship on Facebook is redefined to be equivalent to a personal, face-to-face friendship. This demonstrates how the Bahá'í must negotiate with online culture and bring online communication in line with traditional religious practice and expectations of behaviour in order for the technology to fit comfortably within accepted community values.

4.4 Communal discourse

Finally, religious communities often develop policies or guidelines that present their official view or perceptions of the Internet and advocate particular uses. The aim of this communal discourse regarding the Internet is not merely instructive for community members; it also serves as an identity narrative – to affirm the values and boundaries of the community. In the case of the Bahá'í community, the Universal House of Justice serves an important role in policing and offering prescriptive guidelines for media activity and has attempted to encourage certain forms of Internet engagement so that members' use will not undermine Bahá'í policies and beliefs. A notable discourse has been produced through the work of the Bahá'í Internet Agency, who provide information on how to use the Internet through issuing a number of white papers on a variety of issues related to online communication, as noted above.

A key role of the Bahá'í Internet Agency is to circulate official statements about Internet communication issued by the Universal House of Justice. These documents advocate a particular relationship between the Bahá'í community and electronic, digital communication technologies, one which supports core communal values, such as unity in diversity and service to humanity. The Internet is framed as offering the community new opportunities and challenges, such that the published and thus accepted wisdom of their religious leaders should be consulted when making decisions regarding the Internet. As stated in the document 'Guidelines for Internet Communication':

> The opportunity which electronic communication technology provides is for more speedy and thorough consultation among friends, and is highly significant. Without doubt, it represents another manifestation of a development eagerly anticipated by the Guardian when he foresaw the creation of 'a mechanism of world intercommunication [...] embracing the whole planet, freed from national hindrances and restrictions, and functioning with marvellous swiftness and perfect regularity'. (BIA n.d.)

Official white papers also provide guidance to individual community members seeking to use the Internet to represent their beliefs and the community online. 'Members are to be mindful of how their online activities bear witness to the Bahá'í faith', according to the document 'Individual initiative on the Internet' (2007). It continues:

> Internet initiatives should of course be carried out in light of Bahá'í principles such as moderation, courtesy, probity, fairness, dignity, accuracy and wisdom [... T]he Internet is yet one more domain in which Bahá'ís should demonstrate etiquette of expression worthy of the approaching maturity of the human race – a maturity founded on the oneness and wholeness of human relationships. (BIA 2007)

Thus, members are exhorted to reflect the community in a positive light through mirroring core values. These white papers often emphasise core Bahá'í beliefs and teachings of religious figures as a basis for online decision making. By releasing statements such as the ones above, the Universal House of Justice attempts to define how the Internet should be used by all practicing Bahá'ís (Universal House of Justice 1995). Such statements not only provide Bahá'ís with guidelines for behaviour within specific online contexts but also affirm core values regarding how individuals should present their community identity in public contexts. For example, individual Bahá'ís are not forbidden to be involved in unofficial forums, but these performances should reflect the character of the community.

In general, the House of Justice has no objection to Bahá'ís participating in public, unmoderated discussions about the faith, whether those discussions take place in person or through some form of electronic communication. The wisdom of participating in particular discussions must, of necessity, depend upon circumstances prevailing at the time. When, through such discussions, the faith is attacked or erroneous information about it is disseminated, it may become necessary for individual Bahá'ís to actively defend it (BIA n.d.).

This is affirmed in a 2009 statement issued by the Bahá'í Internet Agency, 'Responding to Criticism and Opposition on the Internet', which states that Bahá'í use of the Internet should reflect the teachings of Bahá'u'lláh:

> Internet initiatives by Bahá'ís should therefore aim to broaden vision concerning challenging spiritual and social questions, shape discourse in a unifying way, and emphasize the potentialities and promise of the present moment in human affairs. When harnessed in this way, the Internet can become a vehicle for promoting mutual understanding and learning, serving others, instilling hope about the human condition, and demonstrating rectitude of conduct. (BIA 2009)

The U.S. Bahá'í Office of Communications also plays a role in framing the Internet as an important sphere in which Bahá'ís are welcome to engage and offers suggestions regarding how this should be done:

> The increasingly participatory nature of Internet activity is providing novel and creative ways of exploring the compelling message of spiritual and social transformation as taught by Bahá'u'lláh, the Founder of the Bahá'í Faith. Bahá'ís around the globe are using the Internet to give expression to the many facets of their belief in an open and imaginative manner, including on blogs and social networking sites. (US Bahá'í Office of Communications 2010)

However, this is a contextualised engagement, as evidenced by the documents provided by the Universal House of Justice that give prescriptive instructions on such topics as how Internet discussion related to issues of Bahá'í faith should be maintained and moderated online as well as how Bahá'í members should behave online as representatives of the community in the online world. Thus, official discourse regarding use of and engagement with the Internet serves as a space to reiterate and strengthen the religious identity of the Bahá'í community. Therefore community documents and policy statements such as those highlighted here help reaffirm community distinctiveness and contribute to the construction or maintenance of a desired public image within the age of the Internet.

5 Reflections on a bounded community's management of new media

Undertaking these four levels of inquiry demonstrates that American Bahá'ís have a distinctive negotiation with the Internet, which is guided by their core beliefs and the particular value of unity and which official sources seek to exemplify through their use of the Internet and how they encourage their members to represent themselves online. Their strict adherence to a certain structure and hierarchy within the offline structure of the community is in many respects simply replicated and encouraged online. As has been shown in this brief exploration, the Bahá'í community's Universal House of Justice has attempted to reconfigure the usage and negotiation of the Internet in an effort to achieve ideological unification of motivations and practices in a context which blends the online and offline contexts. Examples of this reconfiguration are evident in the creation of the Bahá'í Internet Agency, which seeks to direct practicing Bahá'ís on how to properly use the Internet in relation to Bahá'í beliefs. Their white papers not only provide guidelines for Internet use but also lead community members back to the teachings of the Báb and therefore reaffirm core community beliefs and frameworks. As the Bahá'í Internet Agency states, 'The principles of our Faith offer valuable guideposts in making use of the Internet. [...] Bahá'ís need to learn as much as possible about these new modes of interaction and determine how the principles of the Faith apply to their use' (BIA 2006b).

This chapter also shows how a bounded religious community often seeks to replicate traditional or accepted boundaries and practises of the larger community online in order to solidify their established social patterns and behavioural expectations. It is the tradition and established understandings of the identity of a community and their authority structures, which guide such groups' engagement with technology. The Internet can introduce new challenges for bounded communities, in that it allows community members to interact outside official forums or systems that enhance individual choice over community accountability or control. Therefore negotiation processes and discourse frameworks surrounding new media become important spaces for religious groups to consciously re-establish the boundaries of the community and culture, or resist and thence negotiate encounter problematic affordances of the technology. Religious groups desiring to maintain a bounded social and moral system must carefully consider the extent to which certain aspects of network culture may run counter to their desired pattern of religious life. Bounded religious communities thus constrain members' use so that it is both in line with community values and enhances desired structures or community identity markers. The religious-social shaping of technology provides a valuable format to study and interrogate these processes of technological negotiation and reveals the distinctiveness of a given religious community that seeks to represent or promote itself in a modern, networked society.

References

ARIS. 2004. "Top Twenty Religions in the United States, 2001." Available at:
http://www.adherents.com/rel_USA.html#religions.
BIA [Bahá'í Internet Agency]. N.d. "Guidelines for Internet communication." Available at:
http://www.bcca.org/bia/Guidelines%20for%20Internet%20Communication.pdf.

–. 2006. "Blogging and the Bahá'í faith: Suggestions and possible approaches." Available at: http://www.bcca.org/bia/Blogging%20and%20the%20Baha%27i%20Faith.pdf.

–. 2006b. "Bahá'í participation on the Internet: some reflections." Available at: http://www. bcca.org/bia/Participation%20and%20the%20Internet.pdf.

–. 2007. "Individual initiative on the Internet." Available at: http://www.bcca.org/bia/ Individual-Initiative.pdf.

–. 2009. "Responding to criticism and opposition on the Internet." Available at: http://www. bcca.org/bia/ Responding%20to%20Criticism%20and%20Oppositio n%20on%20the%20 %20 %20 %20 %20Internet.pdf.

Bahá'í Library. N.d. "Development and monitoring of Internet forums by the International Teaching Center of the Universal House of Justice." Available at: http://bahai-library. com/uhj_monitoring_Internet

Berry, Adam. 2004. "The Bahá'í faith and its relationship to Islam, Christianity and Judaism: A brief history." *International Social Science Review* 79 (3/4): 137–151.

Campbell, Heidi. 2010. *When Religion Meets New Media*. London: Routledge.

Cole, Juan. 1998. "The Bahá'í faith in America as panopticon 1963–1997." *Journal for the Scientific Study of Religion* 37 (2): 234–248.

–. 1990. "The Bahá'ís of Iran." *History Today* 40 (3): 24.

Cohen, Anthony. 1985. *The Symbolic Construction of Community*. London: Routledge.

Howard, Robert G. 2000. "Online ethnography of dispensationalist discourse: Revealed verses negotiated truth." In *Religion on the Internet: Research Prospects and Promises*, edited by J. K. Hadden and D. E. Cowan, 225–246. New York: JAI Press.

Internet World Statistics. 2011. "Statistics by country." Available at: http://www.internetworldstats.com/list2.htm

Linklater, Andrew. 1998. *The Transformation of Political Community: Ethical Foundations of the Post-Westphalian Era*. Columbia, SC: University of South Carolina Press.

Livio, Oren, T. Weinblatt, and T. Keren. 2007. "Discursive legitimation of a controversial technology: Ultra-orthodox Jewish women and the Internet." *The Communication Review* 10 (1): 29–56.

MacKenzie, Donald, and Judy Wajcman. 2001. *The Social Shaping of Technology: How the Refrigerator Got its Hum*. Milton Keynes, UK: Open University.

National Spiritual Assembly of the Bahá'ís of the United States. 2010. "Core Beliefs of the Bahá'í faith." Bahá'í Faith United States Official Website. Available at: http://www.bahai.us/core-beliefs.

Piff, David, and Margit Warburg. 2005. "Seeking for truth: Plausibility on a Bahá'í email list." In *Religion and Cyberspace*, edited by M. Hojsgaard and M. Warburg, 86–101. London: Routledge.

Shandler, Jeffery. 2009. *Jews, God and Videotape: Religion and Media in America*. New York: NYU Press.

Smith, Peter, and Moojan Momen. 1998. "The Bahá'í faith 1957–1988: A survey of contemporary developments." *Religion* 19 (1): 63–91.

U.S. Bahá'í Office of Communications. 2010. Personal email communication. 6 December.

Universal House of Justice. 1995. "The character of Internet discussion." Available at: http:// bahai-library.com/uhj_character_Internet_postings.

Waldinger, Roger D. 2007. "The bounded community: Turning foreigners into Americans in 21st century Los Angeles." *Ethnic and Racial Studies* 30 (7): 341–374.

Warburg, Margit. 1999. "Baha'i: A religious approach to globalization". *Social Compass* 46 (1): 47–56.

Weinberg, Matt. 2008. "True Bahá'í. 'Baha'i Internet Agency: the dangers of Facebook friends.'" Available at: http://www.truebahai.com/2008/03/bahai-Internet.html.

Wellman, Barry. 1979. "The community question: The intimate networks of East Yorkers." *American Journal of Sociology* 84 (5): 1201–1231.

–. 1988. "The community question re-evaluated." In *Power, Community and the City*, edited by Michael Peter Smith, 81–107. New Brunswick, NJ: Transaction Books.

Anita Greenhill and Gordon Fletcher

11 Life, Death and Everyday Experience of Social Media

1 Introduction

Much attention has been given to the development of social media and its relationship to 'our' everyday experiences (e. g., Galloway 2004). The application of the traditional notion of a face-to-face 'friend' is regularly questioned in critical literature discussing social media use and social networking (Ellison et al. 2007; Tong et al. 2008), and studies have also indicated that at least younger generations have the ability to work with multiple media simultaneously, which makes social media an increasingly central aspect of their daily experience (Thomas 2007; Ware 2008).

The complexities and intricacies of social networking are exemplified and emphasised by those social networks that have explicitly formed around mourning, the remembrance of life and unfortunate death. However, while these special interest social networks are the most visible and easiest to observe in the context of cultural rituals concerning death, all of the most popular social networks (including, for example, *Facebook* and *Bebo*) have been used as sites for the conduct of these rituals (Carroll and Landry 2010; McCrudy 2010; Fearon 2011). This chapter is an interpretative and observational examination of gonetoosoon.org – a website that encourages family and friends, as well as complete strangers, to create memorials, befriend others who have created memorials and to leave digital tributes. We have utilised gonetoosoon.org as the basis for analysis as a representative harbinger of digitally based activities for contemporary mourning rituals. Reimers (1999: 147) emphasises that an 'aspect of rituals, and especially of *rites de passage*, is that they unite participants [...] with each other'. This observation is made in the context of death and mourning, but it could equally define the pivotal purpose of social networks more generally and is a preliminary rationale for the close association of specific actions, such as social network participation, with cultural practices, including mourning. Myerhoff foreshadows the advent of digitally based mourning by arguing that the unifying aspects of ritual also create an association 'with situations and collectives beyond themselves, such as relatives at other places, ancestors, and rising generations' (Myerhoff 1984: 306). Taken together, Reimer's and Myerhoff's two statements effectively define the *raison d'etre* for gonetoosoon.org.

In this chapter, we introduce the concept of 'thananetworking'. This term is consciously applied in order to dually recognise that the practices being described are a subset of social networking more generally as well as that these practices have a relation with dark tourism or thanatourism (Seaton 1996; Slade 2003; Stone 2005). By exploring thanatourism and thananetworking practices, we see the persistence of an ongoing human desire to understand and rationalise death. Thanatourism most commonly cites Jim Morrison's graveyard in Paris and Elvis Presley's Graceland as two examples of tourist activity that has been built around the early, untimely deaths of these performers (Ryan and Kohil 2006; Stone and Sharpley 2008). The human (living) ordering and respect for death provided by graveyards constructs a defined venue for entertainment (Rugg 2000: 264). The activities and actions associated with visiting these venues form the basis for thanatourism – shifting and expanding the concept of pilgrimage to a form of entertainment, a cultural practice that extends beyond religious observance and an action that assists in defining a place. Thananetworking has evolved from the opposite direction – to a similar observable outcome – adapting the ostensibly entertainment-focussed medium of social networking to the purpose of pilgrimage and, significantly, taking the ordering principle of memorialising conventionally found in graveyards into a different domain. Looking at thananetworking is an examination of mourning practices found within digital environments. These are observable in all social media networks as well as in specialised sites, including the site of our focus, gonetoosoon.org.

2 Belief and ritual

Story-telling interlocks with other practices as a mechanism for the reinforcement of prevalent and dominant cultural understandings. Stories provide reference to a plethora of common contemporary operations and experiences that ensure an integrated belief system. The belief in some form of continuity of existence after death amongst most widespread mainstream religions is equated with the survival and perpetuation of a conscious soul after death (Levene 2009). *GoneTooSoon* and other online memorials are not challenging the nuclear core of traditional beliefs, but rather are appending and expanding on ancillary beliefs; this is simplistically evidenced, for example, by the extended use of 'angelic' imagery and ASCII art on *GoneTooSoon*. For the majority of memorials on *GoneTooSoon*, the relationship is to a 'core' set of Christian beliefs that are clearly evident and shaped by the technical capabilities of the site itself, which would make the construction of any 'non-Christian' memorial potentially problematic.

GoonTooSoon also presents an 'alternative' perspective to the mainstream reporting of death and murder that similarly brings an ancillary representation to the core and mainstream of media reporting. The shifting and diminishing power of traditional media in relation to everyday practice is equally important in understanding how mourning practices have come to be associated with new actions and spaces of experience. Many of *GoneTooSoon*'s memorials capture and record (through a form of unintentional serialising) recent British social history, including knife crime in London, gun crime in Manchester, various hate crimes, the abduction and subsequent murder of teenage girls across England and the murder of prostitutes by men seeking fame as 'modern day' Jack the Rippers. The sensational deaths heavily reported by mainstream media overshadow memories of individual lives and threaten personal memorials of life with recollections of death and violence. These forms of memorialising create a form of social memory that potentially brings the fame originally sought by the perpetrators of the murders. Doss (2002: 69) recognises the importance of this interrelationship of media and mourning in relation to 'terrorist' attacks on US territory: 'The images, artefacts and rituals of these visibly public death-shrines in Oklahoma City and Littleton framed issues of memory, tribute and collectivity in contemporary America; their visual and performative dimensions clearly embodied a vast collaboration of mourners and media'. Rituals of memorialising and mourning within ostensibly Christian societies have become more and more spectacular as the actions associated with them have shifted beyond the boundaries of the formal graveyard, private household or wake to occupy more public spaces, including road-sides and social networks. The potential outcome for the association of mourning with the constant cultural desire for participation in and observation of spectacle is an obsession that approaches the teleological fatalism well-evidenced historically in a range of cultures, but most famously in Pharaonic Egypt (Meskell 2001). The contemporary need for all life experiences to be articulated in the form of (social) media spectacle that was predicted by Debord (1995) also influences the ways in which death is mourned – and particularly deaths that fall outside the 'norm' of old age.

The *GoneTooSoon* memorial website – as well as many of the memorials found on other popular networking sites such as *Facebook* and *Bebo* – articulates the interrelationship of grieving practices, expressed through actions such as social networking, with the imperatives of fame-oriented culture as well as the fundamental duality of life and death. Similarly the increasingly wide boundaries of acceptability and decency within contemporary culture (Thompson 2011), itself influenced by cultural obsessions with fame and exacerbated by the ready availability of network technologies, mean that many memorials are detailed and graphic in focusing on the details of the person's death rather than those of life. This has been aggravated on *GoneTooSoon* with the addition of memorials focused on some of the media's most highlighted murders in recent UK history by the site's 'Admin', which has no direct family or friendship connection with the individuals recognised by the memorial.

By utilising the methods of ethnographic observation and examining the combined evidence offered through document analysis and direct presence in the spaces that evidence thananetworking cultural practices, this chapter explores the complexities and intricacies of social networking around mourning, the remembrance of life and of sensational death. While recognising that there is a shift in specific cultural actions (moving from the use of a gravestone to forms of digital *momento mori*), there remains a continuity of cultural practices at a number of levels (including recording vital details and the relationships of the person remembered). This chapter extends the theoretical proposals of boyd and Potter (2003) where the 'real and virtual' spaces of social networking are barely separated, arguing that cultural practices shape and mediate cultural experiences, irrespective of the place in which they are undertaken. Culture and the practices through which it is expressed continue to change and evolve, irrespective of the mediating presence of wires and networks. The differences – if differences are to be sought – between traditional and contemporary practice of mourning are found in the speed, frequency and accessibility of specific actions. This difference has provided immediate higher visibility for social campaigns founded as a memorial to a deceased family member, such as S.O.P.H.I.E (www.sophielancasterfoundation.com) – a modern version of the traditional miracle – a form of bringing back from the dead a loved one, in name at least. An equally significant question raised by the popularity of gonetoosoon.org is how digital spaces offer wider potential for the construction of associations through simple linkages and mutual mourning. When the relatives of murdered teenagers – whose deaths become well documented through mass and social media – associate themselves through tributes with the deaths of celebrities, the meaning of this association and the role it performs in the individual personal grieving process becomes problematised. This observation echoes Doss (2002: 64), who claims:

> Contemporary debate surrounding abortion, AIDS, euthanasia and gun control, however, as well as increased popular interest in 'good death', the afterlife and bereavement therapy, suggest the questioning and perhaps the lifting of certain death-related taboos. By extension, visibly public material culture rituals pertaining to death and grief suggest broad and diverse interests in 'reclaiming' death, in making death meaningful on personal, individual levels.

Riches and Dawson (1998: 144–5) claim:

The portrayal of death in modern society serves a cultural and symbolic purpose. Individuals whose lives have been unremarkable may gain fame if their death is extraordinary. Newsworthiness lies in the 'sensational' nature of the death and in [audiences'] identification with the 'ordinary' lives it has devastated. These stories contain messages about how individuals grieve, offering the public examples of socially appropriate reactions (Walter, 1996) whose lives have been unremarkable.

These processes and approaches to death have evolved to become increasingly clearly articulated within the *GoneTooSoon* environment and are the underpinning basis for thananetworking.

3 Contemporary culture and death

Discussions of the rituals and practices associated with death and dying are well-rehearsed and remain a source of continued interest for a broad range of social science researchers (Hart et al. 1998; Gibson 2004; Gibson 2007). As more time is spent in the digital domain and a variety of intimate and public cultural displays are extended into these spaces, it is increasingly appropriate to critically examine what links to traditional rituals and practices are being displayed in the virtual domain. This examination necessarily includes consideration of the mechanisms by which mythological belief systems are constructed, reconstructed and perpetuated. We take up this examination by exploring the problematisation of ritualised actions and cultural meanings being presented online that have been reconstructed from conventional and traditional rituals associated with death. In particular, within thananetworking practice there is an identifiable blurring of the meanings of fame and infamy and of the boundaries between public and private forms of grieving and emotional displays. Thananetworking, along with roadside memorials and other memorialising of death, also moves the conduct of mourning rituals beyond clearly defined domestic or 'sacred' places. Doss (2002: 80) sees this as a cultural shift: 'The visual and material culture of grief in contemporary America seems to suggest heightened popular commitment to shift the discourse on death from medicine to culture, and distinctive efforts to make death meaningful – memorable – on personal and public levels'.

Reimers (1999: 154) highlights another rationale for the move to memorialising through thananetworking:

Markers of social position violate what in the funeral law is designated as 'good grave culture'. The meaning of this expression is ambiguous. On the one hand, it is stated as a major rule that the bereaved should be free to decide the appearance of the gravestone. On the other hand, it is up to graveyard authorities to decide the boundaries within which the bereaved can make these choices. These limitations, at least at modern cemeteries, usually prescribe that every gravestone be kept within a clear shape, size and design.

Thananetworking overcomes one form of constraint regarding the construction of formal memorials, but in doing so presents other constraints. What is, or is not, possible within the ecosystem of *Facebook*, *Bebo* or *GoneTooSoon* represents a different series of specific constraints to action. However, in contrast to 'good grave culture', these restrictions are generally 'technical' in nature rather than existing in relationship to other memorials or to received notions of what represents 'good taste' for a memorial and respect. The most obvious shift is from a necessity for brevity, with a single photograph (if this is allowed at all) and a specified number of words or letters, to an active encouragement for textual and visual elaboration through photographs, clipart, ASCII art and extended narratives.

This understanding leads directly to the questions posed by our research. Are the actions and communications found on memorial websites (such as gonetoosoon.org) contemporary enactments of continuing belief practices?

4 *GoneTooSoon:* a site description

Gonetoosoon.org is a social network. It encourages its participants to inscribe thoughts and memories as well as photographs and their own creative work. This description does not provide any distinction from *Facebook*, *Bebo*, *LinkedIn* or even *Twitter* or one of the many readily available blogging systems. What distinguishes *GoneTooSoon* is the focus upon mourning and the memorialising of individual death – the key distinction that we utilise as the basis to claim that thananetworking represents a specifically identifiable sub-category of social networking. While members of the site can themselves have a profile, the focus of the site is upon the memorials created for deceased individuals. In effect, living members 'friend' these memorials and create networks with the living members of this site through the memorials of the deceased. In this sense, the dead take priority in the *GoneTooSoon* space and represent the 'hubs' of the social network of the living.

There are few restrictions within the site – anyone can create memorials to anyone, and in the case of celebrity deaths there are often a number of separate memorials that form separate hubs within distinct sub-networks of members. The ability for anyone to create a memorial results in a disproportionate number of memorials for 'famous' people – as the financial and etiquette restrictions of a physical memorial are removed within the *GoneTooSoon* space (an observation that should also be contrasted with the audacious public grief displays such as the £100,000 Michael Jackson memorial unveiled in early 2011 outside Fulham Football Club's stadium by the club's owner Mohammed Al-Fayed). Importantly, the memorials of *GoneTooSoon* provide significantly more detail about the life and death of the individual than a physical memorial. This capacity provides one of the close connections of thananetworking with thanatourism.

Thanatourism involves visiting the burial site of an individual, where the rationale for visiting is tied to the story that makes the individual famous, infamous or at least notable, rather than any personal connection to the individual who is buried (Walter 1996). *GoneTooSoon* constructs and mythologises an individual's identity after his or her death and, in many cases, creates similarly detailed and expansive stories as those found at thanatourism sites. This also connects thananetworking to the mass celebritisation of everyday life – the desire to know about the famous, or at least those who are currently figuring prominently within mainstream media reporting (McAvan 2010). This desire to know is tied into the compelling features of social networking, including the ability to 'befriend' people who are famous and the capacity to express and show this association. But social networking, particularly in its conceptualisation as the Read/Write Web or Web 2.0, is also about the desire to inscribe and actively engage in the construction of meaning (Latour and Woolgar 1986). This invitation and desire to constantly record and annotate association results in the *GoneTooSoon* memorials actively contributing to a more general blurring of fame, infamy and notoriety, while also contributing to the ongoing construction of an individual's fame after death. The ability of social media to continue to actively construct an individual's identity after death raises a number of contradictions and engages these individuals with a range of broader issues, including the degree to which a public individual has active control over his or her identity and the veracity of any given identity. The presence of an aging population coupled with the creation of generations of 'digital natives' increases the likelihood that memorialising in this way will increase. This further raises concerns about the digital assets of the dead and what happens to these assets after an individual dies. The rise of thananetworking highlights that there is no individual or family control over a 'social' memorial, and in many respects control has been passed over to the 'Admin' of the various social networking sites. Doss (2002: 70) similarly recognises this complexity and contradiction in roadside memorials:

> The relationship between mourning and material culture is timeless, of course, and both older and contemporary American monuments testify to human desires to capture and represent memory, to pay tribute, to validate certain historical, political and social perspec-

tives, and to grieve. Yet the spontaneous, often impermanent, and distinctly 'unofficial' nature of many of these roadside shrines, grassroots memorials, offerings and ritualistic behaviours seem less concerned with producing a critique of historical moments and tragic events than [with] catharsis and redemption. This may relate to the nature of trauma itself, and to the ways in which memory can fail because of traumatic events and episodes of child abuse, civil war, torture, disease, natural disasters or the murder of family members and loved ones.

The mythologising of the dead by the living can be considered as an attempt to further define their own living identity (Doss 2002: 76). Within fame-oriented culture, this identity work includes attempts to define relationships with people – both living and dead – who are, or were, famous as well as with individuals popularly defined as 'good' or popular. Within *GoneTooSoon*, this ongoing identity work constructs relationships around remembrance and grieving that in turn mediate and connect like-minded living individuals.

Our analysis of observational data from gonetoosoon.org included identifying and tagging events and instances of activities associated with ritualised practice, examples of storytelling activity and when community participants endeavoured to become associated with the celebration or mourning of the 'famous' dead. This body of evidence was subsequently scrutinised and examples extracted to exemplify the belief practices and social relations enacted within these communities.

5 Famous deaths vs. deaths of the famous

A visible feature of *GoneTooSoon*, and arguably a key source of its appeal, is the range of 'famous deaths' that it records and memorialises with a degree of detail that would not conventionally be found within newspaper or television reporting. These memorials contrast significantly with 'deaths of the famous' – which is more regularly the focus of thanatourism research – including retrospective memorials that reference deaths that occurred before the establishment of the site. Famous deaths are also increasingly marked by the development of a campaign or a charity that remembers the victim and takes up issues surrounding the nature of the famous death itself. It is within the collection of famous deaths that the visible creation of thananetworks is situated.

We offer the following series of vignettes to assist in defining the nature and impact of famous deaths that are documented through *GoneTooSoon*.

5.1 Ben Kinsella

Ben Kinsella was the school-aged victim of a knife crime in London in 2008 as well as the half-brother of the former Eastenders actress Brooke Kinsella. 'Lisa', who joined *GoneTooSoon* in August 2008, created the memorial and has never logged on since (benkinsella.gonetoosoon.org). There have been over 3,400 visits since the memorial was created. There are nine photographs on the memorial, but only two of the photos are of Ben, including one of the images that had been heavily used by the media immediately after he was murdered. Two of the photographs are of the family after the murder; one is of a march with a banner, "Why Ben?", while the remainder of the images are memorial cards that to varying degrees bear Christian references. There are also fifty candles that have been 'lit' for Ben. Living members of the *GoneTooSoon* community have been lighting these candles continuously since 2008. In contrast, the six tributes that have been left are confined to the month immediately after Ben's death.

Since 2008 the Kinsella family, but most notably Brooke, has been involved in campaigning against knife crime with the foundation of the Ben Kinsella Trust (benkinsella.org.uk), a television documentary and support for the increase in prison sentences for knife crime. Brooke Kinsella has subsequently received an MBE (Member of the Order of the British Empire) for her campaigning against knife crime in London and elsewhere.

5.2 Robert Knox

Robert Knox was a hopeful actor who appeared as an extra in one of the Harry Potter films. He was also a victim of a knife attack in London in 2008. The memorial (robert-knox.gonetoosoon.org) was created by 'Donna', who has also created memorials for Steve Galsworthy, a pub landlord from Bournemouth who was stabbed by a gang in 2007; Richard Frank Cutler, who died in World War II aged 23 (her grandfather); Danielle Perrin, the mother of a child at Donna's child's school who was the victim of knife crime in 2008 in Poole; and Keith Cutler (her brother), who died in 1962, eight years before Donna was born. She has also created other memorials for violent crimes around Bournemouth (including an attack on the same street as Steve Galsworthy's pub). The Robert Knox memorial has been visited over 2,700 times since it was created and has received 122 candles since then. Other memorials also exist for Robert – though none have been created by members of his direct family. The photos on Donna's memorial include one of Robert on the set of Harry Potter, two portraits and two photos of the flowers, gifts and balloons left at the site where he died. The memorial includes a lengthy description of the attack and the subsequent court case drawn from another website, evidenced by the bracketed word 'advertisement' left within the body of the description.

5.3 Sophie Lancaster

Sophie Lancaster was the victim of a hate attack in Rossendale in 2007 (not Lancaster, as the memorial claims) (sophie-lancaster.gonetoosoon.org). Sophie and her boyfriend were attacked by a group of youths, primarily because they wore 'goth' fashions. Sophie rushed to support her boyfriend, who was initially attacked, and as a consequence suffered head injuries that placed her in a coma from which she never recovered.

This memorial was created by 'Admin Gts', who have created over 600 other memorials. There have been over 4,600 visits to the memorial since 2007 and 255 candles left to date. There are 41 photographs included in the memorial, but only two feature Sophie and these are themselves duplicates. The majority of the remainder are memorial cards, many with overtly Christian imagery – including a celebration of Sophie's two-year anniversary as an 'angel'. Others feature the face of Bonnie Barratt (and 'Jackie'), while another has an image of 'Sharon' wearing the armband of the S.O.P.H.I.E. campaign. Both 'Sharon' and 'Jackie' are active contributors to GoneTooSoon. 'Sharon' has created five memorials and 'Jackie' has created nine.

Since Sophie's death, her family has created S.O.P.H.I.E. and the Sophie Lancaster Foundation (sophielancasterfoundation.com), which has campaigned for a widening of the definition of 'hate crime' and been actively involved in fundraising, primarily within the North West of England through arts events and concerts.

These three short vignettes reveal the relationship of actions and efforts to express feelings of injustice and powerlessness brought about by each individual loss, and these are consolidated around the memorials found on *GoneTooSoon* as well as elsewhere. In all of these examples, *GoneTooSoon* is not the site or focal point of memorial or remembrance for the family of the murder victims, but rather a space for more distant personal friends and strangers to express grief and association and to recount the details of the famous murder. The individual distance from the specific death opens up the degree to which an individual's death and more broadly their life can be mythologised. The photos on Sophie Lancaster's memorial are wide-ranging in their meanings and their sentiments, making it evident that they are more a reflection of the poster's attitudes and worldview than necessarily those of Sophie Lancaster's lifestyle or her own beliefs. Similarly, tributes (such as 'Sorry Sophie, hadn't been on here for quite some time until recently but you are always in my heart and thoughts. Love Gill xxx') convey more about the day-to-day commitments of the living and the way in which memorials such as those for Sophie are a place to pause and reflect, away from these commitments. These latter examples of actions and sentiments mirror those expressed in more traditional places for mourning.

Other tributes are more clearly theological in their intention, such as messages on Sophie's memorial that use conventional Christian iconography in ASCII art form. All of these tributes can be read as ways of mourning defined by the personal context of the mourner. The majority of the tributes, candle messages and photographs on the memorials do not directly reflect the individual grief of personal loss or the social and cultural disruptions caused by death. However, it is part of thananetworking that personal grief and disruption can be identified through networks sharing mourning for the dead, whereby the grief is expressed and distributed across multiple sites and through differing actions, as members of *GoneTooSoon* build a network by adding other memorials to their personal 'gardens' as well as creating new memorials. These forms of solidarity enable the potential for circuits of exchange, whereby the sharing of reciprocal respect and the mutual honouring of memories can be spread across a range of memorials. Reciprocation from other grieving site members often comes in the form of giving candles or tributes, often with a reference back to their own cause for grief.

The development of a thananetwork as a distributed network of grieving also enables the mythologising of individuals who have died and retrospective identity work that is invariably in a favourable light. In our research, the case of 'Jackie' is both indicative and an exemplar. As the mother of a murder victim, 'Jackie' is one of the most notably active members of the *GoneTooSoon* community and is active on a number of the memorials that have a connection with her daughter's own circumstances, specifically the murders of known sex-workers by men seeking some degree of fame or notoriety. This association also highlights the way in which mythologising is intimately tied to the construction and representation of innocence.

6 The construction of innocence, fame and memory

'Jackie' was the mother of Bonnie Barratt (bonnie-barratt.gonetoosoon.org), a sex-worker with addictions who was murdered in 2007 by Derek Brown, a Preston truck driver who wanted to become the 'modern Jack the Ripper'. Alongside the memorial that 'Jackie' has created to Bonnie, there is also a memorial to Xiao Mei Guo, the other woman murdered in Whitechapel by Derek Brown, as well as to Stephen Booker, a victim of knife crime in 2000. Bonnie's memorial, in contrast to counts of the previous examples, has since had over 42,000 visits and over 22,500 candles lit (with the newest candle always lit 'minutes ago'). 'Jackie' has left over 10,800 tributes and lit 8,600 candles while she has been an active member of the site – approximately ten tributes and eight candles a day since she joined. However, she has created no new memorials since 2008. The fact that 'Jackie' has clearly actively worked at establishing a network on GoneToo-Soon around the memorial she has created for her daughter is evidence of the importance of reciprocated exchanging of candles and tributes, which assist in the establishment of an active thananetwork formed through practices that are based around remembrance of the dead. The description of Bonnie Barratt's memorial has been altered a number of times since 2008, initially with a description of the circumstances of the death and then the subsequent court case. This developed rapidly to include a series of notes for other victims of violent crime as well as the beginning of a campaign called F.A.M.E. (Families Against Murders Escalating). This campaign is then continued on other web pages (www.myspace.com/474417923 and fame-barratt.webs.com/). While the MySpace site is relatively unpopulated, the fame-barratt.webs.com site is primarily a long list of images of murder victims directly drawn from GoneTooSoon. As part of establishing the F.A.M.E group, 'Jackie' asked through the memorial to her daughter on *GoneTooSoon* in 2009, 'PLZZZZ ANY ONE ON MY GARDEN WHO HAD SOME ONE MURDERD CAN I USE THERE PIC TO PUT ON F.A.M.E BANNER IF YOU DONT MIND CAN YOU PLZZZ LET ME NO ASAP PLZZZZZ' (*sic*).

The MySpace site describes the circumstances of Bonnie's life from Jackie's perspective:

> To many My daughter was seen as "No Angel", as she was trapped in voilent relationship and a life of drugs and prostitution, but to me she will always be My beauitful daughter and mother to my young grandson who was robbed of his mum before his life had really began. (*sic*)

> Bonnie was taken after she had made up her mind to turn her life around and get back to the person she used to be, she wanted to stop the drugs She wanted her life back and wanted to make it up to her family. She made plans to improve her life but she never got the chance. (*sic*)

However, references and details to Bonnie's life have become scarcer since 2009, and increasingly 'Jackie' has introduced large amounts of ASCII art in creating her tributes on other memorials with increasingly straightforward references to

Christian iconography. The creation and maintenance of these memorials is simultaneously a mechanism for remembering the individual while constructing, through the separation of time, a myth around his or her life.

For 'Jackie', mythologising individual lives is a fraught activity. In 2008, the day after the conviction of Steven Wright and the murder of Anneli Anderton, she left a candle with the note, 'r.i.p my heart go out to your family as my daughter was murder and othe lady was to in 2007 there bodys have not been found yet' (*sic*, annelli-alderton.gonetoosoon.org – the name is misspelt on the memorial). One of the photographs on Anneli's memorial is from 'Jackie' and is a sombre cartoon-style image of the Bible with the annotation, 'r.i.p. no more pain xxx' (*sic*). There are many parallels to the circumstances of the Anneli Anderton and Bonnie Barratt murders and their lives beforehand. However, Anneli's memorial was created by 'Admin GTS' in 2006 and has received less attention than many more recent memorials. The photographs include only two images, both of which are low resolution, and the main image used on the memorial is drawn from the CCTV image of Anneli on the day she died. This image has been a cause of contention, as a proportion of the small number of tributes that have been left indicate: 'i met annelli just 4days before she was horribly murdered and she seemed a very nice women i hope she is happy and i would like 2 say that this isnt a very nice pic off her she looked a lot different very pretty r.i.p' (*sic*). These tributes also attempt to begin the process of reconstructing a public identity that contrasts with the one created by mainstream media:

> You did not deserve to die. you were so, so much more than a 'prostitute' and 'drug addict' as the papers keep calling you, you were a beautiful young mum who ended up in the horrible world of addiction. I have been there and even though it changes you so much, the litle girl you once were is always still there. I really hope your mum can see this and that she remembers you for the girl you were before addiction took over because that is the real annellli. (*sic*)

Unlike many of the other infamous murders from Suffolk or more broadly across the UK through the 2000s, Anneli is not remembered with a foundation or campaign, and there is no other visible online presence remembering Anneli. These differences are reminiscent of those found at well-tended or poorly tended physical graves.

As a consequence of her own circumstances and her conscious choice to utilise *GoneTooSoon*, 'Jackie' is contributing to the maintenance, remembrance and ongoing mythologising of a number of women who parallel her own daughter's situation, as well as extending the stories portrayed publicly and through the media as 'innocent' deaths – rather than the description regularly attached to

Anneli as 'tragic'. The examples of Ben Kinsella and Sophie Lancaster confirm that *GoneTooSoon* is not the only location for thananetworking and that maintenance of the memory of deceased individuals is being conducted through other websites – primarily the websites and actions of the respective foundations that are the memorialising and mythologising spaces of the more direct families of the victims.

7 Conclusion

Beliefs and grieving practices provide a lens through which it is possible to explore the everyday interactions found on the *GoneTooSoon* network. While in no way do we claim that the exemplars we have employed provide a full or complete representation of *GoneTooSoon*, what we have identified within the *GoneTooSoon* community in describing the actions and interactions of the online grieving process is what we describe as thananetworking. Thananetworking itself employs many of the practices of storytelling identified in anthropological studies of traditional cultures. What is distinctive in the actions of thananetworking, however, are the links that can be identified between contemporary forms of narrative and the association of thananetworking with the expectations found in the construction of celebrity within fame culture. These explorations lead us to consider what building a profile means for memorialising the life and death of an individual and what its subsequent upkeep and maintenance mean for both the living and dead. Personal separation and temporal distance from a specific death opens up the degree to which an individual's death, and more broadly the entirety of his or her life, can be constructed as something with meaning rather than a meaningless tragedy.

By exploring everyday practices on these sites, we see that the *GoneTooSoon* site provides a human response to the uncontrollable events of a life and death, by and for those connected through a desire to associate with fame, or at least famous death. In contrast, the response of families is seen in the establishment of foundations, for example those developed by the families of Ben Kinsella and Sophie Lancaster. In both of these examples, continued engagement and activity rallying against the specific actions that brought about the death of the eponym of the foundation gives friends and relatives of the bereaved a sense of hope that the death was not in vain. In both of these examples, the eponymous individual has a narrative crafted around his or her life that implies that they are representatives of the opposite sentiments to the type of crime that killed them, without necessarily giving any specific examples of this opposition from the individual in life. In contrast, through the thananetwork, post-mortem analysis and presentation of a life is employed by families and friends, as well as 'fans', to construct a mythology of life that is partially premised on the lives of others, brought into complementary orbits through the reciprocal actions of thananetworking. The example of Bonnie Barratt and her mother 'Jackie' is indicative of this attempt to respond to unexpected death. In death, Bonnie Barratt's life has become associated with those of the women murdered in Suffolk as well as more loosely with those of the Soham murder victims[1] and other young women. This storytelling is an active rewriting of Bonnie Barratt's life and the lives of others from a position of being in a vulnerable situation as sex-workers and drug-users. Mainstream media choose to use the euphemism of a 'tragic' death, in contrast to one of 'innocent' death. This, however, is the point – for the family – of constructing this type of tale.

A socio-anthropological explanation also shows that there is an active attempt to rationalise the events associated with death in a way that enables those influenced by it to express their hopes and to establish a form of faith in which these hopes can be realised. This is most readily evidenced in the association of 'famous deaths' with foundations subsequently organised by the families. However, in contemporary culture, this is also where the important parameter of fame intersects with more traditional forms of memorialising and even ancestor worship, in that collective cultural memory increasingly blurs with the concept of fame. Thus preservation of the memory of an individual necessitates constructing them with some form of fame – even if this fame rests solely on the circumstances of their death. Initially, Bonnie Barratt's murder had relatively minimal reporting, but through the actions of 'Jackie' and her use of *GoneTooSoon* to record the details and progress of the police investigation and subsequent successful court case on Bonnie Barratt's memorial, the story continued and awareness of the story became wider. Bonnie Barratt's name and story have been shared across the network, with tributes, candles and memorials that 'Jackie' has created on *GoneTooSoon*, in effect carrying the story of her daughter beyond the initial media reports and into direct association with the grief and mourning of others. The commitment of individual time to continue this memorial and the scale of the work being undertaken by 'Jackie' ensures that the myth and the memorial continue to build, even years after the initial murder.

---

1 The murder of two girls, Holly Wells and Jessica Chapman, by a school caretaker, Ian Huntley (BBC 2003).

References

BBC. 2003. "Huntley guilty of Soham murders." 17 December. Available at: http://news.bbc.co.uk/1/hi/uk/3312551.stm.

boyd, danah, and J. Potter. 2003. "Social network fragments: An interactive tool for exploring digital social connections." *Sketch at SIGGRAPH*. San Diego, California: ACM July 27–31.

Carroll, Brian, and K. Landry. 2010. "Logging on and letting out: Using online social networks to grieve and to mourn." *Bulletin of Science, Technology and Society* 30: 341–349. DOI: 10.1177/0270467610380006.

DeBord, Guy. 1995. *Society of the Spectacle*. London: Zone Books.

Doss, Erika. 2002. "Death, art and memory in the public sphere: The visual and material culture of grief in contemporary America." *Mortality* 7 (1): 63–82.

Ellison, Nicole B., C. Steinfield, and C. Lampe. 2007. "The benefits of Facebook 'Friends': Social capital and college students' use of online social network sites." *Journal of Computer-Mediated Communication* 12: 1143–1168.

Fearon, Jordan. 2011. *The Technology of Grief: Social Networking Sites as a Modern Death Ritual*. Available at: etd.ohiolink.edu/view.cgi?acc_num=antioch1307539596.

Galloway, Anne. 2004. "Intimations of everyday life." *Cultural Studies* 18 (2): 384–408.

Gibson, Margaret. 2004. "Melancholy objects." *Mortality* 9 (4): 285–299.

–. 2007. "Death and mourning in technologically mediated culture." *Health Sociology Review* 16 (5): 415–424.

Hart, Bethne, P. Sainsbury, and S. Short. 1998. "Whose dying? A sociological critique of the 'good death.'" *Mortality* 3 (1): 65–77.

Levene, Nancy. 2009. "Memento mori: Gary Lease and the study of religion." *Method and Theory in the Study of Religion* 21: 139–156.

Latour, Bruno, and A. Woolgar. 1986. *Laboratory Life: The Construction of Scientific Facts*. Princeton, N.J.: Princeton University Press.

Meskell, Lynn. 2001. "The Egyptian ways of death." *Archeological Papers of the American Anthropological Association* 10 (1): 27–40.

McAvan, Em. 2010. "The postmodern sacred." *Journal of Religion and Popular Culture* 22 (1). Available at: http://www.usask.ca/relst/jrpc/pdfs/art221.–PostmodernSacred.pdf.

McCurdy, Patrick. 2010. "The king is dead, long live the king: Meditations on media events and Michael Jackson." *Celebrity Studies* 1 (2): 236–238. DOI: 10.1080/19392397.2010.482303

Myerhoff, Barbara. 1984. "Rites and signs of ripening: The intertwining of ritual, time and growing older." In *Age and anthropological theory*, edited by D. Ketzel and J. Keith, 305–330. Ithaca, NY: Cornell University Press.

Reimers, Eva. 1999. "Death and Identity: Graves and funerals as cultural communication." *Mortality* 4 (2): 147–166.

Riches, Gordon, and Pam Dawson. 1998. "Spoiled memories: Problems of grief resolution in families bereaved through murder." *Mortality* 3 (2): 143–159.

Rugg, Julie. 2000. "Defining the place of burial: What makes a cemetery a cemetery." *Mortality* 5 (3): 259–275.

Ryan, Chris, and R. Kojil. 2006. "The buried village, New Zealand – An example of dark tourism?" *Asia Pacific Journal of Tourism Research* 11 (3): 211–226. DOI: 10.1080/10941660600753240.

Seaton, Anthony. 1996. "Guided by the dark: From thanatopsis to thanatourism."
International Journal of Heritage Studies 2 (4): 234–244. DOI:
10.1080/13527259608722178.

Slade, Peter. 2003. "Gallipoli thanatourism: The meaning of ANZAC." *Annals of Tourism
Research* 30 (4): 779–794. DOI: 10.1016/S0160–738303.00025–2.

Stone, Philip. 2005. "Consuming dark tourism: A call for research." *eReview of Tourism
Research* 3 (5): 109–117.

Stone, P., and R. Sharpley. 2008. "Consuming dark tourism: A thanatological perspective."
Annals of Tourism Review 35 (2): 574–595. DOI: 10.1016/j.annals.2008.02.003

Thomas, Sue, C. Joseph, J. Laccetti, B. Mason, S. Mills, S. Perril, and K. Pullinger. 2007.
"Transliteracy: Crossing divides." *First Monday* 12 (12). Available at:
firstmonday.org/htbin/cgiwrap/bin/ojs/index.php/fm/article/view/2060/1908.

Thompson, John B. 2011. "Shifting boundaries of public and private life." *Theory, Culture and
Society* 28 (4): 49–70. DOI: 10.1177/0263276411408446.

Tong, Stephanie T., B. van der Heide, L. Langwell, and J.B. Walther. 2008. "Too much of a
good thing? The relationship between number of friends and interpersonal impressions
on Facebook." *Journal of Computer-Mediated Communication* 1 (3): 531–549.
DOI: 10.1111/j.1083–6101.2008.00409.x.

Walter, Tony. 1996. "A new model of grief: Bereavement and biography." *Mortality* 1 (1):
7–25.

Ware, Ianto. 2008. "Andrew Keen vs. the emos: Youth, publishing, and transliteracy." *Media
and Culture* 11 (4). Available at:
journal.mediaculture.org.au/index.php/mcjournal/article/view/41.

12   List of Contributors

Nathan Abrams is Professor of Film Studies at Bangor University in Wales. He has published extensively on Jewish film and new media, including most recently *The New Jew in Film: Exploring Jewishness and Judaism in Contemporary Cinema* (Rutgers University Press, 2012). He is also the founding co-editor of *Jewish Film and New Media: An International Journal.* He is currently working on two book-length projects; the first explores ethnicity in the films of Stanley Kubrick, while the second is titled *The Hidden Presence of Jews in British Film and Television* (contracted to Northwestern University Press).

Sally Baker is an independent scholar. Her initial career was in biomedical science, but later she followed her long-standing interest in the social sciences, publishing widely on the sociology of education. At present her research is primarily concerned with two broad areas: national identity and neoliberal welfare reform. Sally's work has led her to an interest in French social theory, particularly the work of Pierre Bourdieu, and she is currently working on new applications and developments of Bourdieusian sociology.

Brian Brown is Professor of Health Communication at De Montfort University. The core of his work has focused on the interpretation of human experience across a variety of different disciplines, including health care, philosophy, education and spirituality studies, exploring how this may be understood with a view to improving practice and with regard to theoretical development in the social sciences.

Heidi Campbell is Associate Professor of Communication at Texas A&M University, where she teaches in Media Studies, and Director of the Network for New Media, Religion and Digital Culture Studies. Her research in religion and new media appears in numerous publications, including the *Journal of the American Academy of Religion, New Media and Society, Journal of Computer-Mediated Communication* and *Journal of Contemporary Religion.* She is the author of *Exploring Religious Community Online* (Peter Lang, 2005) and *When Religion Meets New Media* (Routledge, 2010) and editor of *Digital Religion: Understanding Religious Practice in New Media World* (Routledge, 2013).

Gordon Fletcher is Senior Lecturer in Information Systems at Salford University Business School, Manchester. His research focuses on specific examples and experiences of digital culture and practice. He has published work around conflict with online finance communities, economies within virtual game worlds and practices of online grieving and mourning. He is currently collaborating with Maria Kutar and Marie Griffiths on work related to the quantification and visualization of individual digital footprints and digital identity. Other work includes the examination of science fiction and the use of science fiction prototyping in business development and innovation.

Drake Fulton is a graduate in Communications from Texas A&M University. He is currently working as an accounting analyst for a non-profit company and aspiring to become a math teacher.

Marie Gillespie is Professor of Sociology at The Open University and Co-Director of the Centre for Research on Socio-Cultural Change (www.cresc.ac.uk). Her research interests include globalisation and culture; media, migration and transnationalism; and South Asian and Middle Eastern diasporas. Her latest book, *Diasporas and Diplomacy: Cosmopolitan Contact Zones at the BBC World Service 1932–2012* (with Alban Webb), was published in 2012. www.open.ac.uk/socialsciences/staff/people-profile.php?name=Marie_Gillespie

Anita Greenhill is Senior Lecturer at Manchester University Business School. She received her PhD from the Engineering & Information Technology Faculty, Griffith University in 2002. Prior to her appointment Anita was employed as a lecturer in Information Systems in the Faculty of Management and Commerce and in the Faculty of Computing & Information Technology, both at Griffith University. Anita has over 60 published articles in various fields of interest and expertise, including Information Systems; Virtual Communities; Sociology; Skills Acquisition in Information Technology; Gender and Information Technology; Information Technology, Policy and Education; and Qualitative Research Methods.

Rebecca Haughey is a graduate in Communication and English from Texas A&M University. She is currently a copy editor and freelance writer for a business-to-business publishing company in New York.

David Herbert is Professor of Religion and Society at the University of Agder, Norway. He was formerly Assistant Professor of Sociology of Religion at the University of Groningen, Netherlands, and Senior Lecturer in Sociology and Religious Studies at the Open University, UK. His main works are *Religion and Civil Society* (Ashgate, 2003), *Religion and Social Transformations* (ed., Ashgate, 2002), *Creating Community Cohesion: Religion, Media and Multiculturalism in North West Europe* (forthcoming with Palgrave, 2013).

Kim Knott is Professor of Religious Studies at Lancaster University. Her research interests include the theorization of space and place; the interrogation of religious and political spaces; spatial metaphors in religious and political discourse; the relationship between religion and non-religion; the 'secular sacred'; media representations of religion; and religion and its intersections with migration, diasporas, diversity and ethnicity. Her recent publications include *Media Portrayals of Religion and the Secular Sacred: Representation and Change* (co-authored with Elizabeth Poole and Teemu Taira, forthcoming with Ashgate, 2013), *Diasporas: Concepts, Intersections, Identities* (co-edited with Seán McLoughlin, Zed Books, 2010), and *The Location of Religion: A Spatial Analysis* (Equinox, 2005).

Gordon Lynch is Michael Ramsey Professor of Modern Theology at the University of Kent. His broad area of research interest is in the cultural study of religion and the sacred in modern Western society. His main focus is on the development of a cultural sociological approach to the study of the sacred, where the sacred is understood as what people collectively experience as taken-for-granted moral realities that exert an unquestionable claim over social life. He has developed this work through two recent books, *The Sacred in the Modern World* (Oxford University Press, 2012) and *On the Sacred* (Acumen, 2012).

Arjen Nauta is a Masters student in Political Science at National Sun Yat-sen University in Kaohsiung, Taiwan. Previously he obtained Bachelors degrees in History and Religious Studies and a Research Masters degree in Religion and Culture at the University of Groningen, The Netherlands. He completed a traineeship at the Dutch Embassy in Libya and studied Arabic in Damascus.

Stephen Pihlaja is Assistant Professor of Language and Literature at the University of Nottingham, Malaysia campus, where he teaches courses in linguistics. His research interests include metaphor, computer-mediated communication/discourse, conversation analysis, impoliteness and inter-religious and inter-cultural dialogue.

Elizabeth Poole is a Senior Lecturer in Media, Communications and Culture at Keele University and Co Programme Director of the BA Media, Communications and Culture. She has written widely in the area of the representation and reception of Muslims in the news and is author of 'Reporting Islam: Media Representations of British Muslims' I.B Tauris and editor, with John Richardson, of 'Muslims and the News Media' I B Tauris. She has recently completed a 2 year AHRC/ESRC research project, with Prof Kim Knott (Leeds), on Media Portrayals of Religion and the Secular Sacred' and a project with Dr Siobhan Holohan (Keele) for the Institute of Strategic Dialogue, 'Muslims in the European Mediascape'.

Teemu Taira holds a Research Fellowship from the Academy of Finland at the Department of Comparative Religion, University of Turku, Finland. He is the author of *Notkea uskonto* (Liquid Religion, 2006), co-author of *Media Portrayals of Religion and the Secular Sacred* (2013) and co-editor of *The New Visibility of Atheism in Europe* (special issue of *Approaching Religion*, 2012). His articles on religion, discourse, media and atheism have been published in edited volumes and journals, including *Religion*, *Culture and Religion* and *Journal of Contemporary Religion*.

Lyn Thomas is Emeritus Professor of Cultural Studies in the Institute for the Study of European Transformations (ISET), Faculty of Social Sciences and Humanities, at London Metropolitan University. Her writings include *Annie Ernaux: An introduction to the writer and her audience* (Berg, 1999), *Fans, Feminisms and 'Quality' Media* (Routledge, 2002) and *Annie Ernaux, à la première personne* (Stock, 2005). She has edited a collection on *Religion, Consumerism and Sustainability: Paradise Lost?* (Palgrave, 2010) and co-edited *The Theory and Politics of Consuming Differently* with Kate Soper and Martin Ryle (Palgrave, 2008). In 2011 she co-authored a research report, *'Suspect Communities'? Counter-terrorism policy, the press and the impact on Irish and Muslim communities in Britain*, with Mary Hickman, Henri Nickels and Sara Silvestri. She has co-edited several issues of *Feminist Review*, including *Religion and Spirituality* with Avtar Brah in 2011.

Index

Printed in Poland
by Amazon Fulfillment
Poland Sp. z o.o., Wrocław